A TEXT BOOK OF

INDUSTRIAL MANAGEMENT

For
Semester VI

**THIRD YEAR DEGREE COURSE IN
ELECTRONICS AND TELECOMMUNICATION ENGINEERING**

As Per New Revised Syllabus of
North Maharashtra University, Jalgaon, (2014-2015)

M. S. MAHAJAN

B.E. (Mech.), M.E. (Produciton Engg.)
Ex-principal, Govt. Polytechnic, Jalgaon
Ex-I/C Principal, Govt. College of Engineering,
Jalgoan – 425002 (M. S.)

INDUSTRIAL MANAGEMENT (NMU)

ISBN 978-93-5164-408-8

First Edition : January 2015
© : Author

The text of this publication, or any part thereof, should not be reproduced or transmitted in any form or stored in any computer storage system or device for distribution including photocopy, recording, taping or information retrieval system or reproduced on any disc, tape, perforated media or other information storage device etc., without the written permission of Author with whom the rights are reserved. Breach of this condition is liable for legal action.

Every effort has been made to avoid errors or omissions in this publication. In spite of this, errors may have crept in. Any mistake, error or discrepancy so noted and shall be brought to our notice shall be taken care of in the next edition. It is notified that neither the publisher nor the author or seller shall be responsible for any damage or loss of action to any one, of any kind, in any manner, therefrom.

Published By :
NIRALI PRAKASHAN
Abhyudaya Pragati, 1312, Shivaji Nagar,
Off J.M. Road, PUNE – 411005
Tel - (020) 25512336/37/39, Fax - (020) 25511379
Email : niralipune@pragationline.com

Printed By :
REPRO INDIA LTD,
Mumbai.

DISTRIBUTION CENTRES
PUNE

Nirali Prakashan
119, Budhwar Peth, Jogeshwari Mandir Lane
Pune 411002, Maharashtra
Tel : (020) 2445 2044, 66022708, Fax : (020) 2445 1538
Email : bookorder@pragationline.com

Nirali Prakashan
S. No. 28/25, Dhyari,
Near Pari Company, Pune 411041
Tel : (022) 24690204 Fax : (020) 24690316
Email : dhyari@pragationline.com
bookorder@pragationline.com

MUMBAI
Nirali Prakashan
385, S.V.P. Road, Rasdhara Co-op. Hsg. Society Ltd.,
Girgaum, Mumbai 400004, Maharashtra
Tel : (022) 2385 6339 / 2386 9976, Fax : (022) 2386 9976
Email : niralimumbai@pragationline.com

DISTRIBUTION BRANCHES

NAGPUR
Pratibha Book Distributors
Above Maratha Mandir, Shop No. 3, First Floor,
Rani Jhanshi Square, Sitabuldi, Nagpur 440012,
Maharashtra, Tel : (0712) 254 7129

BENGALURU
Pragati Book House
House No. 1, Sanjeevappa Lane, Avenue Road Cross,
Opp. Rice Church, Bengaluru – 560002.
Tel : (080) 64513344, 64513355,
Mob : 9880582331, 9845021552
Email:bharatsavla@yahoo.com

JALGAON
Nirali Prakashan
34, V. V. Golani Market, Navi Peth, Jalgaon 425001,
Maharashtra, Tel : (0257) 222 0395
Mob : 94234 91860

KOLHAPUR
Nirali Prakashan
New Mahadvar Road,
Kedar Plaza, 1st Floor Opp. IDBI Bank
Kolhapur 416 012, Maharashtra. Mob : 9855046155

CHENNAI
Pragati Books
9/1, Montieth Road, Behind Taas Mahal, Egmore,
Chennai 600008 Tamil Nadu, Tel : (044) 6518 3535,
Mob : 94440 01782 / 98450 21552 / 98805 82331, Email : bharatsavla@yahoo.com

RETAIL OUTLETS
PUNE

Pragati Book Centre
157, Budhwar Peth, Opp. Ratan Talkies,
Pune 411002, Maharashtra
Tel : (020) 2445 8887 / 6602 2707, Fax : (020) 2445 8887
Pragati Book Centre
Amber Chamber, 28/A, Budhwar Peth,
Appa Balwant Chowk, Pune : 411002, Maharashtra,
Tel : (020) 20240335 / 66281669
Email : pbcpune@pragationline.com

Pragati Book Centre
676/B, Budhwar Peth, Opp. Jogeshwari Mandir,
Pune 411002, Maharashtra
Tel : (020) 6601 7784 / 6602 0855
PBC Book Sellers & Stationers
152, Budhwar Peth, Pune 411002, Maharashtra
Tel : (020) 2445 2254 / 6609 2463

MUMBAI
Pragati Book Corner
Indira Niwas, 111 - A, Bhavani Shankar Road, Dadar (W), Mumbai 400028, Maharashtra
Tel : (022) 2422 3526 / 6662 5254, Email : pbcmumbai@pragationline.com

www.pragationline.com

info@pragationline.com

PREFACE

This book has been written with a specific aim of providing a text book on **"Industrial Management"** for Third Year Degree Course in Electronics and Telecommunication Engineering as per the new revised syllabus of North Maharashtra University, Jalgoan.

The need of such a book was felt due to the fact that the students at large find themselves confused and lost while referring so many books available on the subject.

Therefore, an attempt has been made to provide the specific subject matter through a single source.

Sincere efforts have been made to present the subject-matter in a simple language and in a style which will enable even an average student to grasp it easily. Typical questions have been added at the end of the each chapter to enhance the utility of this book.

The author is thankful to Shri. Dineshbhai Furia, Shri. Jigneshbhai Furia, Shri. M. P. Munde, Shri. P. M. More, Mrs. Prachi Sawant, Mrs. Manasi Pingle and other staff of Nirali Prakashan for bringing out this book in the shortest possible time.

The author is also thankful to Sau. Meena Mahajan for extending her co-operation from time to time.

Although, extreme care has been taken to avoid mistakes and misprints, yet some of them might have crept in. The author shall be highly obliged, if the errors are pointed out by the readers.

Any constructive criticism and suggestions will be appreciated by the author for enhancing the utility of this book.

For more details readers are requested to refer my books:

1) Industrial Engineering and Production Management
2) Statistical Quality Control.

January 2015   M.S. Mahajan

Pune

SYLLABUS

Unit-1: Basics of Management (09 Lectures, 16 Marks)
a) Introduction, definition of management,
b) Scientific management
c) Function of management
d) Principles of management
e) Level of management, Managerial skill/roles
f) Relation between Administration, Management and Organisation.

Unit-II: Organisational Structures (09 Lectures, 16 Marks)
a) Principles of organisation. Design of organisation.
b) Forms of organisation - Line, Line and staff.
c) Types of ownerships - Partnership, Proprietorship.
d) Joint stock company, Private limited, Government Ltd., Public Ltd.
e) Co-operative organisation
f) Public sector and Joint ventures

Unit-III: Personal Management (09 Lectures, 16 Marks)
a) Factors affecting man power planning.
b) Source of recruitment, Talent acquisition.
c) Education and training methods of training workers.
d) Lavour welfare, Communication in industries.
e) Suggestion system, Discipline in industry.
f) E-business and E-governances.

Unit-IV: Financial Management (09 Lectures, 16 Marks)
a) Definition and function of financial management.
b) Capital structure. Fixed and working capital. Role of SEBI (Securities and Exchange Board of India).
c) Sources of Finance. Loans from Banks. Trade credit. Public deposits.
d) Wants, Utility, Demand.
e) Supply, Elasticity of demand and supply.

Unit-V: Quality Management and Industrial Act (09 Lectures, 16 Marks)
a) Definition of Quality, Quality control.
b) Process control. Total quality concepts.
c) ISO 9001 – 2000.
d) Factories Act, Industrial accidents, Industrial safety.
e) Rights patents, Trademarks, Copyrights.

❖❖❖

CONTENTS

UNIT I: BASICS OF MANAGEMENT   1.1 – 1.36

UNIT II: ORGANISATIONAL STRUCTURES   2.1 – 2.44

UNIT III: PERSONAL MANAGEMENT   3.1 – 3.42

UNIT IV: FINANCIAL MANAGEMENT   4.1 – 4.40

UNIT V: QUALITY MANAGEMENT AND INDUSTRIAL ACT   5.1 – 5.56

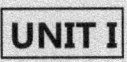

BASICS OF MANAGEMENT

1.1 INTRODUCTION

The history of management goes back to the dawn of human civilization, when human being started group activities for the attainment of some common objectives. Wherever a group is formed and a group activity is organised to achieve certain common objectives, management is needed to direct, co-ordinate and integrate the individual activities of a group and secure team work to accomplish organisational objectives. The need for efficient management is highly felt in business activities. The objectives of all businesses are attained by utilizing the scarce resources like men, materials, machines, money etc. The basic economic objectives of business activity are profit maximization or continuous growth and survival. It is only efficient management which helps in achieving these objectives economically by effective utilization of the scarce resources.

Management is a universal process in all organised economic activities. It is found in every walk of life where the economical and intelligent application of scarce resources are involved. It is not merely restricted to shop, factory or office. It is necessary for a business firm, Government enterprises, education and health services, military organisations, trade associations and so on. In fact, management is an operative force in all complex organisations trying to achieve some stated objectives.

It can be generalized that no enterprise can enjoy a successful existence and survival without the competent management. The slow rate of economic growth of under-developed countries is due to the poor management. Peter Drucker has rightly remarked that there are no underdeveloped countries, there are under-managed countries. According to Kolin Clark, an eminent economist, the low rate of economic growth of under-developed countries is not due to the dearth of capital, but it is due to the dearth of the management talents.

1.2 VARIOUS DEFINITIONS OF MANAGEMENT

Management has been defined by different thinkers in a number of ways. For our understanding management may be viewed as what manager does in a formal organisation to achieve the objectives.

Some of the important definitions of management are as under :

1. Management has been called by *Mary Parker Foller* — 'the art of getting things done through other people.' This definition throws light on the fact that managers achieve the organisational goals by enabling others to perform, rather than, performing the task themselves.

Management, in fact, encompasses a wide variety of activities that no one single definition can capture all the facets of management, given its dynamic nature.

2. "Management may be defined as the art of applying the economic principles that underline the control of men and materials in the enterprise under consideration".

— *Kimball and Kimball*

3. "Management is the force that integrates men and physical plant, into an effective operating unit". — *Keith and Gubelline*

4. Management is principally a task of planning, co-ordinating, motivating and controlling the efforts of others towards a specific objectives". — *James Lundy*

5. As *Appley L.* in his book has written - "Management is the attainment of pre-established goals by the direction of human performance along pre-established lines." According to *Appley L.* "Management is essentially personnel management. We do not build automobiles, airplanes, refrigerators, radios etc. We build men and women and these human resources build products. Human resources are our great assets. They have unlimited potential. Hence, it is but natural that management must give special attention to the development of human resources".

6. *P. Drucker* in his book 'Practice of Management' has defined, "Management is a multi-purpose organ that manages a business, manages a manager and manages workers and work".

Drucker stresses three jobs of management - (i) Managing a business; (ii) Managing managers; and (iii) Managing workers and work. Even if one is omitted, we would not have management any more and we also would not have a business enterprise or an industrial society. According to Drucker, the manager has to balance and harmonise three major functions of the business enterprise. Hence, a manager is a dynamic and life-giving element in every business. Without efficient management, we cannot secure the best allocation and utilization of human, material and financial resources.

7. "Management is knowing exactly what you want men to do, and then seeing that they do it by the best and cheapest ways" — *F.W. Taylor*

8. "Management is defined as the creation and maintenance of an internal environment in an enterprise where individuals, working together in groups, can perform efficiently and effectively towards the attainment of group goals." — *Koontz and O'Donell*

According to this definition, management is an art of creating favourable performance environment enabling the group to attain stated objectives and management is the body of organised knowledge, i.e., Science which underlies the art.

9. Quoting from *American Management Association* - "Management is guiding human and physical resources into dynamic organisation units, which attain their objectives to the satisfaction of those served and with high degree of morale and sense of attainment on the part of those rendering service."

10. According to *Henri Fayol*, the father of modern management thought, "Management is to forecast and to plan, to organise, to command, to co-ordinate and to control". It attempts to describe management in terms of what a manager does and not what management is.

11. The definition given by *James A. F. Stoner*, covers all the important facets of management. According to him, "Management is the process of planning, organising, leading and controlling the efforts of organisation members and of using all other organisational resources to achieve stated organisational goals".

The definition suggests :

(i) Management is a continuous process.
(ii) Several inter-related activities have to be performed by managers, irrespective of their levels to achieve the desired goals.
(iii) Managers use the resources of the organisation, both physical as well as human, to achieve the goals.
(iv) Management aims at achieving the organisations' goals by ensuring effective use of resources.

It is evident that the emphasis is on achieving the objectives by using the inputs like materials, machinery, money and the services of men.

12. A precise definition of management can be stated as: "Management is a social process involving co-ordination of human and material resources, through the functions of planning, organising, staffing, leading and controlling, in order to accomplish stated objectives".

There are five parts to a definition of management, as a social process:

(i) First, the co-ordination of resources;
(ii) Second, the performance of managerial functions as a means of achieving co-ordination;
(iii) third, establishing the objective or purpose of management process, i.e., it must be purposeful managerial activity;
(iv) fourth aspect is that, management is a social process i.e., it is the art of getting things done through other people; and
(v) the fifth is its cyclical nature i.e., an ongoing (continuous) process which represents planning–action–control–re-planning cycle.

This definition of management is applicable to all forms of group efforts in all forms of organisations; i.e., profit or non-profit enterprises. It is also applicable to all levels of management in an organisation.

1.3 SCIENTIFIC MANAGEMENT BY F.W. TAYLOR

Scientific management is an attempt to determine and apply the facts and laws that are essential for efficient running of an enterprise.

The utility of scientific methods to problems of management was first of all introduced by F. W. Taylor in America (1865-1915). He is regarded as a "father of scientific management".

Scientific management may be defined as,

"The art of knowing exactly what is to be done and the best way of doing it".

Scientific management is the result of applying scientific knowledge and the scientific methods to the various aspects of management and the problems that arise from them.

The Aims of Scientific Management:

- It tries to make the best use of production resources (men, materials, machines, capital etc.)
- It discovers the economical and efficient methods of production so as to reduce effort and eliminate wastage of time and motions.
- It provides right man for right job through scientific selection and training of workers, shop supervisors etc.
- It results in improvement in the quality and rate of the output by research, quality control and inspection devices.

The Scientific Management involves:

(i) Scientific study and analysis of work

(ii) Scientific selection and training of employees, and

(iii) Standardization of raw materials, working conditions and equipment.

Principles of Scientific Management by F.W. Taylor

Taylor through his principles of management initiated a system in which there would be an effective and fruitful co-ordination and co-operation between the management and the workers.

1. Development of science for each element of work: Analyse the work scientifically, rather than using thumb rule. It means that, an attempt is made to find out what is to be done by a particular worker, how he is to do it, what equipment will be necessary to do it. This information is provided to the worker so as to reduce wastage of time, material etc. and improve the quality of work.

2. Scientific selection, placement and training of workers: This principle states that select the workers best suited to perform the specific tasks, and then train them within the industry in order to attain the objectives of the enterprise. This eliminates the possibility of misfits in the organisation and ensures better working. Workers should also be trained from time to time keep them informed of latest development in the techniques of production.

3. Division of labour (Separation of planning function from doing function): Division of work in smaller tasks and separation of thinking element of job from doing element of the job, this is the principle of specialisation. It is essential for efficiency in all spheres of activities as well as in supervision work. To be more effective and efficient, Taylor, the founder of scientific management introduced functional organisation, in which one foreman was made incharge for each function.

4. Standardization of methods, procedures, tools and equipment: Standardization helps in reducing time, labour and cost of production. The success of scientific management largely depends upon standardization of system, tools, equipments and techniques of production.

5. Use of time and motion study: Taylor introduced time and motion study to determine standard work. Taylor undertook studies on fatigue incurred by the workers and the time necessary to complete the task.

Taylor suggested that for increasing production rate, the work of each person should be planned in advance and he shall be allotted a definite work to complete by a given time by using a predetermined method.

6. Differential wage system: Taylor's Differential Piece Rate Scheme provides an incentive for a worker to achieve high level of optimum output. It distinguishes the more productive workers from less productive workers and motivates them to produce more. Taylor believed that if labour is suitably rewarded and is satisfied with job, he will work whole heartedly to achieve the objectives of the enterprise.

7. Co-operation between labour and management: Management also strives to get the thinking of management changed so as to make the management feel that mutual respect and co-operation between the workers and the management helps in providing proper and efficient leadership. The labour starts thinking that, it is their work and they must put their heart and soul in the work assigned to them. In fact, the main job of scientific management is to revolutionize the mind of the both workers and management for mutual benefit and also for the benefit of the enterprise.

8. Principle of Management by Exception: In order to make effective utilisation of time of top managers, Taylor suggested that only major or significant deviations between the actual performance and standard performance should be brought to the notice of top management. Top management should pay more attention to those areas of work where standards and procedures could not be established and where there is a significant variation between standard performance and actual performance.

1.4 PRINCIPLES OF MANAGEMENT (14 PRINCIPLES OF HENRY FAYOL)

Administrative theory of management was introduced by Henry Fayol. He established the pattern of management and the pyramidal form of organisation. He pointed out that technical ability is more demanding on the lower level of management, whereas managerial ability is more important on the higher level of management.

Henri Fayol analysed the process of management and divided the activities of an industrial undertaking into six groups:

1. Technical activities (*production, manufacture, adaptation*)
2. Commercial activities (*purchasing, selling and exchange*)
3. Financial activities (*optimum use of capital*)
4. Security (*protection of property and persons*)
5. Accounting (*stock taking, balance sheet, costing, statistics*)
6. Managerial (*planning, organising, commanding, co-ordinating and controlling*)

Fayol's Principles of Management

In 1916, H. Fayol described a number of Management/Organisation principles in his book – 'General and Industrial Management'. These principles constitute the theory of management or administration of business enterprises.

Based on his management experience, Fayol listed the following *fourteen* principles of management:

1. Division of work: This is the principle of specialization. Division of work should be according to work, department, job etc. Both technical and managerial activities can be performed in the best manner only through division of labour and specialization. It can ensure maximum productivity and efficiency in all spheres of activity.

2. Authority and responsibility: The right to give order, the right to command, is called authority. The obligation to accomplish objectives or expected results or performance is called responsibility. They are interrelated and exist together. In any management process, delegation of power, utilisation of authority and fixation of responsibility are key to success.

3. Discipline: No organisation can work smoothly without discipline, it is the very core of administration. The rules, regulations, policies and procedures must be honoured by all the members of organisation. Discipline is imposed by administration. It requires good superiors at all levels, clear and fair agreement on rules, regulations, procedures. There must be penalties (punishment) for non-obedience or indiscipline.

4. Unity of command: In order to avoid confusion and conflict, each individual should receive orders and instructions only from one superior and should be accountable to one superior only. Unity of command provides responsible leadership, better guidance and direction, good co-ordination and disciplined performance.

5. Unity of direction: All members of an organisation must work together to accomplish common or same objectives. Their efforts shall be directed towards one common super goal.

6. Emphasis on subordination of personal interest to general or common interest: It means that the common interest of the organisation must be given more importance than the interest of the individual. The organisation will collapse when personal interest become supreme than the general interest.

7. Adequate remuneration to personnel: The persons working in the organisation should be paid suitably and adequately. This will help to maintain their interest in the work and the enterprise. Exploitation of employees in any manner must be eliminated. A wage policy should be based on adequate financial and non-financial incentives.

8. Centralization: The decision for centralization would naturally vary from organisation to organisation. However, there must be a good balance between centralization and decentralization of authority and power. Extreme centralization and decentralization must be avoided.

9. Scaler chain or line of authority: An organisation chart should be prepared for better communication and effective co-ordination. It shows the flow of authority and responsibility from top to bottom.

10. Order: "A place for everything and everything in its place" is a best norm, for material management, which also holds goods for management of men also, that is, 'a place for everyone and everyone in his place'. This is essential for successful execution of orders received from the top. Order or system alone can create a sound organisation and efficient management.

11. Equity: An organisation consists of human beings, a group of people working together for some common objectives of the enterprise. Hence, there should be equity justice and kindness on the part of managers to create loyalty and devotion among subordinates. Unbiased, meaningful and equal treatment should be the motto of a management in its relations with employees.

12. Stability of workers: Security of income and employment is a pre-requisite of sound organisation and management. This will reduce unnecessary labour turnover, and increase efficiency by having stable working force.

13. Initiative: This principle allows subordinates to utilize their initiative. Initiative is a freedom to think plan and to execute. The employees should be allowed to take initiative, of course, under watchful eyes. Initiative brings self-confidence in a worker which is essential for improving efficiency of the organisation.

14. Esprit de Crops (Team spirit): According to this principle "Union is strength". Management should not adhere the principle of 'divide and rule' instead it should try to achieve co-operation and team spirit in the employees. Pride, loyalty and sense of belonging is essential for efficient working and the prosperity of the organisation.

1.5 LEVELS OF MANAGEMENT / SKILLS / ROLES

In an organisation, all those who are responsible for the work of others are usually, known as managers. Though their primary task remains the same, getting the things done by other people, there is a wide variation in their authorities and responsibilities. These differences are largely due to the differences in the levels of management. In any organisation, the total management job requires many skills and talents. Obviously therefore, the job of manager is divided and sub-divided. Such an arrangement implies levels of management. Levels of management, in fact, refers to a line of separation between different positions drawn with a view to distinguish each other in respect of their duties, responsibilities, rights and authorities.

The three levels of management that are commonly found in an organisation are:

(a) Top Management

(b) Middle Order Management

(c) Lowest Level or Supervisory Management.

(a) Top Management:

Top Management constitutes the highest level in the management hierarchy. This is the policy-making level in any organisation. This level consists of small group of executives, Board of Directors, Chairman, Managing Director, Personnel Manager, Chief Executive etc. Top Management is responsible for the overall management of the organisation. They define the aim of the company, establish the primary objectives, policies and strategies to be pursued to achieve these objectives. They also formulate the plans of organisation and procedure, inaugurate the board programme, and approve specific major projects in the programme. They provide direction to the organisation by guiding the organisations interactions with its environment.

(b) Middle Order Management:

Middle order management occupies a central place in the hierarchy. It is concerned with execution of the detailed policies and plans determined by top management (Administration) through the framework of organisation. Middle order management is answerable to top management. Its main functions are: (i) to plan (ii) to guide (iii) to supervise (iv) to co-ordinate (v) to exercise control over the lower level management. It often functions as a link between top management and lower level management.

(c) Lowest Level or Supervisory Management:

This is the lowest level in the hierarchy of management. Managers at this level function under the control and direction of the middle order management. Their functions are also to plan, to guide, to supervise and to exercise control, but all these functions are performed to get work done from the operating staff. This level of management takes orders from the middle order and explains them to the workers at operating level. In fact, this level of management is accredited with the responsibility of getting the work done and is made accountable to those who occupy the middle order management. This level includes Foreman, Supervisor, Superintendent, Inspector etc.

The following graphical account makes the above hierarchy more clear:

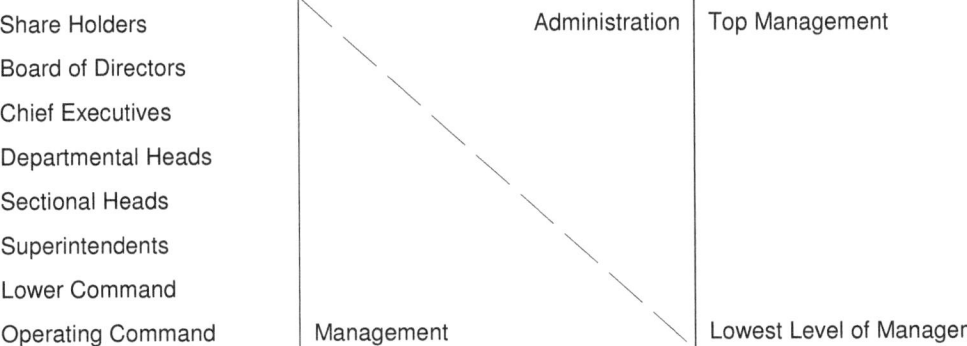

Fig. 1.1: Levels of management

J. Beaty has divided the levels of management into five groups or activity levels as represented in the table:

Table 1.1

Level	Represented By	Function
1. Top Management	(a) Board of Directors (b) Managing Directors (c) Chief Executives (d) General Manager (e) Secretary	(a) Determine the objectives. (b) Establishing Policies. (c) Monitoring performance. (d) Judging the results.

Contd...

2. Upper Middle Management	(a) Production or Works Manager (b) Finance Manager (c) Personnel Manager (d) Materials Manager (e) R & D Manager	(a) Establishment of organisation. (b) Selection, training/ placement of staff. (c) Assigning duties to subordinates. (d) Design operating policies and operating routines. (e) Exercise control over the sub-ordinates.
3. Middle Management	(a) Superintendents (b) Departmental heads	(a) To plan details of operation. (b) To co-operate with top management for the smooth functioning of organisation. (c) To active co-ordination between various departments. (d) Development of manpower for the organisation by imparting training.
4. Lower Management	(a) Foreman (b) Supervisors	(a) To act as a link between management and the workers. (b) Direct supervision of the workers. (c) Arrangement of material, tools, facilities etc. for production.
5. Working	(a) Workers (b) Service Staff (c) Security Staff	(a) Carry out the work assigned to them.

1.5.1 Managerial Skills (Skills of Management)

Managerial skills is the ability of a manager to make a smooth functioning team of people working under him. Management job is different from other jobs. It involves obligation to make effective utilization of human and material resources. It requires sound judgement to handle complex situations. Further, the nature of the job becomes increasingly complex at each higher level, because of the increase in the scope of authority and responsibility. Thus, the skills required in management are different in nature at different management levels. Each higher level requires increased knowledge, broader perspective and greater skills. Manager has to reconcile, co-ordinate and appraise the various viewpoints and talents of people working under him towards the organisation goals.

The skills required of a successful manager, whether he is working in a business organisation, an educational institute or a hospital, can be classified as under:

[I] Technical Skills

[II] Conceptual Skills

    (a) Decision-making skills

    (b) Organisational skills

{III] Human Relation Skills:

    (a) Communication skills

    (b) Motivating skills

    (c) Leadership skills

[I] TECHNICAL SKILLS

Technical skills refers to the ability to use methods, processes, tools, equipment, techniques and knowledge of a specialized field. It is primarily concerned with the ways of doing things. It refers to the proficiency in handling methods, techniques and related to a specific field of activity. Technical skills are most important for lower level managers, because by nature, their job involves supervision of the workers on the shop floor. Effective supervision, guidance, direction and co-ordination of the work performed by the subordinates, therefore depends on the technical skill possessed by the lower level managers. Any supervisor without a sound knowledge of the job cannot make an effective supervisor. Such supervisors are not respected by the workers at the shop floor. The relative importance of the technical skills, as compared to the other skills, diminish as one moves up to a higher levels of management.

Fig. 1.2 illustrates the Managerial skills required at different levels of management.

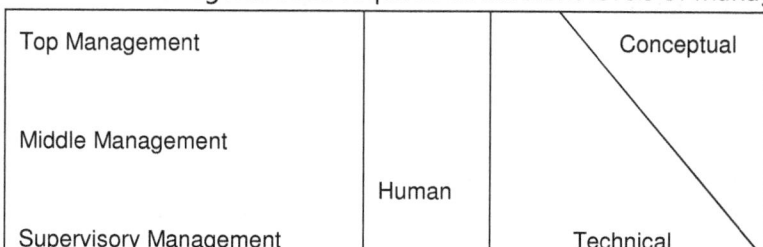

Fig. 1.2: Managerial skills

[II] CONCEPTUAL SKILLS

Conceptual skill is the ability to see the organisation as a whole, to recognize inter-relationships among different functions of the business and external forces and to guide effectively the organisational efforts. It is easier to learn technical skills than the conceptual skills. Conceptual skill extends to visualizing the relation of the organisation to industry, to the community and to the political, economic and social forces of the nation as a whole, and even to forces which operate beyond the national boundaries. It is the creative force within the organisation, which is concerned with design and problem solving. A high degree of conceptual skill helps in analysing the environment and in identifying the opportunities and threats.

  (a) **Decision-making Skills:** Decision-making skill is the ability of a person to take timely and accurate decisions. This requires mental ability, sound knowledge and presence of mind.

  (b) **Organisational Skills:** This helps in manpower planning i.e. for selecting people for different type of activities. It means placing right men for the right job.

[III] HUMAN RELATION SKILLS

Human skills are primarily concerned with persons as contrasted with 'things'. Human skill refers to the ability to work effectively with others and build co-operative group relations to achieve organisational objectives. It is the ability to work with, understand and motivate people. He understands why people behave as they do and is able to make his own behaviour understandable to them. He can foresee their reactions to possible courses of action and is able to take their attitudes into account.

  (a) **Communication Skills:** It is the ability to pass on information to others. Improper, insufficient and poorly expressed information, can create confusion and annoy the subordinates.

  (b) **Motivating Skills:** Motivating skill inspires people to do what the manager wants them to do.

1.6 RELATION BETWEEN ADMINISTRATION, MANAGEMENT AND ORGANISATION

In the study of the management literature the use of the terms of Management and Administration has been a controversial issue and some of the writers do not find any difference between the two terms. While there are writers who maintain that Administration and Management has got two different functions.

According to *Oliver Sheldon* "Management is a lower level function and is concerned with the execution of policies laid down by administration".

But English authors like *Brech and others* have written that "Management is a wider term which includes administration".

At the outset it should be made clear that in practice the three words Administration, Management and Organisation are neither synonymous nor interchangeable. They have their own field of operation. Administration determines the objectives and policies of the enterprise. Management carries out these policies to achieve objectives of the enterprise. For Administration and Management to function effectively, there must be proper structuring of the enterprise and this is known as organisation (structure). Organisation can be termed as a keystone on which any enterprise is based.

Administration gives proper direction. Management properly executes, it is an execution function. And, organisation is an effective machinery for accomplishing company objectives in a team spirit. In brief, it can be said that, "Management carries out the policies of Administration through the framework of the organisation".

Organisation is the process of dividing work into convenient tasks and duties and then grouping such duties in the form of departments and posts, deligating authority to each post and of appointing qualified staff to be responsible to ensure that the work is carried out as planned.

The following table illustrates a clear distinction between Administration, Management and Organisation:

Table 1.2

No.	Administration	Management	Organisation
1.	It is the process of determining the objectives to be achieved.	It is the process of planning the work as per the objectives laid down by the administration.	It is the process of dividing the work into different tasks and duties as planned.

Contd...

2.	It lays down the policies and principles.	It executes the policies and programmes.	It organises the work.
3.	It prepares the framework under which one is asked to work and execute.	It supervises and controls the execution of assigned work.	It draws out the line of authority and determines the line of action.
4.	It provides: (i) direction (ii) guidance, and (iii) leadership	It co-ordinates activities.	It delegates the authority and fixes responsibility.
5.	It is the first and provides guidelines to the management and organisation.	It comes second, follows the administration and derives strength from administration.	It occupies the third place and solely responsible for what the management has planned and administration has set.

1.7 FUNCTIONS OF MANAGEMENT

Management is an on-going activity consisting of number of functions. The important functions of management are:

1. Planning
2. Organising
3. Directing
4. Controlling
5. Decision-making
6. Co-ordinating
7. Motivation

1.7.1 Planning

Planning is the most basic of all management functions. Planning means thinking before doing. In other words, planning is the preparation for action. Every manager plans, no matter at what level he operates. It is a function to decide about what, where, when, who, why and how a particular activity should be done. It sets the objectives of the business, determines the different course of action to achieve these objectives, evaluates each course of action and decides about the best course of action under the given conditions. It thus provides direction to the enterprise.

Planning defines the goals, sets the policies, procedures, programmes, develops strategies so that the objectives of the enterprise can be attained most efficiently. It analyses all the difficulties that are likely to occur in running the business and decides in advance, how these difficulties can be overcome.

Planning is a rational, economic, systematic way of making decisions today, which will affect the future. Planning helps to have an optimum utilisation of the available resources. Without planning, the activities of an enterprise may become confused, haphazard and ineffective. For example, if a company making refrigerators, does not plan in advance as to how many refrigerators and of what capacity are to be made before summer starts and if it does not procure necessary materials, tools, supplies and personnel in time, it cannot approach the production target and hence may not run profitability.

Planning includes forecasting, formulation of objectives, policies, programmes, schedules, procedures and budgets. Generally, long range planning is undertaken by top management personnel.

Some of the definitions of planning given by different writers are as follows:

"Planning is deciding in advance what to do, how to do it, when to do it and who is to do it. Planning bridges the gap from where we are, to where we want to go. It makes it possible for things to occur which would not otherwise happen". — *Koontz and O'Donnell*

"Planning is the thinking process, the organised foresight, the vision, based on facts and experience that is required for intelligent action". — *Alfred and Beatty*

"Planning is deciding in advance, what is to be done. It involves the selection of objectives, policies, procedures and programmes from among alternatives". — *M. E. Harley*

A careful analysis of these definitions reveals that:

(i) Planning involves visualising future course of action and putting it in a logical way.

(ii) It involves thinking and analysis of information.

(iii) It is concerned with determination of objectives and goals in the light of future.

(iv) It involves development of alternative courses of action to achieve such objectives.

(v) It involves decision-making i.e. selection of best course of action among these alternatives.

(vi) Its objective is to achieve better results.

(vii) It is a continuous and integrated process.

Objectives of Planning

The important objectives of planning are:

1. Planning Helps in Effective Forecasting: The first and the most important objective of planning is forecasting. Effective planning anticipate future and prepare themselves to meet the challenges of the future. A well thought out plan solves many of the problems associated with the uncertain future. Continuous planning by management shows precisely, what the enterprise wants to achieve in a given period as well as how it intends to accomplish the objectives formulated in advance.

2. Planning Provides Certainty in the Activities: Planning decides the policies, defines the procedures and makes the rules for the activities of all the employees of the organisation. This helps in bringing certainty in the activities of the organisation.

3. Planning Provides Performance Standards: A good plan specifies clearly the targets to be accomplished. For example, five year plan of a company may prescribe that rate of return on shareholders' investment must double with five years from 15% to 30% per annum. The performance of the company is measured and controlled on the basis of such a specific standard. The specific objectives decided in advance, themselves become standards on the measuring tools.

4. Planning gives a Specific Direction to the Organisation: When you plan the events, you make them happen in a particular way. As a plan, a decision regarding a future course of action it specifies the sequence of events to be performed. It thus gives the specific direction to all the activities of an organisation by preparing the outlines of these activities well in advance.

5. Helps the Organisation to tune with the Environment: In general, organisations that plan, have been the winners against the non-planners. Planning helps the managers to control the events, rather than being controlled by them. A manager can establish through planning, a profitable relationship with the environment and minimize risk and insecurity.

6. It Provides Economy in the Management: Planning establishes the co-ordination among all the activities of the organisation. It guides the management and all the employees of the organisation in their activities. It helps in maintaining effective control and discipline. It checks all types of wastages and thus, brings an economy in management.

7. It is very much Helpful in Preparing the Budgets: Planning helps the management in accomplishing pre-determined budgets of the enterprise in a logical manner.

8. The Need for Planning Arises from Constant Change: A business enterprise lives in a dynamic and complex environment. Economic, social, political and technological trends must be noted and their influence must be taken into account in the plans and policies from time to time. An enterprise and its environment are mutually interdependent - interacting with each other continuously. Management through comprehensive business planning, can anticipate, meet and adopt creatively to everchanging environmental conditions and demands. It helps the management to assure the survival of the organisation under keen competition and changing environment.

9. Planning is Directed towards Efficiency: The main purpose of planning is to increase efficiency. The guiding principle of a good plan is the maximum output and profit at the minimum cost. *"Planning is the foundation of most successful action of the enterprise"*. It aims at efficiency. Planning is an intellectual activity, the main aim of which is (a) to suggest the best way of doing things; and (b) planning is linked to goals and objectives. Thus, planning is directed towards efficiency by achieving the objectives, through determination of best course of action.

It should be noted that

— "Failure to plan is planning to fail".

— "Planning is outlining a future course of action in order to acheive an objective".

— "Planning is looking ahead".

— "Planning is getting ready to do something tomorrow".

— "Planning is a trap laid down to capture the future".

Steps in Planning

The details of planning may differ, depending upon the specific requirements of a particular business. However, in all types of businesses, planning process involves certain necessary steps, summarised as follows:

1. Determination of Objectives:

Planning is not possible without definite objectives. If the objectives of the business are clearly defined, then only it is possible to plan for future. Planning in fact, begins with decisions about what the organisation wants to achieve during a specified period. It is always desirable to express the objectives/goals in quantitative terms for all the key areas of the business like production, profit, productivity, market share etc. The time frame in which the objectives have to be achieved, must also be specified. Thus, what, how and with what resources, are a few important questions that should be answered at this stage. After determining the overall objectives of the business, it is necessary to fix up departmental objectives and the objectives for sub-departments and sections. These objectives are in harmony with overall objectives of the business.

Since goal/objective setting is the essential step in planning, managers who fail to set meaningful goals will be unable to make effective plans. If Telco is able to retain its prominence in the Heavy Commercial Vehicles Segment, it is because, all the employees of the organisation know that the primary objective is retaining the leadership in the industry.

2. Forecasting to Assist Planning:

Establish planning premises and constraints: Planning premises, in simple are the assumptions made about the various elements of the environment. Planning assumptions or premises provide the basic framework in which plans operate. Thus, it is a forecast of conditions - both internal and external to the organisation.

Internal premises: The important internal premises include sales forecasts, policies of the organisation, resources of the organisation, skills, attitudes and beliefs of the people. Each of these elements is a critical success factor. For instance, the accuracy of the sales-forecast, influences the procurement of resources, production, scheduling and the marketing strategies to be adopted to achieve the objectives.

External premises: Important external premises relate to all those factors in the environment outside the organisation. They include technological changes, general economic conditions, Government policies and attitudes towards business, socio-cultural changes in the society, political stability, degree of competition in the market, availability of labour, material, power etc.

It is evident that some of these factors are tangible, while others are intangible. Though accurate premising is difficult, anticipating future situations, problems and opportunities would definitely help the managers in reducing the risk; though not completely eliminating it.

3. Decide the Planning Period:

In some cases plans are made for a short period, varying from a few months to a year, while in some other cases, they are made to cover a longer period. The period may extend to 5-10 years and even more. Companies normally plan for a period that can be reasonably achieved. The lead time involved in the development and commercialisation of a product and time required to recover the capital investment (pay-back period) influence the choice of the length of the plan. Again, in the same organisation, different plan periods may exist for different purposes. Operational plans focus on the short-term, strategic plans focus on the long term.

4. Collection, Classification and Processing of Information:

All relevant information pertaining to factors that affect planning is collected. Information must be classified, analysed and processed. It helps interpretation and the establishment of cause and effect relationship.

5. Deciding Alterative Courses of Action:

The objective can be fulfilled by more than one course of action. For example, if we want to increase the profit, we can increase the price, we can increase the sales keeping the price constant or we can reduce the cost of production by adopting improved techniques, reducing waste and by optimum utilisation of resources. We can raise capital by selling shares or by borrowing from financial institutions. All such possibilities must be explored during the planning of business.

6. Evaluation of Alternative:

The advantages and disadvantages of each alternative are then weighted against the other alternatives. Cost benefit analysis is made to evaluate each feasible alternative.

7. Selection of Best Plan:

After the evaluation of different alternative plans in terms of results; the best, feasible and economical plan is selected.

8. Subsidiary Plans to aid Master Plan:

After deciding the main plan, subsidiary plans are constructed to successfully implement the master plan. To implement the master plan each department head prepares a plan of his department.

9. Controlling Plans:

Plans and subsidiary plans are first tried on a pilot basis to test the possibility of their success. The plan is then implemented. It is constantly monitored and results are obtained as feedback from time to time. The drawbacks or shortcomings are removed as early as possible. Future plans are framed in the light of this experience.

Advantages of Planning

1. **Maximum utilization of resources:** Through proper planning, it is possible to have a maximum utilization of resources. All efforts are directed towards the desired goals, and an effective sequence of activities is accomplished. Activities can be co-ordinated so as to achieve the pre-determined goals or targets.

2. **Minimisation of unproductive work :** As a result of planning unproductive work is minimized. Since the planned activities are subjected to a careful scrutiny and only necessary activities are taken up to accomplish the specified work.

3. **Reduces uncertainty:** Planning provides opportunity to a business manager to foresee various uncertainties which may be caused by changes in Technology, taste and fashion of the people etc. and the management can be prepared to face the change with reasonable success. It involves anticipation of future events and therefore, helps in reducing uncertainties. Management of change is based on planning.

4. **Basis for managerial action:** Planning compels managers to visualize the whole picture of business clearly and completely. This enables the management to see important relationships, gain full understanding of each activity, and plan the managerial actions.

5. **Basis for control:** Planning also provides a basis for control. Planning involves not

only the time for starting and finishing of each activity, but it also determines objectives and lays down standard of performance. Thus, there is a close relationship between the function of planning and controlling.

6. Avoids bottlenecks in production: Production planning analyses all the problems likely to arise in manufacture and decides in advance as to how these difficulties can be overcame.

7. Planning encourages innovation and creativity: Planning is basically a deciding function of management. It helps innovative and creative thinking among the managers because many new ideas come to the mind of a manager when he is planning. It creates a forward looking attitude among the managers.

8. It improves motivation: A good planning system ensures participation of all members and all managers which will improve their motivation. It improves the motivation of workers because they know clearly what is expected of them.

9. Facilitates effective delegation of authority: Planning facilitates effective delegation of authority of act, removes communication difficulties, provides proper machinery for co-ordination and integration of all functions.

10. Planning gives competitive edge to the enterprise: This is because planning may involve expansion of capacity, changes in work methods, changes in quality, anticipation of taste and fashion of people and technological changes, preparedness to meet uncertainties etc.

Limitations of Planning

Though planning facilitates various management functions and brings orderliness, stability and continuity of operation, it suffers from certain limitations as follows :

1. Limitations of forecast: Planning future oriented activity which is based on forecast. As the period of planning increases the accuracy of forecast diminishes. Planning looses its value if reliable and adequate data is not available.

2. Costly affair: Planning is quite a costly and time consuming process. Unlimited amount of time is spent on forecasting, preparing estimates, collecting information and facts for analysis, evaluating alternatives etc.

3. Influence of external factors: By the time plan is established, the environment may change and this requires complete revision of the plan. Moreover, sudden outbreak of war, government control, natural calamities and many other factors are beyond the control of the management. They make the successful execution of plans very difficult.

4. Resistance to change: The human element in organisation always resists change, they are more concerned about the present rather than the future, which is uncertain. Planning being forward looking is always affected by this resistance to change. Sometimes, planners themselves do not like change and on other occasions they are afraid to bring changes as it will create resistance on the part of the workers. This attitude makes the planning process ineffective.

5. Rigidity and inflexibility: Planning implies strict adherence to predetermined policies, procedures and programmes. This restricts individuals freedom, initiative and desire for creativity and causes delays in decision-making.

Following measures may be adopted to overcome the limitations of planning:

1. Set realistic and achievable goals.
2. Communicate assumptions, on which, plans are formulated to all the people and departments concerned.
3. Encourage and make people participate in the planning programme so as to ensure the right commitment.
4. Ensure proper co-ordination between the short-term and long-term plans. They should not be considered as mutually exclusive.
5. Encourage creativity in planning. Creativity helps in identifying the best alternatives.
6. Pay attention to the resources position of the organisation so as to ensure the availability as and when required.

1.7.2 Organising

Organising is the process of establishing a structure for the organisation so that it helps the manpower of the oganisation to function systematically, to fullfil the organisational goals effectively.

Organising is the process by which individuals, groups and facilities are combined in a formal structure of tasks and authority.

Organising provides a framework of management or a mechanism for positive integrated and co-operative action by many people, in a joint effort to implement plan. Planning decides what management wants to do, while organising provides an effective machine for achieving the plan or objectives.

The process of organising consists of

1. Identifying and grouping the activities of an enterprise that are necessary to achieve the objectives of the business.
2. Assigning the group of activities to individual managers.
3. Providing them with authority and responsibility for carrying out these activities.
4. Co-ordinating the effort of individual managers so that there is no wasted effort or duplication of work.

The organising process is shown in Fig. 1.3.

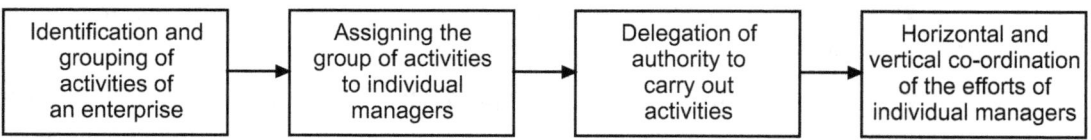

Fig. 1.3 : Organising process

Steps in Organising

The various steps for developing an effective organisation for an enterprise are as follows :

1. Determining clearly the objectives of an enterprise.
2. Listing the various activities functionwise, such as marketing, production, personnel, accounts etc. The activities within a broad function are further grouped into separate subfunctions, e.g., the activities pertaining to marketing may be grouped into activities related to subfunctions of sales, purchasing, stores etc.
3. Dividing the activities under each function/subfunction which can be done by a single individual.
4. Defining the individual's duties, responsibilities, powers and accountability clearly, so that each person knows what he is expected to do in terms of attainment of objectives of the enterprise or of department/section.
5. Delegating powers to the individual to enable him to carry out his responsibility.
6. Providing adequate facilities such as office, furniture, equipment etc. to the individuals to discharge their duties in a proper manner.
7. Clearly defining the relationships between peoples and methods of co-ordinating them.

1.7.3 Directing

According to *Drucker*, "Directing is that part of management process which actuates the organisational members to work effectively and efficiently for the attainment of organisational objective".

Directing consists of the process and techniques utilized in issuing instructions and making certain that operations are carried out as originally planned.

In other words directing means,

(i) Telling employees what to do and how to do their work and
(ii) Seeing to it that they do it that way.

Directing is of great importance for the success and survival of the industry. This is an important managerial function, because the managerial decisions are put into action through effective direction. Actual activity starts only when manager issues directions to his subordinates as to what is to be done and how it should be done.

Directing consists of guiding and supervising the subordinates in their activities. Only giving orders is not directing.

Directing involves motivating, guiding, inspring and supervising subordinates towards company objectives. Good planning may ensure the achievement of the predetermined objectives only when human efforts, largely diverse are co-ordinated, guided and directed for the accomplishment of the objectives. This however, is a difficult task, since manpower resources are difficult to manage. In fact, the directing ability of the manager in the organisation determines its effectiveness. Therefore, the person who directs must have dynamic leadership. This work is done by the Director or General Manager or Managing Director.

Supervision is necessary in order to ensure that :

(a) the work is going on as per the plan established.

(b) the workers (or subordinates) are doing work as they were directed to do.

The position of the director (person who directs) in a factory is like a captain of a ship. Directions are not only to be given, but also to be obeyed. Hence they must be definite, clear cut, understandable, communicable and practicable. As far as possible these must be in writing.

Characteristics of Directing

- Directing is a vital managerial function in the management process.
- It stimulates the employees to execute the plans and policies in order to achieve the desired results.
- It is performed at all levels of management, but particularly important for the operating management levels concerned with routine operations. It includes assignment of jobs, explaining procedures, providing instructions on the job, issuing orders and directives and seeing that errors are rectified in time.
- It makes it possible for the managers to direct, motivate and lead their subordinates to their assigned work with interest for attaining the objectives of the organisation.
- Directing helps employees in utilizing their full potential for increased productivity and achieving job satisfaction.

- The five aspects of directing function are :
  - Supervision
  - Leadership
  - Motivation
  - Communication and
  - Co-ordination.

1.7.4 Controlling

Introduction

In management literature, the word "Control" has a special meaning. It means setting standards, measuring actual performance, and taking corrective action. It is more than mere evaluation, appraisal or correction. It measures performance against goals and plans, indicates where deviations exist and helps accomplishment of objectives. It serves to determine personnel responsible for deviations to take necessary steps to improve performance. In short, control means setting standards, measuring performance and corrective action with a view to achieve best results.

Definitions

According to *Henry Fayol*, "Control consists in verifying whether everything occurs in conformity with the plan adopted, the instructions issued and the principles established".

According to *Koontz and O'Donell*, "Controlling implies measurements of accomplishment against the standard and the correction of deviations to ensure attainment of objectives according to plans".

Ernest Dale in his book 'Theory and Practice of Management' has stated that —

"The modern concept of managerial control envisages a system, that not only provides historical record of what has happened to the business as a whole, but also pin points the reasons, why it has happened and provides data that enable the chief executive or the departmental head to take corrective steps, if he finds, he is on the wrong track".

According to *E.F.L. Breach*, "Control is checking current performance, against predetermined standards, contained in the plans, with a view to ensuring adequate progress and satisfactory performance".

Necessity of Controlling

Controlling is essential in order to ensure that every activity is carried out according to the plan and directions. The orders may be mis-interpreted or delayed due to lack of control. Control enables a manager to keep a check and co-ordinate the activities of his subordinates, so as to meet the objectives of the company, economically and effectively. Any variation between actual performance and the laid down goals and objectives can be immediately detected and corrective action can be taken by the manager, so as to prevent such variations in future. Control is effected through organisation structure. Controlling is a continuous process of measuring actual results of the operations of an organisation, in comparison with the standards laid down as a guide.

The function of control is to match actual performance with the plans, and to point out defective works, to rectify them and prevent recurrence.

Controlling is therefore, necessary to ensure that orders are not misunderstood, rules are not violated and objectives have not been unknowingly shifted.

Control is thus an important function of management. Without control, a manager cannot do the complete job of managing. All other functions are preparatory steps for getting the work done and controlling is concerned with making sure that there is proper execution of these functions. It ensures work accomplishment, according to plans. It is essential feature of scientific and successful management.

Essential Steps in Controlling Procedure

There are three essential steps in the process of control:

1. Setting Standards: Standards are fixed against which, results can be measured. The standard established for the company as well as the individual departments may be stated in terms of output, quality, costs, production targets, time standards, sales quotas etc. These standards should be clear and meaningful. It is essential to identify responsibility for standards with definite individuals in the organisation.

2. Checking and Reporting on Performance: There are three methods of checking performance

(a) Prior approval by the executive to allow the work to proceed as planned.

(b) Personal observation by the executive to get realistic picture of the actual performance.

(c) Checking the unexpected.

Only when unexpected results occur, there is a need for reports and corrective action. In the absence of such reports, the management assumes that all activities are proceeding as planned.

3. Taking Corrective Action: The actual performance is compared with the plan. If there are any deviations, then the reasons for deviations are found out and analysed. Then necessary steps are taken to get back on plan.

Types of Control

Based upon the objectives, controls can be classified as:

1. **Physical control :** Physical control seeks to control quality and quantity, e.g. so many units of output must be produced during the course of a month etc.

2. **Financial control :** Financial controls are expressed in monetary terms e.g. cost per unit of production, cost of material, labour, indirect expenses etc.

3. **Budgetary control :** In budgetary control, physical and financial standards for future are determined and results are compared against these pre-determined standards.

Besides above classification, controls can be classified on the basis of activities of the organisation: Policy control, Quality control, Inventory control, Overall control etc.

Objectives of Controlling

The main objective of controlling is to ensure a high degree of efficiency of the business. This very objective helps the manager to attain the goals of the organisation in a systematic and effective way.

The following are the objectives of controlling:

(i) To ensure high efficiency of the business.

(ii) To understand what had happened or is happening, why and by whom is happening.

(iii) To ensure effective and proper communication between the management and workers at all levels - to achieve the objectives of the organisation.

(iv) To keep proper check and control over direct and indirect expenses.

(v) To reframe organisational goals, policies and objectives.

(vi) To find out the various deviations from the planned and proposed targets and to take necessary corrective action.

(vii) To make sure that all the activities are performed according to the pre-determined plans.

1.7.5 Decision Making

A decision can be defined as "a course of action consciously chosen from available alternatives for the purpose of a desired result".

Decision making means to decide the future course of action for the organisation, over short or long terms. It is necessary to take decisions throughout the business cycle, for achieving maximum returns on the assets of the business enterprise. Decision making is necessary to solve business problems; for example, Inventory control decisions, Marketing decisions, deciding volume of production, capital investment decisions, stock decisions etc. In other words - "The decision is the point at which plans, policies and objectives are translated into concrete actions". Planning leads to sound decision and implies decision-making i.e. selection from among alternatives of a course of action. Decision is at the core of planning.

Decision making under certainty is comparatively easy. Decision making under uncertainty requires that the person responsible for making decisions should use his judgement and experience about future events. He must make sure that, which outcomes are most likely than others and combine his knowledge with the consequences associated with the various decisions. While taking decision under uncertainty the management should be willing to take a calculated risk.

Stages in Effective Decision Making

(a) Define the Problem: Define the problem clearly and precisely. Before any attempt is made to take decision, it is important to identify the real problem. Correct diagnosis is the first phase of effective decision making. It is also necessary to establish the objectives of the decision.

(b) Classify the Objectives and identify the Problem Environment: The objectives established are marked and listed as per their weightage and importance for the organisation. The real problem and the situation in which the problem exists are identified.

(c) Search for Alternative: Identify the feasible alternatives for consideration, as solution of the problem.

(d) Select Evaluation Criteria: To compare the various alternatives, it is necessary to select evaluation criteria, such as; cost effectiveness, performance, quality, output etc.

(e) Select the Best Alternative: The various alternatives are evaluated as per the criteria selected. From the results of evaluation, a suitable and economical course of action is selected under the existing conditions in the factory. It is necessary to ensure that the decision will accomplish the purpose and it will be acceptable to those who must implement it.

(f) Feedback: Decisions are made for the future. They are made by human beings and thus there is every possibility of their being wrong. The organisation must therefore, have a sound, fool-proof feedback system; such feedback would help in determining how the decisions are working out in action.

Characteristics of Decision Making

1. It is a continuous process. Decisions are necessary on numerous issues and problems in each area of business.
2. The question of decision making comes into picture only when there are alternatives.
3. Decision making is always purposive, in that decisions should aim at achieving some purposes.

4. It is an intellectual process, supported by sound reasoning and judgement. To make decision means, to make a judgement regarding what one ought to do in a certain situation after considering thoroughly the available alternative course of action.

5. Decision making is all pervasive, in the sense, that all levels of managers take decisions, though the impact and scope of decisions vary.

6. It is always related to a situation in which a manager may take one decision in a particular set of circumstances and another in different set of circumstances.

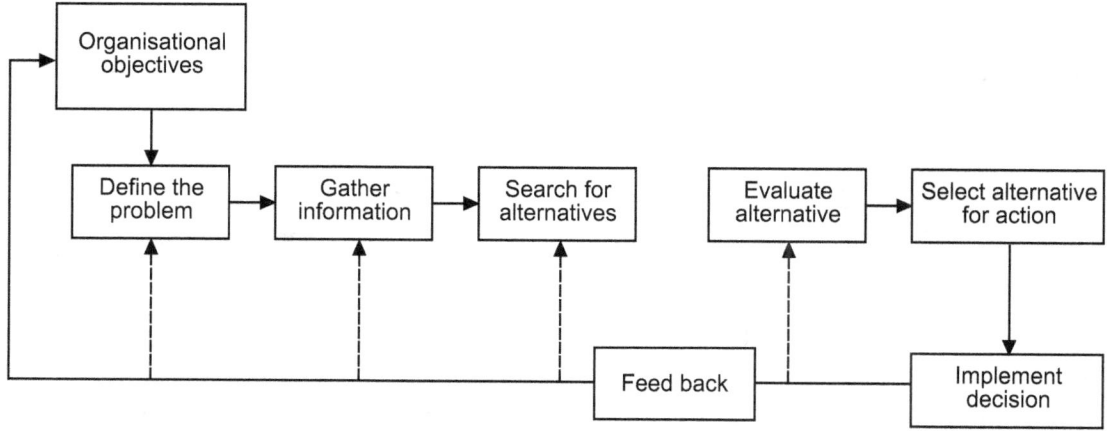

Fig. 1.4: Decision making process

Types of Decisions

Decisions may be of different types. Some of the important types of managerial decisions are as follows:

1. Major and Minor decisions
2. Programmed and Non-programmed decisions
3. Strategic and Tactical (Routine) decisions
4. Policy and operation decisions
5. Long-term, departmental and Non-economic decisions
6. Individual and group decisions
7. Organisational and Personal decisions

1. Major and Minor Decisions: These can be categorised on the basis of their intensity. For example, purchase of a new automatic machine of worth 50 lakhs is categorised as major decision, while purchase of stationary (pencil, papers, pens etc.) for office use will be the minor decision.

2. Programmed and Non-programmed Decisions:

(a) Programmed decisions: These are classified on the basis of procedures adopted. Programmed decisions are routine and repetitive and are made within the framework of organisational policies and rules. These policies, procedures and rules are established well in advance to solve recurring problems in the organisation.

For example, the problem relating to promotion of employees is solved by promoting those employees who meet established promotion criteria. These criteria are established by promotion policy and the managers have only to decide which employees meet criteria for promotion and decision is made accordingly.

Programmed decision are easy to make and can be taken quickly because they are taken according to established policy already made. These type of decisions are subjected to quantitative assessment and can be easily programmed into a computer. Now-a-days the programmed decisions are made through management information systems (MIS), making use of computers.

(b) Non-programmed decisions: Non-programmed decisions are used for unstructured, unique ill-defined situations of non-recurring nature. In such decisions various alternatives cannot be decided in advance. A common feature of non-programmed decisions is that, they are unique and non-recurring and therefore, readymade solutions are not available. Non-programmed decisions involve high risk, cannot be easily subjected to quantitative assessments involve greater expenditure of resources and cannot be programed into a computer. For example, new product decisions acquisition and merger considerations allocation of organisations resources, decisions about a failing product line etc. represent non-programmed decisions.

The non-programmed decisions are made on the basis of judgement, intuition, insight and experience of the managers. The systematic approach to problem solving and decision making is useful for non-programmed decisions. Moreover these decisions are of high importance because of their long-term consequences. Hence, these are made by managers at higher levels in the organisation.

3. Strategic and Tactical (Routine) Decisions: Strategic decision relate to policy matter of the orgnaisations. It is one which is made during the current time period but whose primary effect will be felt during some future time period. Examples of strategic decisions are change in product mix, expansion of business, decision regarding plant location, issue of public equity shares or debentures, automation, introduction of new production line etc. These decisions are taken by higher level management.

In a strategic decision following characteristics are present:

1. Strategic decision is a major one which affects organisational structure, objectives, facilities and finances.
2. It contributes directly to the achievement of organsational objectives, and other decisions are derived from it.
3. A strategic decision may involve major departure from earlier one concerning some organisational practices; for example, change in product mix, use of automation etc.
4. The strategic decision has normally three elements.
    i) A course of action or plan which specifies the work to be done to achieve the result, known as action element.
    ii) The desired result or objective to be achieved through the implementation of the decision.
    iii) A commitment, which directs some part of the organisation to undertake the course of action, makes the personnel involved responsible for attaining the objectives and allocates resources to them i.e. commitment element.
5. The strategic decision is normally a non-programmaed decision, which is made under the condition of uncertainty. This is because strategic decision is to be taken in the context of environmental factors which are quite dynamic and uncertain.

Tactical or Routine Decisions or Operational Decisions: These decisions are made within the framework of strategic decisions and are designed to implement the well set policies and procedures.

Tactical decisions relates to day-to-day working of the organisation. The various features of tactical decision are as follows:

1) Tactical decision is a operational decision which relates to day-to-day operations of the organisation and has to be taken frequently. The decision is mostly repetitive in nature. For example, purchase of raw materials, assigning duties to employees etc.
2) It is programmed decision. The decision is programmed through the prescription of policies, rules, procedures etc. When the case for decision making comes, the decision maker simply applies those prescriptions and decides the things.
3) The outcome of tactical decision is of short-term nature and affects a narrow part of the organisation.
4) The authority for making these decisions can be delegated to lower-level management.

4. Policy and Operation Decisions: Policy decisions are very important for the survival and growth of the organisation. Policy decisions are taken by the top management, they have a long-term impart on the business operations.

Operational decisions relate to day-to-day operations of the enterprise and are taken at lower or middle management level. For example, whether the piece rate system or time rate system is to be followed in the factory for calculating the wages to the workers is the policy decision and is required to be taken at higher level. While, the calculation of the actual wages to be paid to the workers is the example of operating decision.

5. Departmental and Non-economic Decisions: Departmental decisions are taken by the departmental heads and relates to the individual departments only.

Non-economic decisions are the decisions relating to non-economic factors such as technical values, moral behaviour, business ethics etc.

6. Individual and Group Decisions: Every manager makes decisions in the organisation either in his individual capacity or as a member of the group. In fact, organisational decisions are combination of individual and group decisions. Both types of decisions have their positive and negative aspects. Individual decisions are taken by a single individual in context of routine decisions where guidelines are already available. These decisions can be taken quickly.

The choice between individual decisions and group decisions depends upon

(i) Nature of problem, (ii) Time availability, (iii) Quality of decisions, (iv) Climate of decision making, (v) Legal requirements.

When a manager makes a decision as an individual, he has to consider the steps involved in decision making and uses techniques of decision making. However, when he has to make decision as a group member he has to consider a group behaviour also. Many specific techniques have been developed for improving group decision making such as brain storming, delphi technique, consensus mapping, nominal group technique etc.

7. Organisational and Personal Decisions: Decisions taken by the managers in their official capacity are called organisational decisions. These reflect the basic policy of the company.

Personal decisions relate to the manager as an individual and not as a member of organisation.

1.7.6 Co-Ordinating

Definition of Co-ordination

Co-ordination may be defined as "an on-going process, whereby, a manager develops an integrated, orderly and synchronized pattern of group effort among his subordinates and tries to attain unity of effort in the pursuit of a common purpose".

"Co-ordination is the orderly arrangement of group effort, to provide unity of action in the pursuit of common purpose". — *Alan C. Reiley and James D. Mooney*

George R. Terry, in his book 'Principles of Management' has said — "Co-ordination deals with the task of blending efforts in order to ensure successful attainment of an objective. It is accomplished by means of planning, organising, actuating and controlling".

According to *Ordway Tead*, "Co-ordination is the effort to ensure a smooth interplay of the functions and forces of all different component parts of an organisation, to the end, that its purposes will be realised with a minimum of friction and a maximum of collaborative effectiveness".

According to *E.F.L. Brech*, "Co-ordination is balancing and keeping the terms together, by ensuring a suitable allocation of working activities to the various members and seeing that these are performed with due harmony among the members themselves".

In simple terms —"Co-ordination is the orderly arrangement of group effort, to provide unity of action in the pursuit of common purpose".

Need for Co-ordination

Co-ordinating means achieving team spirit and unity of action amongst the subordinates for achieving the common objectives. In a business unit, work is performed by numerous individuals, in various work centres. The individuals are doing numerous different jobs; many of them are highly specialised in their own work. It is the function of management to see that the individuals in the organisation operate as a team.

Consider, for example, a cricket team having the best players known, may find it difficult to win, if there is a lack of co-ordinated effort. Similarly, the success for a commercial enterprise, is based on the collective efforts of individuals. If properly co-ordinated, these individuals supplement each other's efforts to the extent that the group can be more productive. If they are not co-ordinated, the individuals, in pursuing their particular duties, may undo or delete the effects of their colleagues.

The need for co-ordination by management, arises particularly because of the existence of:

(i) Several persons at work.
(ii) Subdivisions and complexity of work.

(iii) Delegation of authority and responsibility.
(iv) Chances of difference between executives and specialists.
(v) Human nature and their problems.
(vi) Growth in size of organisation.

Tools of Co-ordination

The usual tools of co-ordination are as follows:
(i) Clear cut objectives.
(ii) Clear cut authority and responsibility of every subordinate, so that he knows his specific duties and obligations.
(iii) Effective communication between the executive and his subordinates, supervisors and workers.
(iv) Good human relationship of the managers with their subordinates.
(v) Co-operation amongst the subordinates and between the executive and the subordinates.

Types of Co-ordination

1. **Internal Co-ordination:** Internal co-ordination means co-ordination among different departments, branches, sections and other parts of an enterprise. It also exists among employees of different departments, supervisory staff, managers, directors and other personnel.

2. **External Co-ordination:** It is mainly concerned with the co-ordination between customers, suppliers, society, government and other outside agencies with whom, the business concern has to deal with.

3. **Vertical Co-ordination:** Co-ordination from top level to the bottom or from bottom to top, for attaining common objective of the business, is called vertical co-ordination.

4. **Horizontal Co-ordination:** Where activities of different departments such as purchase, sales, accounts, finance etc. are knit together is called horizontal co-ordination.

1.7.7 Motivation

Definition

Motivation means "inspiring people to intensify their desire and willingness to perform their duties effectively and co-operate for the achievement of common objectives of the business".

Motivation is the mental preparation of an individual to do a specific job. It is a desire to do something. According to *Michael J. Jucius*, "Motivation is the act of stimulating someone or oneself to get a desired course of action, to push the right button to get desired action".

As putforth by *Brech*, motivation is a gentral inspiration on process which puts the members of the team to do their work effectively, to give their loyalty to the group, to carry out properly the tasks they have accepted and generally to pay an effective part in the job that the group has undertaken.

As mentioned by *Dalton Emcfarland*, "The concept of motivation is mainly psychological. It relates to those forces operating within the individual employee, or subordinate which inputes him to act or not act in certain ways".

Motivation and leadership are the master keys to successful management of any enterprise. They are also responsible to ensure productivity of human resources. Motivation can set a person into motion, to carry out certain activity. Motivation assumes unique importance in modern business management. Democratic leadership heavily relies on motivation of employees, through financial and non-financial incentives. Effective communication and participation enhance the power of motivation. Feedback of information (upward communication) is necessary for effective motivation and direction.

Fundamentals of Motivation

The first fundamental thing is that a peron wants to exist and survive and for this, he needs basic necessities of life e.g., food, cloth, shelter, education and medical aid etc.

The second fundamental of motivation is the desire to achieve a goal, for satisfaction or bliss. Basically people are motivated to put in sincere efforts if they are assured of fulfilling their needs such as psychological needs, social needs, security needs, ego (needs for self-respect) etc.

Types of Motivation

Motivation can be classified into two categoreis:

1. Intrinsic or Internal motivation
2. Extrinsic or External motivation

1. Intrinsic Motivation: The inner urge of a man for achieving a goal is called "Intrinsic or internal motive". There is no outside complusion for doing a wok in such cases. A person who works with internal motive is a self-motivated person. He is mentally prepared to do job and hence intrinsic motivation is more effective.

Employees are intrinsically motivated when they genuinely care about their work look for better way to do it. An intrinsic motivation emerges from work performance when the employee experiences sense of accomplishment on doing good work. It is achieved when people experience feeling of choice competence, meaningfulness and progress. Thus, job satisfaction emerges out of the performance associated with these features.

Examples of intrinsic motivation are interests, emotional attachments, burning desires, fighting spirit for some noble cause. For example, a patriot sacrifices his life for the sake of motherland, a scientist may be totally absorbed in his research work due to his inner desire of mental satisfaction.

2. Extrinsic Motivation: An extrinsic motivation is intangible form that is provided to employees after the work performance. Extrinsic motivation results from some material benefit in the form of pay increase salary, bonus, praise and so on; which motivates the workers to do their jobs more effectively and efficiently.

Some times extrinsic motivation may also emerge from fear of loss of job, punishment etc. which will motivate the workers to do their jobs more effectively.

Functions of Motivation

Motivation performs the following three functions:

1. It originates action.
2. It directs activities in the direction of goal.
3. It helps to continue the activities till the goal is achieved.

Importance of Motivation

Motivation is needed to create interest, initiative, enthusiasm, loyalty and willingness to work. As a result of this, motivation helps to improve the productivity. The importance of motivation could be seen under these heads.

1. Arouse desire to work: Person may be capable of doing a work, be efficient, possess the necessary skill etc., still he cannot do the work allotted to him in right time, in right quantity and of right quality unless he is motivated to do so.

Workers not properly motivated may not mentally accept the orders or directions with the result the objectives of the company may not be achieved efficiently and effectively.

2. Appropriate use of factors of production: An organisation may have best instruments, equipments, tools, raw materials in sufficient quantity. But these factors can only be used appropriately (effectively) through sound motivation system.

3. Reduction in labour turnover: Labour does not try to go to another organisation if properly motivated. Not only this, the talented personnel from other organisations are also attracted to join the organisation in which motivation schemes are utilized.

4. Increase in production and productivity: Motivation increases the desire to work whole-heartedly and hence leads to increase in production and productivity.

5. Basis of co-operation: Motivation increases job satisfaction, so the workers' interest, loyalty for the organisation increases. This helps to maintain good employer-employee relations and develops the sense of co-operation.

Thus, without motivation, the workers will not discharge their duties efficiently. There will be high rate of absenteeism, poor quality of production, higher degree of turnover. Effective motivation is the secret of improved quantity and quality.

EXERCISE

1. Define management. Give at least four definitions.
2. What is scientific management? Describe the Taylor's principles of scientific management.
3. Describe 14 principles of management by Henry Fayol.
4. Describe the various levels of management with their functions/roles.
5. What is managerial skills? Describe the skills required for a successful manager.
6. Differentiate between Administration, Management and Organisation.
7. Define planning. State its objectives.
8. State and describe the various steps in planning.
9. State the advantages and limitations of planning.
10. Define organising. State the essential steps in organising.
11. Explain directing as a function of management.
12. Define controlling. Describe its importance in managing the business.
13. What is 'Decision Making' ? Describe the various steps involved in decision making.
14. Name the various types of decisions. Explain any two of them.
15. Differentiate between
    i) Programmed decisions and Non-programmed decisions.
    ii) Strategic decisions and tactical or routine decisions.
16 Define controlling. State is objectives and necessity.
17. Define co-ordination. Explain the need of co-ordination in an organisation.
18. Define co-ordination. State the various types of co-ordination and the tools for co-ordination.
19. Define motivation. Explain the importance of motivation in an industry.
20. Define motivation. Dedifferentiate between Intrinsic Motivation and Extrinsic Motivation.

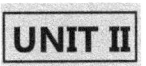

ORGANISATIONAL STRUCTURES

2.1 ORGANISATION

Introduction

Every business needs to be organised for effective and efficient performance. Once the objectives, strategies and necessary plans to carry out are formulated, the next phase in management process is that of organisation. Organisation is thus a function of management which basically deals with the establishment of organisation structure. To start and run a business, the essential requirements are men, materials, machines and money. Organisation is a co-ordination of these factors in such a way that maximum output is obtained efficiently and effectively with minimum total cost. Organisation in fact is a backbone of management, which establishes relationship between people, work and resources. A clear understanding of the objectives and strategies of an organisation enables structuring, functioning and performance of an organisation. Organisation involves division of work among people whose efforts must be co-ordinated to achieve specific objectives and to implement pre-determined strategies.

Necessity of Organisation

The increasing size of the manufacturing plant, introduction of most complex methods of production, tough competition between the enterprise and labour problems has necessitated every factory to be well organised, in order to produce required quantity of the products of the required quality, at the required time with minimum production cost.

A well designed organisation structure with qualified personnel in all key positions achieves execution, co-ordination and control of all policies and functions of the firm.

The importance of organisation can be judged from the following words of *A. Carngie*, an American industrialist.

"Take away all our money, great works, ore mines, and coke ovens but leave our organisation and in a few years, I shall have established myself. In fact the success or failure of any enterprise largely depends on the nature of organisation".

Advantages of Good Organisation

A good organisation offers the following advantages:
(i) It establishes responsibility for accomplishment of certain objectives.
(ii) It eliminates jurisdictional dispute between individuals.
(iii) It provides for easier communication and helps in developing executives.

(iv) It helps in equitable distribution of work and function.

(v) It assists in measuring a person's performance against his responsibilities.

(vi) It permits expansion and contraction without seriously disrupting the existing structure.

(vii) It prevents duplication of work.

(viii) It ensures good co-operation and higher morale.

(ix) It makes organisational growth possible with adequate control and without over-burdening the top executives.

(x) It ensures optimum utilization of resources at minimum possible cost.

2.2 DEFINITIONS

The following are some of the useful definitions of organisation:

1. "Organisation is a process of (i) identifying and grouping the work to be performed, (ii) defining and delegating the responsibility and authority and (iii) establishing the relationships for the purpose of enabling people to work most efficiently together in accomplishing objectives". — *Louis A. Allin*

2. "Organisation is the form of every human association for the attainment of a common purpose". — *Mooney and Reily*

3. "Organisation is a system of co-operative activities of two or more persons". — *Chester Barnard*

4. "Organisation is a process of defining and grouping the activities of the enterprise and establishing the authority relationship among them". — *Haimann*

5. "Organisation involves the grouping of activities necessary to accomplish goals and plans, and assignment of these activities to appropriate departments and positions for authority delegation and co-ordination". — *Koontz and O' Donnel*

6. "Organisation is the process of combining the work which individuals or groups have to perform with facilities necessary for its execution, that the duties so performed provide the best channels for efficient, systematic, positive and co-ordinated application of available effort". — *O. Sheldon*

7. "An Organisation is the rational co-ordination of the activities or roles of a number of people for the achievement of some common explicit purpose or goal, through division and labour and function, and through a hierarchy of authority and responsibility". — *E. H. Schien*

8. "An Organisation consists of people who carry out differentiated tasks which are co-ordinated to contribute to the organisation's goals". — *G. Dessler*

2.3 STEPS IN ORGANISATION (DESIGN OF ORGANISATION)

As already stated, design of organisation consists of :

- Determination of activities necessary to accomplish goals and plans.
- Grouping of these activities and assignment of these activities to appropriate departments.
- Delegation of authority and responsibility to carry out the work with proper co-ordination, and
- Preparing the organisation chart which shows the organisation structure.

The logical steps involved in the process of organisation design are:

1. Determination of Objectives, Strategies, Plans and Policies: Organisation is a tool which is applied for the attainment of the objectives of the business. The objectives should be clear, precise and complete because the entire organisation is to be built around the objectives of the enterprise. Objectives decide the purpose of organisation and the nature of work to be accomplished through the organisation.

2. Determination of Activities: The next step is to determine activities needed to execute these plans and policies and accomplish the objectives. From the objective of the company the principle activities are determined. The work load is broken down into component activities that are to be performed by all the employees. The activities are so split to determine the job which can be performed by an individual.

3. Separation and Grouping of Activities: It is necessary to classify and group the activities in the best possible way. To attain the benefits of specialization and division of labour, every company, will separate its activities on the basis of primary function — finance, engineering, purchasing, production, sales and industrial relations. All the similar or directly related activities are grouped together in the form of departments. They can be further subdivided into sections. For example, the manufacturing function and the department handling it may be subdivided according to the products, processes or type of equipment ; and the selling department may be subdivided according to the territory, type of product or class of customers. The subdivision should be definite and avoid overlapping.

All groups must have approximately same workload. If there is expansion of certain activities in one group, sub-grouping or rearrangement of certain activities should be done. In small business unit, purchasing, storekeeping, machine operations, repairing, quality control are combined in one group, viz. production activities while in large scale industries there are separate purchase department, stores, maintenance, quality control department etc.

4. Delegation of Authority: The right given to superior for directing and guiding the actions of his subordinates to extract the work from them (smoothly and efficiently without any friction) is called "Authority".

Authority is necessary for the performance of the job and therefore authority is delegated to the subordinates for enabling them to carry out their work smoothly and efficiently.

Authority in other words is "the right to command and exercise one's absolute power which compels others to behave in a desired way". The authority, always flows from superior to subordinates. For example, the works manager, by virtue of his authority, directs a foreman to arrange production of a job in this shop and the foreman in turn exercises his authority over his workers and directs them to produce the same.

5. Delegation of Responsibility: Responsibility must always be accompanied by the authority. Responsibility may be described as the obligation and accountability for the performance of delegated duties. A superior is always accountable for the acts of his subordinates. Therefore, responsibility always flows from subordinates to superior. A worker has the responsibility to perform a task as directed by foreman. The foreman, in turn, is under obligation to manage to do as directed by his superior (the production superintendent). In any organisation, the superior is held responsible for the actions of his subordinates and the subordinates are accountable for the work to their superiors. Effective management necessitates a clear flow of formal authority and responsibility.

6. To Establish Interrelationships: The grouped activities are placed in the overall organisation structure at appropriate level. It is necessary to integrate or tie these groups of activities: (a) through authority relationship horizontally, vertically and laterally, and (b) through organised information or communication systems i.e., with the help of effective co-ordination and communication.

By integration of activities we have unity of objectives, team work and team spirit. It establishes harmony of efforts of different individuals and groups avoiding the conflicts arising out of it.

7. Providing Physical Facilities and Proper Environment: It is necessary to provide right type of physical facilities and create environment for the smooth running and prosperity of the organisation. Physical facilities may include machinery, tools, equipments, infrastructure etc. Right environment means proper lighting, ventilation, heating, cooling arrangements at the workplace, reasonable hours of work, rest pauses, safety devices, job security, job satisfaction and above all human approach by the management.

8. Preparation of Organisation Chart: An organisation chart is then prepared. Organisation chart is a graphic means or record which shows the formal organisation structure. It shows the formal superior-subordinate relationships. A chart is a blueprint of company. It shows who supervises and controls whom and how the various units / departments or sections are interrelated. It gives visual ideas about formal relationships by showing the main line of authority, the main lines of communications, and the flow of authority (downwards) as well as the flow of accountability (upwards) throughout all the levels and management hierarchy.

2.4 PRINCIPLES OF ORGANISATION

Efficiency of the enterprise depends on the organisational structure. Some of the important principles to be followed for developing sound and efficient organisation structure are:

1. Consideration of Unity of Objectives: The objectives of the enterprise influence the organisation structure. The organisation is a mechanism to achieve the objectives of the business. In view of this, the objectives must be clearly defined for the entire enterprise, for each department and even for each position in the organisation structure. There must be unity of objectives so that all efforts can be concentrated on achieving the set goals at minimum cost.

2. Principle of Specialization: Effective organisation must include specialization. Precise division of work facilitates specialization. The organisation structure should be formulated in such a way that the activities of the enterprise are divided according to functions. Work should be distributed among the persons very carefully on the basis of their skill, experience and ability to do that work.

3. Principle of Authority: Authority empowers the superior to make a subordinate to do the work. Everybody in the organisation, from top level downwards should be given some authority to secure co-operation from subordinates. Lines of authority should be clearly established in the structure of organisation in order to avoid overlapping actions, omission of acts etc.

4. Principle of Co-ordination: The organisational structure should be such that different departments co-ordinate with each other to achieve the common goals. Co-ordination is necessary for unity of action i.e., to facilitate integration of the basic managerial function.

5. Principle of Unity of Command: According to this principle, each sub-ordinate should have only one superior and dual sub-ordination should be avoided. For example, X is the boss of Y ; Y is accountable to X. Y is the boss of Z ; Z is accountable to Y. Thus, no one in the organisation should have more than one boss. This principle avoids the possibility of conflicts in instruction and develops a sense of personal responsibility for the work.

6. Principle of Span of Control: The number of persons who are directly responsible to the executive is called the *span of control*. No single executive should have more people looking to him for controlling and guidance than he can reasonably manage, because (a) The time at the disposal of the executive is limited (b) He has limited available energy/capacity. The number of persons which can be effectively supervised by a single executive should be limited to six in average firm. However, where the operations are routine or automatic, executive can direct a large number upto 20.

2.5 FORMS OF ORGANISATION

The organisation structure is a skeleton of a framework that divides the total activities into related groups, develops superior and subordinate relationship among the persons by prescribing the authorities.

Thus, it indicates the hierarchy (persons arranged according to rank), authority structure and reporting relationships (who should report to whom).

The organisational structure differs from industry to industry. It usually depends upon:

(i) Size of the organisation.

(ii) Nature of the product being manufactured.

(iii) Complexity of the problems being faced.

There are *four* main types of organisation structure:
- Line Organisation
- Line and Staff Organisation
- Functional Organisation
- Project Organisation

2.5.1 Line, Military or Scalar Organisation

This is the simplest and earliest type of organisation. It is also called as Military or Scalar Organisation (Fig. 2.1).

In this type of organisation, the line of authority flows directly from top to bottom and the line of responsibility from bottom to top in opposite direction. In line organisation, the business activities are divided into *three* groups:

(i) Finance or Accounts,

(ii) Production,

(iii) Sales (Distribution).

Each of these departments is subdivided into certain self-contained departments or sections. Each departmental head has complete control over his section and he is fully authorized to select his labour, staff, purchases of raw materials, stores and to set the standards of output etc. The responsibility of each departmental head is clearly defined. Each department works as a self-supporting unit.

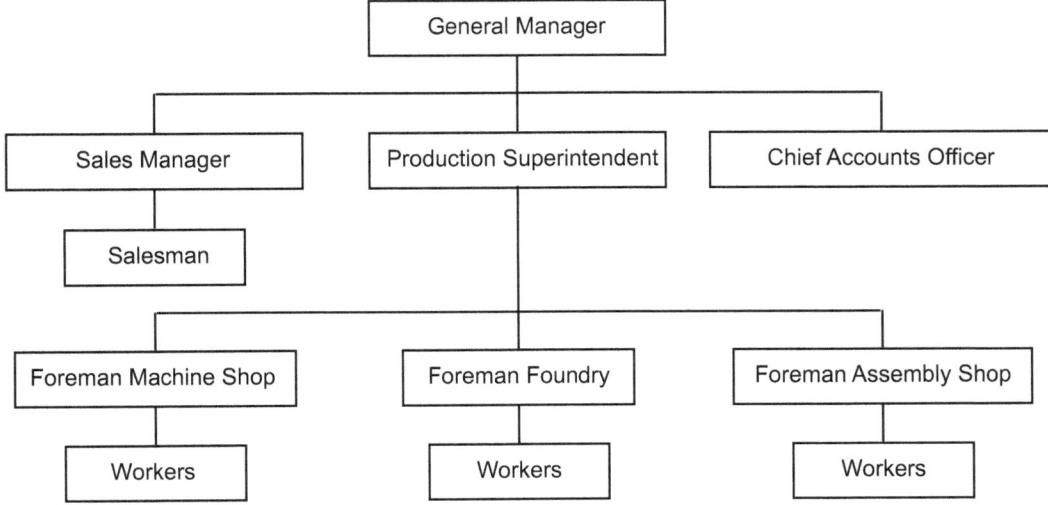

Fig. 2.1: Line organisation

The following diagram shows the chart of the organisation. The General Manager is the overall in-charge. The whole work is divided into *three* sections *viz. Production, Distribution* and *Finance* and given into the charge of each departmental head. The line of authority flows from General Manager (G.M.) to three departmental heads, from there it moves down to the labour through lesser and lesser superior bosses. However, the line of responsibility flows in opposite direction i.e., labour is responsible to the foreman, each foreman is to the production superintendent and these executives independently are responsible to the General Manager. In this type, all men of the same authority level are independent of all others similarly situated.

Advantages

1. **Simplicity:** It is easy to establish and simple to understand. The entire activities are broadly grouped into departments. The departmental head has the sole authority over his department. The different departmental heads are put at the same level of authority, each having a complete command over his department.

2. **Clear cut Authority and Responsibility:** The delegation of authorities and assignment of responsibilities are clear and precise. There are no chances of authority conflicts and shifting of responsibilities.

3. **Strong in Discipline:** Due to unity of command and unified control it is possible to maintain strict discipline. There is a clear cut authority and responsibility. The duties and responsibilities of each individual are clearly defined.

4. **Unity of Command:** It establishes clear cut superior-subordinate relationships. Each subordinate is responsible to only one superior. This develops a sense of responsibility and loyalty.

5. **Quick Decisions:** The entire management is in the hands of one individual namely General Manager, quick decisions and speedy actions are therefore possible.

6. **Rapid Communication:** There is a clear channel of communication, which results in rapid communications of orders, suggestions and instructions.

7. **Co-ordination:** The complete responsibility is in the hands of the heads and therefore effective co-ordination within the department is obtained.

8. **Development of All-round Executive:** The departmental head has to look after all the activities of his department, therefore, it encourages the development of all round executive at the higher level of authority.

9. It is flexible to expand or contract and stable.

Disadvantages

1. **Undue Reliance:** The success of the enterprise depends upon the caliber and ability of few departmental heads. Loss of one or two capable men may put the organisation in difficulties.

2. **Personal Limitations (Lack of specialization):** In this type or organisation an individual executive is supposed to discharge different types of duties. He cannot do justice to all different activities, because he cannot be specialized in all trades.

3. **Overload of Work:** Departmental heads are overloaded with various routine jobs, hence they cannot spare time for important managerial functions like planning, development, budgeting etc.

4. **Dictatorial Way:** In line organisation, too much authorities centre around line executives. Hence it encourages dictatorial way of working.

5. **Duplication of Work:** Conflicting policies of different departments result in duplication of work.

6. **Unsuitable for Large Concerns:** It is limited to small concerns.

7. **General Interest of Enterprise may be Over-looked:** Departments may work for their self-interest and may sacrifice the general interest of the enterprise.

8. **Scope of Favourism:** As the departmental head has the supreme authority, there are chances of favourism.
9. **Wastage of Materials and Man hours:** Because of lack of specialization perhaps there may be more wastage of materials and man hours.

Applications

Line organisation can work satisfactorily under following conditions:

(i) Small enterprises free from complexities.

(ii) Automatic and continuous process industries such as paper, sugar, textile etc.

(iii) Where few activities are to be performed.

(iv) Less number of workers are employed.

(v) Where the work is routine e.g., Government department.

2.5.2 Line and Staff Organisation

Line and staff organisation is that in which the line heads are assisted by specialist staff.

If the firm is of large size, managers cannot give careful attention to every aspect of management. They are busy with ordinary task of production and selling. Hence staff is deputed to do the work of investigation, research, recording and advising to managers. Thus, the staff brings specialization by assisting the line officers. The line maintains discipline and stability, staff provides experts information and helps to improve overall efficiency. Thus, the staff are thinkers while the line are doers.

Usually the staff has no administrative authority. They serve only in advisory capacity in their field of specialization.

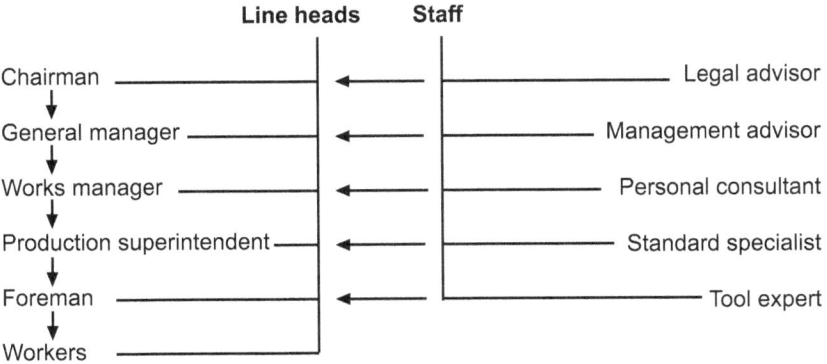

Fig. 2.2: Line and staff organisation

Advantages

1. **Planned Specialization:** The line and staff is a duplex organisation, dividing the whole work into creative plan and action plan. The creative plan is concerned with original thinking and the action plan takes care of the execution of work. Line executives therefore, have enough time to organize, control and supervise the production effectively.

2. **Well-defined Authority and Responsibility:** The line officers have definite responsibility and authority. The subordinates receive order only from one superior. Therefore, it is possible to maintain strict discipline.

3. **Availability of Specialized Knowledge:** The staff with expert knowledge provides opportunities to the line officers for adopting a rational multidimensional views towards a problem. Therefore it helps to take sound decisions.

4. **Adaptability to Progressive Business:** This type of organisation contains good features of both line as well as functional organisation. Specialized staff can devote their time for planning, method study research, collection of data etc. Therefore, line and staff organisation is most suitable for progressive and flourishing business. Most of the industries in India today are using this plan after slightly modifying it to meet their specific needs.

5. **Less Wastage:** There will be less wastage of material.

6. **Improved Quality:** Quality of the product will be better.

Disadvantages

1. **Chances of Mis-interpretation:** Although the expert's advice is available, yet it reaches the workers through line supervisors. The line officers may fail to understand the meaning of advice and there is always a risk of misunderstanding and misinterpretation.

2. **Chances of Friction:** There are bound to be occasions when the line and staff may differ in opinion may result in conflict of interests and prevents a harmonious relationship between the two.

3. **Ineffective Staff in the Absence of Authority:** The staff have no authority to execute their own advice. Their advice is not a binding on the line officers. Therefore, the advice given by specialists may be ignored by line heads.

4. **Expensive:** The overhead cost of the product increases because of high salaried specialized staff.

5. **Lithargic Staff Officer in the Absence of Accountability:** The line officer is accountable for the success or failure of his action, not the staff officer. This may make the staff officer indifferent. He may not stretch his talents to give the right advice.

6. **Loss of Initiative by Line Executive:** If they start depending too much on staff it may loose their initiative drive and ingenuity.

Application

Line and staff organisation is generally followed by all Government and Private concerns involving complicated processes or operations i.e., big steel plants, heavy electricals, electricity boards, large manufacturing plants etc.

2.5.3 Functional Organisation

F.W. Taylor suggested functional organisation, because it was difficult to find all-round persons qualified to work at middle management levels in the line organisation.

Functional organisation divides managerial activities, so that each head from the works manager down has few functions to perform as possible and is able to become specialist in these. Authority from top to down is delegated according to the function. In this type of organisation, specialists like production engineer, design engineer, maintenance engineer, purchase officer etc. are employed.

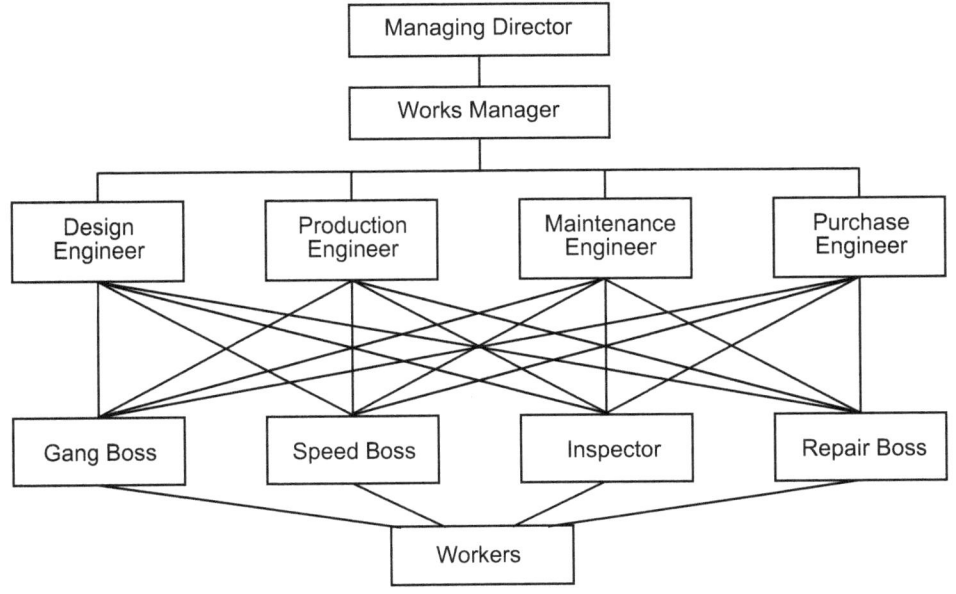

Fig. 2.3: Functional organisation

Each specialist is supposed to give his functional advice to all other foremen and workers. Taylor divided the responsibility of shop supervision among several foreman, each specially qualified and in charge of certain aspect of work. Each specialist is authorised to give orders to workers, but only in regard of his field of specialization.

Fig. 2.3 illustrates a typical organisation chart of functional organisation. The Specialists, Design Engineer, Production Engineer, Maintenance Engineer, Purchase officer gives functional advice to all foreman (supervisors) and guide them in their respective field of specialization only. The shop supervisors (e.g., gang boss, speed boss, inspector and repair boss) supervise and help the workers, each foreman assisting only in his particular function. The gang foreman directs the setting up of tools into machine and the efficient movement from machine to machine. The speed foreman instructs workers in proper use of cutting tools and machine operations so that they may reach a specified rate of output. The inspection foreman regulates the quality of the work. The repair foreman supervises upkeep and maintenance, and guides the workers regarding routine lubrication, cleaning and upkeep of machines.

Advantages

1. **Separation of Work:** In functional organisation, mental work has been separated from routine work. The specialist has been given the authority and responsibility for supervision and administration pertaining to their field of specialization unnecessary over-loading of responsibilities is thus avoided.

2. **Specialization:** Specialization and skilled supervisory attention is given to workers. The result is increased in rate of production and improves quality of work.

3. **Narrow range with high depth:** The narrow range of activities enables the functional expert to develop in-depth understanding in his particular area of activity.

4. **Ease in Selection and Training:** Functional organisation is based upon expert knowledge. The availability of guidance through experts make it possible to train the workers properly in comparatively short span of time.

5. **Standardised Operations:** The work of subordinates is divided into standard parts. Expert knowledge is available for each part. The job requirements of each part are definite, clear and few.

6. **Reduction in Prime Cost:** Since for every operation expert guidance is there, wastage of material, is reduced and this helps to reduce prime cost.

7. **Scope for Growth and Development of Business:** This type of organisation presents ample scope for the growth and development of business.

8. **Standardization:** It helps mass production by standardization and specialization.

Disadvantages

1. **Indiscipline:** Since the workers receive instructions from number of specialists (which may be conflicting) it leads to confusion to whom they should follow. Therefore, it is difficult to maintain discipline.

2. **Shifting of Responsibility:** It is difficult for the top management to locate responsibility for the unsatisfactory work. Everybody tries to shift responsibilities on others for the faults and failures.

3. **Kills the Initiative of Workers:** As the specialized guidance is available to the workers, the workers will not be using their talents and skill, therefore their initiative cannot be utilized.

4. **Overlapping of Authority:** The spheres of authority tends to overlap and gives rise to friction between the persons of equal rank.

5. **Lack of Co-ordination between Functions:** Except the function in which he is specialized he is absolutely indifferent to other functions. Therefore, there is a lack of co-ordination of function and efforts.

6. **Increase in Cost:** High salary is paid to the experts employed. This increases the total cost of the job.

2.5.4 Project Organisation

Depending on the authority that is given to the person responsible for the project, the project organisation may take one of the following forms:

- Line and staff organisation (project manager as a staff assistant to chief executive).
- Project manager as a specialized staff function.
- Matrix organisation.

1. Project Manager as a Staff Assistant Chief to the Executive

Fig. 2.4 shows an arrangement in which the project manager serves as a staff assistant to the chief executive. The project manager, in this position, has no authority. He does not make any decision for the project, nor does he provide any staff service to the functional departments. The project manager merely collects information and communicates the same to the chief executive. He may influence some decisions taken by the chief executive or by functional departments, but he cannot himself make any decisions which can become binding for others. This arrangement may be chosen by a chief executive who wants to directly control the project but cannot devote much time to keep track of details.

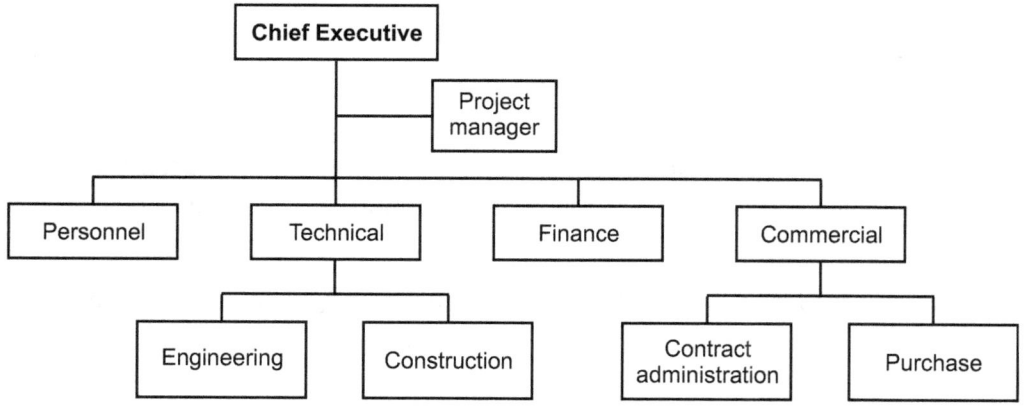

Fig. 2.4: Project manager as a staff assistant to the chief executive

2. Project Manager as a Specialized Staff Function

The project manager, in this case, will be a specialist in project management tools and techniques, and in view of his superior knowledge relating to scheduling, budgeting and information systems, he is in the best position to advise other functions. He can carry out service activities like collection and transmission of data, follow-up of one functional group to service another group, maintain records, measure progress, analyse progress and prepare progress reports. He may advise the functional groups but a final decision would rest with the functional groups. He does not have any authority which can shape the destiny of the project.

Most companies tend to use this arrangement when project management is used for the first time in the company as this does not require much change in the working of the organisation.

2.6 TYPES OF OWNERSHIP

Modern business is carried out by the following types of ownership organisations (form of business organisation):

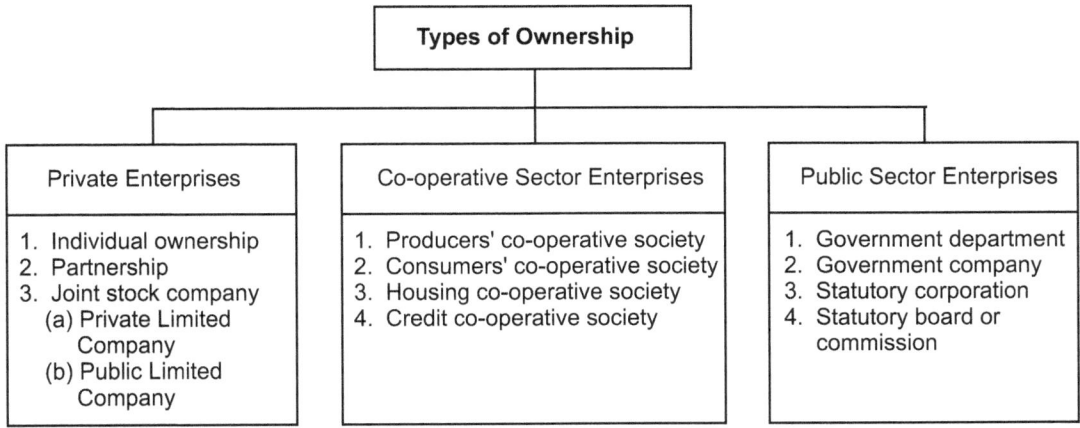

Fig. 2.5: Types of ownership organisation

2.6.1 Individual Ownership (Proprietorship)

This is the simplest and oldest form of business organisation.

In this type of enterprise the individual entrepreneur supplies the entire capital (even if he has to borrow). He organises and manages the business himself, and takes the entire risk. The entire authority and responsibility in the matter of decision making, policy making and working belongs to him and all profits and losses are of his own. If necessary he can employ some persons to assist him. This type of business can be started by any one having initiative, tact, selling aptitude and little capital to enter into business. It is owned, managed and controlled by only one man, hence it is also called as one man business.

Legal Liability: His legal liability covers all his possessions. The creditor can collect his personal property.

Applications

This form of ownership is most satisfactory in the following cases:

1. For small scale business requiring small capital which can be spared by one man, for example, agriculture, small scale industries, cottage industries, retail trade, handicrafts, professional services, commercial shops etc.
2. Where the risk covered is not too heavy.
3. Where management by one man is possible.
4. Where local market is available.

Advantages

1. **Simple and easy:** This type of ownership is simple in nature and easy to manage. The labour knows for whom they are working and to whom they are accountable.

2. **Least legal formalities:** It does not involve much legal formalities or other complicated procedure to start the business. Only a formal licence from the local authority is necessary.

3. **Quick decisions and prompt actions:** The whole business is controlled by one man, therefore, he can take and implement the decisions quickly and in right time. Quick decisions and prompt action enable the entrepreneur to take advantage of business opportunities for gains.

4. **Quality production:** Since the owner takes all the risks, he gives personal attention and supervision to the products made. This may result in reduction in waste and better quality products.

5. **Better labour relationship:** Since the business is small, the number of workers are less and the owner comes in close contact with the workers. This helps to maintain good employer-employee relationship.

6. **Personal attention to customers:** Since the business is small it is possible to pay personal attention to customers and their requirements and to give them entire satisfactions by overcoming their complaints about the product.

7. **Small capital:** Since capital required is small, talented men of small means can start independent business of their own and earn living.

8. **Maintenance of secrecy:** The individual entrepreneur can easily maintain the secrets of the business as he only know everything of his enterprise.

9. **Incentive:** The direct relationship between efforts and rewards acts as an incentive to the owner to put his best efforts to manage the business efficiently and increase his earning. Self-interest can be a driving force to secure economy and efficiency.

10. **Flexibility:** The individual ownership is highly flexible as it is capable of adjustment to the requirements of changing business conditions.

Disadvantages

1. **Limited capital:** Due to limited capital it is not possible to expand the business even if it is much profitable.

2. **Unlimited liability:** In case the owner is not able to pay the debts, the same can be recovered out of the sale of his business assets and personal property. The individual owner will have to think twice before adopting new and risky ventures, latest and

new methods etc. as his private property is constantly in danger of meeting the debts and obligations of his business.

3. **Personal limitations:** The individual owner has to control all the aspects of his business alone. He cannot be expert in all techniques like management, sales, engineering, processes etc. Further growth and expansion of business may not be possible due to want of proper and adequate organising power.

4. **Small income:** Inspite of all efforts, such a business can yield only a small income. The resources are limited. Many profitable ventures are ruled out.

5. **Cannot compete with a big business:** Since the business is small, it cannot compete with a big business producing the same articles.

6. **Short life:** If the owner dies, the business may collapse. Because, his successors may be incapable or not interested in this type of business. Disability, prolonged illness or death of owner may result in the business coming to standstill or its closure unless his successors take the interest and ability to run the business.

7. **Division of labour is not possible:** The owner as well as the worker has to perform variety of activities, therefore they cannot be specialized in a particular activity.

8. **No economies of large scale:** Economies of large scale manufacturing, buying and selling cannot be obtained on account of small size organisation.

2.6.2 Partnership Organisation

Sometimes the one man business reaches such a stage of development that it becomes impossible for one man to control the business and to contribute the necessary capital. The original entrepreneur may become too old for work. It would seem essential to take a younger person into a partnership to prevent the firm from decaying. Partnership may also be formed to start a new business altogether. Partnership is usually formed to combine capital, labour and varied specialized skills or abilities.

Partnership business is owned by two or more persons (upto 20) who share the powers, responsibilities and profits according to an agreement reached amongst themselves.

A person may possess exceptional business ability, experience, talent but no capital, he can have a financing partner. A financier may need a managerial expert as well as a technical expert and all of them may combine to set up a business with common ownership and management by mutual agreement to form a partnership business.

According to Indian Partnership Act 1932, Partnership is defined as,

"the relation between two or more persons who have agreed to share profit of a business, carried on by all or any of them acting for all".

Formation

Partnership can be formed either verbally or by written agreement but to avoid the possibility of conflict at a later stage, it is advisable to enter into written agreement. The written agreement is known as "Partnership Deed". The partnership deed contains the terms and conditions relating to partnership and the regulations governing its internal management. It also lays down the rights and duties of the partners. The deed is a duly stamped and sealed document containing the terms of contract is also registered in a Court of Law. Thus, a partnership deed enjoys legal status and it serves as legal evidence in future to settle any dispute or differences.

The partnership deed should have the following details:

1. Name of the firm.
2. Nature of business.
3. Date of starting partnership.
4. Duration of partnership.
5. Rate of interest on capital invested, if any.
6. Money contributed by each partner.
7. Allotment of managerial functions among the partners.
8. Share of profit and losses.
9. Salary, if any allowed to managing partners.
10. The basis for the inclusion of any new partners.
11. The amount which can be withdrawn by each partner.
12. The aim of partnership as well as the manner in which it can be dissolved.
13. Accounts of the firm and authority for signing cheques, bills of exchange etc.
14. Provision of Arbitration for settling the disputes that may arise in future. In absence of any agreement, profits and losses are shared equally as per the provisions of the Indian Partnership Act, 1932.

The partners have to prepare a statement which will have the following particulars:

1. Name of the firm.
2. Place of business — principal place and branches, if any.
3. Name and addresses of all partners.
4. Date of joining the firm in case of every partner.
5. Duration, if any.

The statement should be duly dated and signed by all partners. It is required to be submitted to the Registrar of Firms along with necessary registration fees. All subsequent changes in the constitution of the partnership incoming and outgoing partners etc. will have to be communicated to the Registrar within 14 days of such alterations.

Types of Partners

1. **General partners:** All the partners who participate in the working of the firm and are responsible jointly with other partner, for all liabilities, obligations and defects of the firm are the general partners.

2. **Limited partners:** The liability for debts of the limited partners is limited to the extent of their contributed capital. They are not entitled to interfere in the administration of the firm.

3. **Active or managing partners:** Active partners are those who take active part in the management and formulation of policies. Sometimes they get salaries in addition to the normal profits as partners.

4. **Sleeping and silent partners:** They do not take any active part in the business. They simply contribute their capital in the business and get their share in the profit of the firm. They are liable for all liabilities of the firm as partners.

5. **Nominal partners:** They lend their reputed name for the company's reputation. They do not invest money and do not take any active part in the management.

6. **Minor partners:** Minor partners are those whose age is below 18 years and associated with the business. Such partners can be allowed only with the consent of other partners. Their liability is limited to their investment only. Within six months of attaining the age of majority, they have to give public notice about their desire to serve or continue their connection with the firm. In such a case, they will be regarded as full-fledged partner with unlimited liability.

Advantages

1. **Easy formations:** The formation of partnership is easier as compared to joint stock companies. Voluntary mutual agreement is enough to start the partnership. Procedure for registration is simple and also registration is not compulsory.

2. **More capital:** Two or more partners combine their resources in partnership, therefore, the amount of capital is larger as compared with individual ownership.

3. **Diverse talent:** In this type of organisation, persons possessing different abilities and skills may come together. Persons having good ideas and experience of business make partnership with rich people. Thus, money and knowledge both are combined to earn profit.

4. **Less possibility of error of judgement:** A problem is examined from more than one point of view, therefore the decision arrived at is likely to be sounder than in one man business.

5. **Prompt decisions:** There are limited number of partners who are in continuous and intimate touch with each other. Therefore prompt decisions can be taken, and organisation can decide on, a suitable course of action before it is too late.

6. **Large economics:** As compared to individual ownership, the advantage of division of labour, specialization, standardization and economics of large purchasing are more.

7. **Personal factor:** Partnership can maintain personal relationship with employees and the customers.

8. **Divisions of labour:** The partners can divide the work among themselves on the basis of their personal capabilities. Therefore they can run the business more efficiently.

9. **Simple dissolution:** The partnership business can be dissolved easily. The partnership is purely voluntary association.

   It can be dissolved by giving 14 days notice to other partners.

10. **Cautious and sound approach:** As the private property of every partner is constantly in danger of meeting all business obligations of the firm, partners will have to think twice before undertaking any highly speculative/risky business.

    The unlimited liability can also act as the best security for raising loans or advances because private property of all partners can be used as additional security in addition to the property and assets of partnership organisation.

Disadvantages

1. **Unlimited liability:** Because of unlimited liability any one partner can be held liable for the whole debt of the firm. This frightens away-the moneyed people. They are reluctant to join those who have ability, skill but no capital.

2. **Short life:** After the death or retirement of any one partner, the partnership may come to an end.

3. **Insufficient capital:** It can raise much less capital as compared to joint stock company. This prevents the expansion of the business to take advantage of increased demand.

4. **Disagreement:** Sometimes due to misunderstanding friction may arise between the partners which adversely affects the efficiency and expansion of the business.

5. **Less secrecy:** A partner may withdraw from the firm and establish his own enterprise with the knowledge of the secrets of the business.
6. **Non-transfer of partnership:** No partner can transfer his interest in the firm to any body without the unanimous consent of other partners.
7. **No direct relation between efforts and rewards:** The profits are shared by the partners. So, there is no incentive for hard working. Sometimes it encourages lavish expenditure.
8. **Lack of public confidence:** As the financial matters are strictly confined to partners only, and in absence of any strict legal control over the affairs of partnership, there is much less public confidence in partnership. It creates suspension in the mind of the outsiders who are dealing with firm.

Suitability of Partnership

Partnership is an ideal form of organisation for small scale and medium size business where there is a limited market, limited risk of loss and limited capital and limited specialization in management is needed. Examples are: wholesale trade, retail trade, commercial forming, small scale industries, local enterprises, warehousing, transport services, professional services, marketing services etc.

2.6.3 Distinction between Individual Ownership and Partnership

No.	Parameter	Individual Ownership	Partnership
1.	Membership	Individual Owner. (One Man Business)	Minimum 2, Maximum 50.
2.	Requirement for its formation	No agreement is required for its formation.	An agreement (Partnership Deed)
3.	Capital	Limited capital contributed by only owner.	Comparatively large capital, contributed by number of partners.
4.	Registration	Not necessary.	Registration is necessary under the Partnership Act 1932.
5.	Risk/Profit	Individual owner has to bear the risk and enjoys the entire profit.	Risk spread out amongst the partners. Profit is shared according to the agreement between themselves.

Contd...

6.	Management	Individual owner has to manage the entire business.	The management of the business is shared by the partners.
7.	Secrecy	The individual entrepreneur can easily maintain the secrets of the business.	A partner may withdraw from the firm and establish his own enterprise with the knowledge and secrets of business.
8.	Soundness of decisions	An individual owner may not be expert in all aspects of business, hence sometimes his decisions may go wrong.	The problem is examined from more than one point of view, hence decisions arrived are likely to be sounder.
9.	Suitability	Suitable for small scale business.	Suitable for small as well as medium scale business.
10.	Division of labour	Not possible.	The partners divide the work among themselves. Division of labour is thus possible to some extent.

2.7 JOINT STOCK COMPANY

The industrial revolution brought about a radical change in the system of production and commerce. With the introduction of factory system, large-scale organisation and mass scale production came into being. With the change in the scale of production from small scale to large scale and with the widening of the market from local to national and international, the individual ownership and partnership firms with their limited capital, short life span, limited managerial skill and unlimited liability failed to meet needs of the time. This resulted in the evolution of joint stock company. The companies are formed and registered under the Indian Companies Act, 1956.

In this type, capital is contributed by large number of persons, in the form of shares of different values. Persons who purchase the shares are called shareholders and the managing body known as "Board of Directors" is elected by the shareholders. The shares are transferable.

A simple but comprehensive definition of the company can be given as under:

"A company is an artificial person having an independent legal entity and a perpetual succession with a distinctive name and a common seal having a common capital divided into shares of fixed value which are transferable and carry limited liability".

Characteristics of Joint Stock Company

The following are some of the characteristics of joint stock company:

1. A company is created by registering or incorporating an association of persons under the Company Act.
2. It has a separate legal existence as distinct from its members.
3. Artificial personality enabling it to exercise certain legal powers.
4. Perpetual life and a very stable existence.
5. It has a common seal on which its name is engraved and this common seal acts as its signature. It is affixed on all important legal documents and contracts.
6. There is a complete separation of ownership from management.
7. Liability of shareholders is limited.
8. Lower tax liability.
9. Easy transferability of shares.
10. There is a wide distribution of risk of loss.
11. Large membership.
12. Statutory regulations as provided in the Indian Companys' Act, 1956.

Joint Stock Company (Definition)

The joint stock company is legal business owned by the shareholders having limited liability, and managed by an elected "Board of Directors". The most important type of business organisation today is the joint stock company. Infact, a business on respectable scale can be organised only in this manner.

Formation of Joint Stock Company

An entrepreneur (promoter) prepares a scheme of business, he secures the co-operation of at least six more persons, because the minimum number of persons to form a company is seven. The promoters of the company prepare the following document:

(a) Memorandum of Association.
(b) Articles of Association.
(c) A list of persons who have consented to be the Directors of the Company along with the consent in writing of such persons.
(d) A declaration by an advocate to the effect that all the requirements of the Act have been fulfilled.
(e) Name and address of promoters.

The memorandum of association contains:

1. The name of the company.
2. Its aims and objectives.
3. The location of head office.
4. The amount of share capital.
5. The kind and value of each share.
6. A declaration that the liability is limited.

Articles of association contains: Rules and regulations governing the internal management of the company. The rights of the shareholders, Duties, Powers of Directors, Regulations regarding rights to vote and issue of capital etc.

These documents are then submitted to the Registrar of joint company. If the Registrar is satisfied that the requirements of the law have been fulfilled, he issues a certificate of incorporation. The company then comes into existence.

Raising Finance: Funds can be taken from banks and finance corporations etc. in the form of loans, or by selling shares and debentures.

Managing the Business: The shareholders elect the directors to manage the business on their behalf. The board of directors only lays down the general policy and discusses major issues. The day-to-day business is carried on by the salaried manager or the Managing Director.

Organisation Structure

The organisation structure of the joint stock company is as follows:

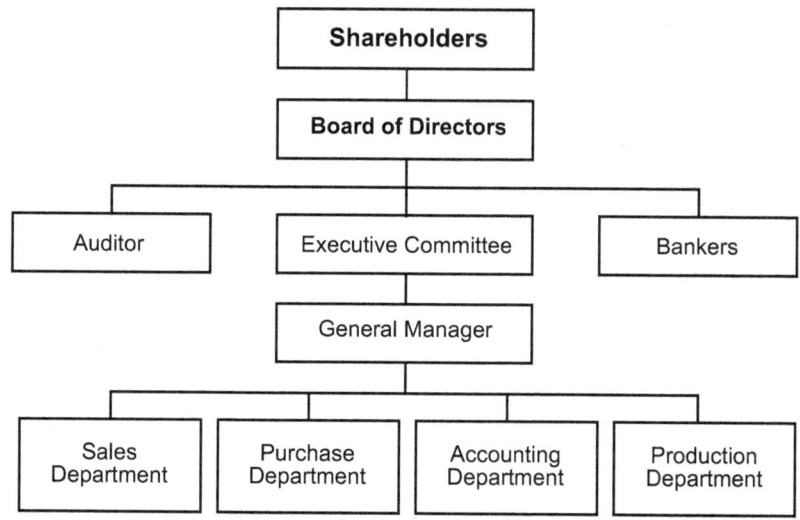

Fig. 2.6: Organisation structure of joint stock company

2.7.1 Types of Joint Stock Company

There are *two* types of Joint Stock company:

1) Private Limited Company, and   2) Public Limited Company.

1) Private Limited Company: This type of company can be formed by two or more members. The maximum number of members is limited to 50 (excluding the employees). The company is registered under the Indian Companys' Act, 1956. In this, the transfer of share is limited to members only and general public cannot be invited to purchase shares.

Normally, the members of such company are friends or relatives. In this system, persons who want to take the advantage of limited liability and at the same time keep the business as private, forms the private limited company. Most of the middle sized industries are run in this manner.

The company need not circulate the Balance Sheet, Profit and Loss Account etc. among its members; but it should hold its annual general meeting and place such financial statements in the meeting. A private Ltd. Company enjoys a separate legal status, continuity of life, benefit of limited liability, larger capital raising power, business secrecy to certain extent and above all the number of privileges and exemptions (not possible for public company) as per Companies' Act.

2) Public Limited Company: As its name indicates, the membership of public limited company is open to general public. The minimum number of persons required to form a public limited company is seven, but there is no upper limit. Such companies can advertise, to offer its shares to general public. Public limited companies are subjected to greater control and supervision of the Government. This control is necessary to protect the interest of the shareholders and the member of the public. Shares are transferable without any prior approval. The affairs of the company are managed by "Board of Directors".

2.7.2 Advantages and Disadvantages of Joint Stock Company

Advantages *of* Joint Stock Company

1. **Economies of large scale:** Joint stock company can take advantage of internal and external economies in buying and selling, lower overhead charges relating to distribution, publicity and administration, research and experiments etc.
2. **Limited liability:** The shareholders have a limited liability. It is limited only to the value of their shares. In case, the company fails, the personal property of the shareholders cannot be claimed by the creditors.
3. **Huge capital:** The capital of the company is raised by the sale of shares. The value of each share is low, this attracts all sorts of people, rich and poor to invest their capital. Therefore, large amount of capital can be raised.
4. **Share transferable:** When the shareholder needs money he can get it by selling his shares.

5. **Economical administration:** The directors have not to be paid salaries but just a fee for attending the Board meeting. Thus, the company can get advice of persons of mature wisdom and good experience at a small cost.
6. **Democratic:** The directors are elected by shareholders in case the shareholders feel that the directors are not working properly they can be removed and new directors chosen in their places.
7. **Permanent existence:** Any number of shareholders may leave it, but the company continues.
8. **Legal control:** The Government exercises control over working of the company. The object is to prevent fraud and to protect the interest of shareholders and the public at large.
9. **Risk spread out:** There are large number of investors and secondly, an individual investor can buy shares of different companies and thus widely distribute his risk of loss.
10. **Mobilization of scarce saving:** Limited liability, transferability of shares and unlimited membership makes the joint stock company a very effective instrument for mobilization of scarce saving of the society towards industrialization.
11. Accelerated economic growth of the country is possible through industrialization.
12. It creates huge employment possibilities.

Disadvantages of Joint Stock Company
1. **Dishonest directors may exploit the shareholders:** The transferability of shares kills the interest of the shareholders, therefore the directors are all in all, they can deceive the shareholders.
2. **Legal complexities:** Its formation, functioning involves very large legal procedures.
3. **It is democratic in theory only:** Due to small capital of each shareholders, transferability of shares and since the shareholders are from different parts of the country, they do not take active interest in the affairs of the company. Therefore, the real power to run and manage the business is in the hands of the directors. The directors, self elected at first manage to get themselves re-elected.
4. **Delay in decisions:** The Board of Directors manages over affairs of a joint stock company and hence quick decisions are not possible. Moreover, there may be disagreement among directors which may hamper the business.
5. **Favourisms:** The directors may show favourism by selecting their own persons for high posts.
6. **Difficult labour relations:** The owners of company have no personal touch with the employees. There are often labour troubles. Inspite of these disadvantages, business on a large scale can only be started and run successfully in this manner.

7. **Lack of initiative and personal interest:** Lack of personal interest on the part of salaried managers may lead to inefficiency and waste (because there is no direct relation between effort and income for them).
8. Concentration of economic power and wealth in a few hands.
9. **Misuse of internal information:** Misuse of internal information by the managing group in bringing wide fluctuations in the market price of equity shares is possible.

Considering both merits and demerits of the company form of organisation, it can be concluded that in the present day world, this form of business organisation is very essential for the industrial development of a country. In the absence of joint stock principle, the exploration of a country's natural resources and its economic and industrial development would not have been possible.

Liquidation

It becomes difficult to run joint stock company if liability becomes much more than assets and when creditors press for payment of loans. In such circumstances, the company has to dissolve or wind up. This is known's liquidation.

Liquidation may be compulsory or voluntary or under the supervision of court. If the resources are not adequate to make the payment, then the assets of the company have to be sold. The amount thus collected is paid to the creditors in proportion of the credit. If some amount is left after payment it is distributed among the shareholders.

2.7.3 Comparison between Private and Public Limited Joint Stock Companies

No.	Particulars	Private Limited Joint Stock Company	Public Limited Joint Stock Company
1.	Membership	The membership is confined to the close friends and relatives of the promoters; they contribute their capital. They cannot invite public to share the capital.	The membership is open to the General Public. Any person interested can contribute and become shareholder.
2.	Limits to Membership	The minimum number of member required is two, while the maximum number is limited to 50.	A minimum of 7 members are required to form the company. There is no limit to the maximum number of members.

Contd...

3.	Election of Directors	There is no need of holding a statutory meeting to elect the director.	The statutory meeting has to be held and the shareholders elect the directors.
4.	Resale of Shares	The shares cannot be resold or transferred without the consent of the company.	The shares cannot be resold or transferred without the consent of the company.
5.	Audit of Accounts	There is no legal provision of the audit of company's account.	The accounts have to be audited legally and circulated among the members of the company.
6.	Minimum Capital	Can be started with any amount without any legal binding.	Minimum lay-down capital is legally required before starting the business.
7.	Name	It has to use words "Private Limited" at the end of its name.	It has to use only the word 'Limited' at the end of its name.
8.	Number of Directors	It has to have minimum 2 directors.	It has to have minimum 3 directors.
9.	Legal Control	There are less legal controls.	Regulations are more strict.
10.	Remuneration of Directors	Restrictions are less for Directors' Remuneration.	Remuneration of Directors is restricted to 11% of the net profits.

2.7.4 Distinction between Partnership and Joint Stock Company

No.	Partnership	Joint Stock Company
1.	In a partnership firm, the liability of the members is unlimited.	Liability is limited to the value of their share.
2.	Minimum number of partners is 2 and maximum number is 20.	In private limited company, minimum number of shareholders is 2 and maximum number is 50. In public limited company, minimum number of members is 7 and there is no maximum limit.
3.	A partnership firm has no separate legal entity.	A joint stock company has a legal existence.

Contd...

4.	Limited capital.	Large amount of capital can be collected.
5.	It is managed by the partners.	It is managed by the elected board of directors.
6.	The partners cannot transfer his share without the consent of all other partners.	In public limited company the shares are transferable ; but not in private limited company.
7.	It has short life. The partnership may come to an end due to death or retirement of any partner.	It has permanent/perpetual existence.
8.	It can be started very easily. Procedure for registration is simple and moreover registration is not compulsory.	Its formation, functioning involves very large legal procedures.
9.	Selfish attitude among partners may create difficulties in business.	Smooth and efficient management is possible as it works on the democratic principles.
10.	There are no restrictions of keeping detailed accounts and they are not required to be submitted to Government.	It has obligation to keep detailed accounts of business and present the balance sheet and audit report (by some authorized Chartered Accountant) to the Government.
11.	It is governed by the Partnership Act, 1932.	It is governed by the Indian Companies Act of 1956.

2.8 CO-OPERATIVE ORGANISATIONS (SOCIETIES)

Small scale and cottage industries were gradually replaced by large scale industries as a result of Industrial Revolution. The wealth began to concentrate in few hands. It divided the society into two classes – the capitalists and the poor. The capitalists tried to exploit the poor through long working hours, poor wages, bad working conditions etc. Similarly, with the expansion of market from the local to national and international boundaries, there appeared very long chain of middlemen and intermediaters in the channel of distribution, trying to link the primary producer and the ultimate consumer. This created extraordinary differences in the two prices, producers' price and the price at which ultimate customers get the product. The hardship suffered by exploited class compelled it to unite for their economic uplift through self and mutual help. The co-operative movement was evolved. The industrial co-operative and consumers co-operative societies were developed in Germany. Later on it spread all over the other countries of the world.

Definition of Co-operative Organisation

Co-operation is a form of organisation, wherein persons, irrespective of caste, creed and religion, voluntarily associate together, as human beings, on the basis of equality for the fulfillment of their common economic interests.

The International Labour Organisation gave a comprehensive definition of a co-operative organisation as follows:

"A Co-operative organisation is an association of persons, usually of limited means, who have voluntarily joined together to achieve a common economic end through the formation of a democratically controlled organisation, making equitable contributions to the capital required, and accepting a fair share of risks and benefits of the undertaking".

Mr. N. Barrow defined co-operative society as:

"A voluntary organisation of persons with unrestricted membership and collectively own funds. Consisting of wage earners and small producers, united on democratic basis for the establishment of enterprises under joint management for the purpose of improving their household or business economy".

A simple definition can be stated as,

"A co-operative society is a voluntary association of economically weak persons who work for achievement of their common economic objectives on the basis of equality and mutual service.

The definitions given above clearly illustrate the distinctive characteristics of the principles of co-operative organisation.

Thus, if we have (i) Common need, (ii) Its full realization by all, and (iii) Willingness to seek the common objective by joint action, the only method is co-operation. Co-operative spirit is the heart of a co-operative society. "Each shall work for all and all for each" is the motto of co-operation.

The members supply the capital, manage the business and share all profits and losses. The main object of co-operative society is to promote self help and mutual assistance among men of moderate means and income, having needs and interest in common. Such men are industrial workers, small artisans, agriculturists and members of middle class.

Mutual trust, mutual supervision, self-reliance, spontaneity and equality are the five pillars of a co-operative organisation and co-operative spirit is the backbone.

Distinctive Features/Characteristics of Co-operative Organisation

Main characteristics of co-operative organisation are as follows:

1. **Voluntary organisations:** Co-operative society is a voluntary organisation. A member can continue his membership as long as he desires and can withdraw his capital and discontinue his membership by giving a notice.

2. **Open membership:** There is no limit to its members. Membership is open to all adults, whether man or woman, rich or poor without any distinction of caste, creed and religion. Value of each share is quite less which a poor can also afford.

3. **Economic and democratic management:** The management is based on democratic lines of equality. Every member can cast only one vote irrespective of the number of shares he may hold. A man having only one share can become the president of the cooperative organisation. Generally, the management is honorary.

4. **Profit is not important:** The objective of co-operative society is to promote self-help and mutual assistance and thus to serve the members and not to earn profit.

5. **Spirit of co-operation:** Under co-operative, service is of primary importance and self-interest is of secondary importance. "Each for all and all for each" is the moto of co-operative organisation.

6. **Unity:** Unity of joint action is the basis of co-operation.

7. **Common interest:** The members come together to fulfill their common interest. It may be a social or economic activity such as agriculture trade, finance, manufacturing etc.

8. **Co-operative status:** A co-operative society has to be registered under separate legislation. It gives a separate legal status and certain exemptions and privileges under the act.

Aims and Objectives of Industrial Co-operatives

As already described, the main objective of co-operative society is to promote self-help and mutual assistance and fulfill their common economic interest. However, some of the objectives of industrial co-operatives may be as follows:

1. To purchase and supply raw-materials, tools and equipment to members.
2. To secure contracts and execute them with the help of members.
3. To market the finished goods of members.

4. To purchase machinery for giving on hire to members.
5. To borrow funds from members and non-members.
6. To grant loans and advances to members on the security of raw-materials and finished goods belonging to them.
7. To undertake all such activities as are conductive or incidental to the accomplishment of the aforesaid objectives and secure material and social progress of all members.
8. From the social point of view, the industrial co-operatives are expected to safeguard the interest of the poorer sections of community against exploitation by the capitalists and lead to equitable distribution of wealth and income.

Formation of Co-operative Societies

In our country, there is a special legislation governing the registration, working and management of co-operative organisations. To start a co-operative society an application is submitted to the Registrar of Co-operative Societies. The application for registration should provide all essential information e.g., name and address of the society, its aims and objectives, particulars of share capital etc. The application should be signed by at least 10 members. The application should accompany duplicate copies of By laws, i.e., rules and regulations governing the internal organisation and management of the society. The Registrar after the scrutiny of the application, if satisfied with the soundness will issue a certificate of registration and the society will be formed. Once the society is duly registered, it can admit new members and also issue it shares.

2.8.1 Types of Co-operative Societies

The various types of Co-operative Societies are:

- Producers' Co-operative Society
- Consumers' Co-operative Society
- Housing Co-operative Society
- Credit Co-operative Society, etc.

1. Producers' Co-operative Society: In this form of co-operative, the workers wish to be their own masters, the business is owned by them. They elect their own managers. They are their own employees. The profit instead of enriching the few individuals, goes to the actual workers. The workers are supposed to put in very hard work. There are no strikes and lock-outs. It prevents the workers from being exploited; and teaches them how to work in team spirit.

This type of ownership is suitable where large capital and much technical and expert knowledge is not needed.

Examples: Agricultural and cottage industries.

Advantages

1. Persons with limited capital (workers) can start a business.
2. It prevents the workers from being exploited.
3. There are no strikes, lockouts etc.

Disadvantages

1. Inadequate capital.
2. Inefficient management.
3. Lack of discipline.

2. Consumers' Co-operative Society: The consumers living in a particular area combine together. Each contributes a small capital. A store is opened in which articles of common use are stocked and sold at reasonable prices. Such co-operative stores are found in many colleges and schools in India.

Advantages

1. Much capital is not needed.
2. The management is simple and honorary.
3. There is legal control and inspection.

Disadvantages

1. They offer very little selection for customers.
2. The honorary office bearers do not take much pains, they are sometimes dishonest.

3. **Housing Co-operative Society:** Housing co-operative societies are formed for the purpose of getting plots or constructing houses for the needy persons, Government provides great facilities (providing loans at low rate of interest etc.) for this purpose.

4. **Co-operative Credit Society:** Its object is to finance the poor cultivators by providing loans at low rate of interest for the development of land, purchase of agricultural machinery, fertilizers etc.

A credit co-operative society may be formed by persons working in the same organisation to provide loans to the members in case of financial difficulties or for purchasing necessities of their life such as cloth, wheat etc.

2.8.2 Advantages and Disadvantages of Co-operative Societies

In general, the advantages and disadvantages of the co-operative organisation are as follows:

Advantages of Co-operative Societies

1. Co-operative societies protect the interest of the weaker section of the community as under:
   (a) Provide better methods and tools of production to small manufacturers and craftsmen.
   (b) Help the farmers in farming and marketing their products efficiently.
   (c) Provide financial assistance at moderate rate of interest.
   (d) Opening super bazaar types of stores gives relief to the weaker section of the society and helps in establishing price level.
2. **Elimination of middleman:** The commodities are purchased directly from the manufacturers and supplied to the members. It thus eliminates the profit of middleman; and the goods can be sold at cheaper rates.
3. **Services motive:** The co-operative sector is based on service motive and therefore, there is no question of profit making, black marketing etc.
4. **Democratic nature:** Its management is democratic, elected by shareholders.
5. **Sense of co-operation:** It promotes a sense of co-operation among the members and also among the people of the locality. Thus, it serves the social purpose also.
6. **Socially neglected class:** Provides occupation and means of earning to socially neglected class like widows, physically handicapped or poor section of the community.

Disadvantages of Co-operative Societies

1. **Lack of co-ordination:** It may suffer due to lack of co-ordination between various members. Conflict may arise in sharing of duties and responsibilities and also in sharing produce and profit.
2. **Chances of undue advantages:** Some of the forceful members sometimes try to take undue advantages and succeed in it.
3. **Favourism:** The executive committee and the employees favour their friends and relatives at the cost of other members.
4. **Limited capital:** Co-operatives are generally association of low income group people. They cannot finance expanding business.

5. **Inefficient management:** The lack of educated and trained persons practically in villages badly affect the successful working of the Co-operative Organisation.
6. **Political influence:** Many a time co-operatives are exploited by the politicians for their selfish gains.

2.8.3 Distinction between Co-operative and Joint Stock Company

No.	Parameters	Co-operative Society	Joint Stock Company
1.	Formation	(i) Under Co-operative Society Act. (ii) Minimum member 10.	(i) Under companies Act. (ii) Minimum members 2 for Private Ltd. and 7 for Public Ltd.
2.	Fundamental Principles	(i) Spirit of co-operation. (ii) Promote self help and mutual assistance among members. (iii) Unity of purpose. (iv) Community interest. (v) Socialist bias.	(i) Spirit of competition. (ii) No need for unity of purpose. (iii) Capitalistic bias. (iv) Large number of shareholders.
3.	Membership	(i) Generally local or regional territory (from limited area).	(i) Wide spread membership.
4.	Capital	(i) Limited	(i) Large capital.
5.	Transfer of shares	(i) A member can withdraw his share capital, shares are not transferable.	(i) Shares are transferable.
6.	Liability	(i) Limited	(i) Limited
7.	Distribution of Profit	(i) Maximum dividends of shares 12 p.c. (ii) Its main purpose is to serve members, profit is not important.	(i) No limit on dividend. (ii) Profit motive.
8.	Privileges	(i) Government gives special privileges to encourage co-operative movement.	(i) No such special privileges on the other hand Government exercises strict legal control.

Contd...

9.	Management	(i) Democratic with equal voting rights ("One Man One Vote").	(i) Democratic unequal voting right ("One Share One Vote").
10.	Contact	(i) Members are generally known to each other. They come together to fulfill their common need.	(i) Shareholders have no contact with each other. They invest money to earn profit.
11.	Life	(i) Short. It may be dissolved if the common need is fulfilled, members lost their interest.	(i) Perpetual or permanent existence.

2.8.4 Distinction between Private Sector and Public Sector

No.	Private Sector	Public Sector
1.	The main objective of private sector is to earn more and more profit. It benefits only the owners.	Social benefit is of primary importance while profit motive is given secondary importance.
2.	The enterprise is owned and managed by individual or a group of individual.	It is owned and managed by the Central or State Government.
3.	There is a limit to the capital which can be raised by private sector.	Government has ample funds and can borrow more if needed, in the money market at lower rate. Hence, large amount of capital can be collected.
4.	It causes concentration of wealth in the hands of few capitalists.	It leads to equitable distribution of wealth and income. Profit is utilized for the welfare of the notion.
5.	Private sector has to face competition in the market.	There is absence of competition generally the projects undertaken needs huge capital and private sector is not attracted to them.

Contd...

6.	Private Sector dominates in the production of consumer goods.	It generally dominates in the production of producer goods.
7.	There are chances of exploitation of general public (workers and consumers).	Public sector enterprises are subjected to greater control and it helps to protect the people from exploitation.
8.	Private sector does not undertake risky ventures or those having low profit margin.	It helps in the growth of industries which require huge capital but useful for the welfare of the nation even though profit margin is less.
9.	Private sector leads to unbalanced growth of industries.	Public sector encourages industrial growth of under-developed regions in the country.
10.	Wastage of material and labour is minimum.	Public sector can rarely attain the efficiency of private sector; wastage and inefficiency can seldom be reduced to minimum.

2.9 PUBLIC SECTOR ORGANISATIONS

Faster and planned economic development cannot be fulfilled by private sector alone. Hence, the public sector has to play a key role to accomplish quick industrialization and rising standard of lining of the people through developing key and basic industries , e.g., Iron and steel industries, aircraft, defence industries, fertilizer industries etc. In our country, the expansion of the public sector was in accordance with Industrial Policy Resolution, 1948 and 1956 and as per the directives of our Five-Year Economic Plans.

The objectives of public sector enterprises can be stated as:

1. Equitable distribution of wealth and income.
2. Balanced economic development through dispersal of industrial location.
3. Adequate employment opportunities.
4. Speedy agricultural and industrial development without the growth of monopolies.
5. Self-sufficiency of the nation modern technology and managerial skills so that in due course our country need not depend on foreign collaboration in capital technology, skill etc.

Public sector includes:

(i) State Enterprises (Government Sector) and
(ii) Public Corporations.

2.9.1 Government Undertaking (State Ownership)

Private ownership causes accumulation of wealth in the hands of few capitalists. These dominating motive to earn more and more profit has led to economic unbalance and neglect of the well being of workers and welfare of community as a whole. The exploitation by the capitalists increased the gap between richer and poorer. The monopolistic tendencies of the Private ownership necessitated the State's participation in trade and industrial fields.

The State ownerships are the business organisations which are owned, managed and run by the Government or local bodies like municipality, district board etc. This is generally done in the case of public utility services like gas, electricity, water supply, bus, railways navigation etc. The railways, post and telegraph are completely owned by Central Government. Some other industries such as ship building, steel industry, electricity generation, railway engine manufacture etc. are owned the Government and also by joint stock companies.

The Government either starts or nationalizes certain industries to prevent economic imbalance in the nation. The social benefit is of primary importance while profit motive is given a secondary consideration.

Advantages

1. Profits go to the Government, and are utilized for the benefit of the society at large. Nation building departments can be liberally financed from the increased resources.
2. Purity of supply is guaranteed. There is no incentive for adulteration for a Government undertaking as there is for private business.
3. Government has ample funds and can borrow more, if needed, in the money market at low rates. This would lower the cost of production.
4. The best talent is attached towards Government service. The Government can, therefore, engage superior staff. The business, therefore, will run better.
5. Government can afford to wait long for an enterprise to yield profit. Big business ventures like iron and steel works, heavy electricals, defence projects can be started.
6. Consumer's interests are properly safeguarded.
7. Government enterprise is subjected to greater control. Public cannot be exploited for long.

Disadvantages

1. Government Officer behaves like a big boss, and a respectable citizen receives no courtesy.
2. The Government servant has not the same incentive to do the best as a man in private service. In government service promotion is by seniority, and not by merit. Therefore Government servants do not work hard.
3. Frequent transfers of Government servants are harmful to the success of the enterprise. There is no continuity of policy.

4. The Government business is all routine and there is little initiative. Economic progress is therefore slow.
5. There is little check on extravagance and inefficiency. There are no shareholders to question the directors in the annual meeting.

In under-developed countries, the public sector (i.e., State enterprise) has to play an increasingly expanding role. It has a special role to play in creating an infra-structure of social overhead capital like means of transport, communications etc. These projects need huge capital, but since they are not productive in the narrow sense, private sector is not attracted to them. But they are of vital importance to the development of the economy hence they have to be undertaken by the State. Therefore state enterprise assumes special importance in an under-developed or developing economy.

Even in the sphere reserved for the private sector, the state can step in, if the private sector is not showing sufficient progress as required by the countrie's needs. There is also a wide field in which both private and public sector can start enterprise. This policy is being given effect to by the Indian Five Years Plans.

2.9.2 Public Corporation

A public corporation is a body created by a Law of Parliament with its powers, duties and liabilities defined in the written law. Public corporations try to combine the public interest of the Government body and the autonomous management of the public sector. These corporations have no profit motive and work for the sake of social welfare.

Characteristics of the Public Corporation

The main characteristics of the public corporation are:

(i) It is created by the separate act passed by the Parliament or State Legislative Assembly.
(ii) It is owned by the Government – either Central, State and or local bodies.
(iii) It is managed by the board of directors nominated by the Government.
(iv) It enjoys complete internal autonomy and is free from parliamentary or political control in the internal and routine management.
(v) It enjoys financial freedom and can raise financial resources independently. It has not to depend on budget appropriations. It has borrowing power. Its bond issue is guaranteed by the Government.
(vi) The employees of the public corporation are not treated as the Civil servants of the Government. The corporation is empowered to follow its own personal polices for recruitment, training, transfer and promotion.
(vii) Its primary objective is to serve the public interest an hence it is accountable to the Parliament for its policy decisions and the resultant functioning.

Public corporation is the best mechanism through which large public enterprise can be administered. Based on the principle of maximum autonomy, consistent with public accountability, eliminating bureaucracy it has introduced public service into community ownership.

Limitations/Disadvantages of Public Corporations
1. It is suitable only for the management of very big enterprises.
2. It needs special legislation and hence its formation is elaborate an time consuming.
3. It is a rigid form of organisation as any change in its constitution will require amendment of the special act.
4. The autonomy of the corporations are only on paper. In reality, the Ministers, Government Officers and Politicians interfere in the working of such corporations.
5. Public corporations possess monopoly and in the absence of competition, these are not interested in adopting new techniques and making improvements in their working.

At present, Insurance, Finance, Industry, Mining, Transport and Trade in many countries are carried on through public corporation.

Examples of Public Corporation are: Air India, Food Corporation of India, Oil and Natural gas Corporation, Road Transport Corporation, Financial Corporation, Industrial Development Corporation, Electricity Board, Damodar Valley Corporation etc.

2.9.3 Joint Venture (Foreign Collaboration)

Joint venture is a typical form of foreign collaboration. It is adopted by a multinational company to expand its business in foreign countries, particularly developing countries. It takes place between two or more units when these units come together for financial, managerial and technical collaboration. Joint venture is a partnership between the corporations of two countries. The foreign partner or collaboration supplies capital, technology as well as managerial and technical personnel to start a project in another country. Multinational companies are particularly interested in expanding their production and markets through joint ventures all over the world.

Forms of Joint Venture

Joint venture may take the following forms:
1. Mixed companies with equal contribution in equity share capital as partners.
2. Joint ownership in which domestic country provides factory premises, buildings, raw-material, power and labour, while other country (foreign country) supply capital, machinery, technical know-how and skill.
3. Jointly operated enterprise in which a foreign company supplies capital goods i.e. in the form of long term credit and the debtor company in a developing country repays the loan in the form of export of output i.e. goods produced.

India's three big steel mills represent joint ventures of the state level with German, British and U.S.S.R. Steel Industries. Hindustan Machine Tools represents a joint enterprise between Indian Govt. and Swiss Machine tools.

Developing countries welcome and encourage formation of joint venture to import capital, skill and technology in order to achieve quick industrialisation and economic development.

To prevent exploitation by multinational partner the terms and conditions of collaboration agreements are subjected to Government scrutiny and approval. Foreign Exchange Regulation Act 1973, exercises rigid control over joint ventures of all multinational companies. Joint venture helps to remove technological gaps and deficiencies.

At the end of 1985 there were 208 Indian joint ventures abroad, of which, 156 were in operation and 52 at different stages of implementation.

Choice of Form of Organisation

As explained earlier, a business enterprise can be organised into several forms. Every form of organisation has its own advantages and limitations. A business mail has to keep in view these advantages and limitations while selecting an appropriate form of organisation. The choice has to be made both at the time of setting up a new enterprise and at the time of expansion or growth of an existing firm.

While launching a new business enterprise, the following factors must be considered for selecting the form of ownership.

1. Nature of business : Service, trade, manufacturing.
2. Scale of operations : Volume of business (large, medium, small) and Size of market area (local, national, international) served.
3. Degree of direct control desired by the owners.
4. Amount of capital required initially and for expansion.
5. Degree of risk and liability and willingness of owners to assume personal liability for debts of business.
6. Division of profits among the owners.
7. Length of life desired by the business.
8. Relative freedom from government regulations (Flexibility of operations).
9. Scope and plan of internal organisation.
10. Comparative tax liability.

However, it must be noted that these factors are inter-related and inter-dependent. For example, the amount of capital required and the degree of risk involved depend upon the nature and volume of business operations. The degree of control and the division of profits are both related to risk and liability. Therefore, an entrepreneur should not consider these factors in isolation. The inter-relationship between these factors should be duly considered.

The suitability of different forms may be classified as under :

1. Proprietorship: Small trading and service like retail stores, workshops, bakeries, restaurants, hair dressing, laundries, tailoring, automobile service and repair shops, auxiliary industries, small scale manufacturing and other enterprises requiring small capital, catering to local markets, involving limited risk and the use of personal knowledge and skills.

2. Partnership and private companies: Medium sized service and trading concerns like wholesalers, transporters, architects, consultants, small scale manufacturing industries, auxiliary industries requiring simple techniques and processes.

3. Public companies: Large scale manufacturing and commercial undertaking like - chain stores, departmental stores, rubber industries, steel industries, power generation etc. requiring heavy investment, specialized talents and complex processes of production and distribution.

2.9.4 Comparative Evaluation of Different Forms of Business Ownership

Forms of Ownership	Sole-proprietorship	Partnership	Private Ltd. Company	Public Ltd. Company	Co-operative Society
1. Ease of Formation	Easiest, no legal formalities.	Easy, only an agreement required	Difficult, some legal formalities are to be followed.	Very difficult, several legal formalities.	Easier legal formalities.
2. Registration	Not necessary	Optional	Compulsory	Compulsory	Compulsory
3. Membership	Single membership, Maximum – 20.	Minimum – 2	Minimum – 2 Maximum – 50	Minimum - 7 No limit	Minimum - 10
4. Legal Status Existence	No separate legal status.	No separate status.	Separate legal status.	Separate legal status/	Separate legal status.
5. Liability of Members	Unlimited, full risk.	Unlimited	Limited	Limited	Limited
6. Capital & Suitability	Limited Capital, small scale size business.	Moderate capital, Suitable for small and medium industries.	Large capital, Suitable for medium scale industries.	Very large capital, Suitable for large scale business.	Limited capital, Suitable for small and medium size business.

7. Management and Control	Quick decisions, Individual owner controls the business.	Unanimous decisions, Limited specialisation, Partners control the business.	Board decisions, Greater specialisation. Ownership and control goes together.	Board decisions. Greater specialisation, Divorce ownership and management.	Divorce between ownership and management.
8. Transferability of Interest	At will	With mutual consent.	Restricted as Articles of Association	Freely transferable	Restricted
9. Stability	Short life	Less stable, May be dissolved by death, insolvency of Partner.	Perpetual existence.	Perpetual existence.	Comparatively short life.
10. Business Secrecy	Perfect secrecy	Secrets limited to partner	Secrets shared by members.	Secrets shared with public.	Secrets limited to members.

EXERCISE

1. Define organisation. State the necessity and importance of organisation in an Industry.
2. Explain the various steps involved in designing the organisation.
3. Describe the various principles of organisation.
4. Define organisation. State the advantages of good organisation.
5. Name the various types of organisation structure and explain any one of them with its merits and demerits.
6. Describe Taylor's functional organisation with its advantages and disadvantages.
7. Why is the line and staff organisation preferred to the line type of organisation in todays Industry? Describe.
8. Differentiate between 'Line organisation' and 'Functional Organisation'.
9. Name the various forms of ownership organisation. State the factors to be considered before deciding the form of ownership to be started.
10. Describe 'Individual Ownership' with its advantages and limitations.
11. Compare Proprietorship with, Partnership Organisation.
12. Describe Partnership organisation with its merits and demerits.

13. Define 'Partnership deed'. State its contents.
14. Describe the procedure to be adopted for starting Partnership.
15. State the characteristics of 'Joint Stock Company' responsible for making it the most important type of ownership of industrial organisation.
16. What is meant by 'Joint Stock Company'? Describe briefly the procedure for forming 'Joint Stock Company'.
17. Differentiate between 'Private Limited Company' and 'Public Limited Company'.
18. Explain the following with reference to Joint Stock Company:
    (i) Formation of Joint Stock Company.
    (ii) Liquidation.
    (iii) Characteristics of Joint Stock Company.
19. Distinguish between 'Partnership' and 'Joint Stock Company'.
20. Define Partnership, describe the different types of partners.
21. Define co-operative organisation. State the characteristics of co-operative organisation. State the objectives of co-operative societies. How they are formed?
22. Name the various types of co-operative societies. Describe:
    (i) Producers' Co-operative Society and
    (ii) Consumers' Co-operative society with their advantages and limitations.
23. State the advantages and limitations of co-operative organisations.
24. State the objectives and explain the role of Public Sector enterprises for developing countries.
25. What is State Ownership? State its advantages and limitations.
26. What is Public Corporation? What are its characteristics?
27. What is Joint Venture? What are the various forms of Joint Venture? Give examples of Joint venture organisation in India.
28. Compare between 'Co-operative Society and 'Joint Stock Company.
29. Amongst various types of organisations, proprietorship ensures quickest growth. Comment.
30. What are the aims of Public Sector Organisation? Are the Public Sector Organisations successful?
31. Stale the advantages and disadvantages of individual ownership. Explain each point in brief.
32. State the objectives, advantages and limitations of co-operative organisations.

UNIT III

PERSONAL MANAGEMENT

3.1 MANPOWER PLANNING

Introduction

Manpower planning is a very important part of the overall planning of a business organisation. It is obvious that a business cannot prosper, unless the right number of employees, having required skills, talents and qualifications is available at right time. Manpower planning is done to fulfill the two main objectives, namely:

(i) To utilize the present employees fully, and

(ii) To fill up future manpower requirements.

The fulfillment of these two objectives is absolutely necessary for the success and survival of any business organisation. Manpower planning is a continuous, dynamic process and manpower assessment should be done every year and revised periodically at fixed interval, keeping in view the yearly manufacturing programme. For effective manpower planning, it is necessary to carry out job analysis.

Definitions

Manpower planning may be defined as, "the scientific process of allocating the right number of right men to be required in future, at right time on the right job".

According to *E. B. Geisler*, "Manpower planning is the process including forecasting, developing and controlling, by which, a firm ensures that it has the right number of people and right kind of people at the right places, at the right time, doing work for which they are economically most useful".

According to *James J. Lynch*, "Manpower planning is the integration of manpower policies, practices and procedures, so as to achieve the right number of the right people in the right jobs at the right time".

According to *Dale S. Beach*, "Human resource planning is a process of determining and assuring, that the organisation will have an adequate number of qualified persons, available at the proper times, performing jobs which meet the needs of enterprise and which provide satisfaction for the individuals involved".

3.1.1 Types of Manpower Planning

Types of manpower planning can be distinguished :

(i) On the basis of the level at which it is done, and

(ii) On the basis of the period, for which it is done.

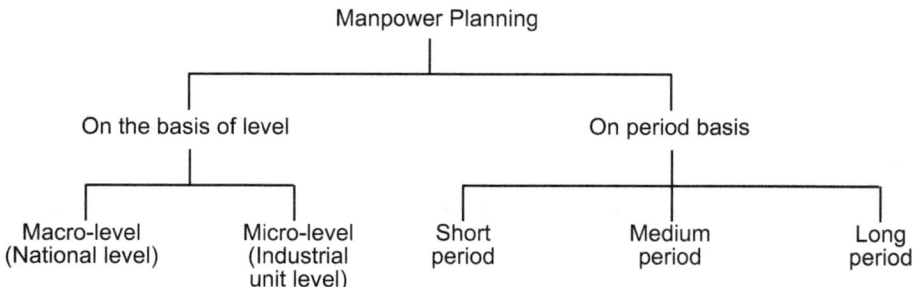

Fig. 3.1 : Manpower planning

In developing country like India, manpower planning is absolutely essential. Manpower planning is done on the national level as a part of the planning, for overall economical development of the country. The objective is to provide more and more opportunities of employment, while utilizing the human resources of the nation most efficiently. In India, manpower planning is a part of overall planning and so its responsibilities lie with planning commission.

Manpower planning at the organisational level is also important, because it decides the various measures to be taken, such as, recruitment, selection, promotion, transfer etc. by an industrial unit. Depending upon the size of the industry, manpower planning may be done at three levels :

(i) At the departmental level,

(ii) If there are number of branches of the industry, planning can be done at the level of each individual branch of the factory.

(iii) At the top level, i.e. by the board of directors of the company.

Short term plans are prepared for the period of one year. Short term plans are made as a part of five year plans at national level. These plans are very useful at company level. Medium term plans are those which are made for 2 to 5 years. At national level, medium-term plans are essentially prepared as a part of financial planning. These plans give special attention towards employment opportunities and training and development of employees. Long-term manpower planning is prepared for a longer period, such as, 10 to 15 years. This is done at national level. It is important to estimate manpower needs of a nation and accordingly to raise educational and training facilities, keeping in view long-term interests of the nation.

3.2 FACTORS AFFECTING MANPOWER PLANNING

The factors affecting manpower planning are :

(i) Working hours　　　　(ii) Number of shifts

(iii) Nature of production　(iv) Product mix

(v) Performance rate　　 (vi) Hours lost.

(i) Working Hours : Manpower requirement is directly related to the working hours per day by the employees.

If the number of working hour is more, less manpower will be required and vice-versa. For example, due to complexity in process and working conditions in a chemical plant, instead of 8 hours per shift, workers may be required to work for six hours in a shift, the manpower planning basis will differ in both the industries.

(ii) Number of Shifts : If the factory is running in shifts, it should be remembered that production falls in the night shifts, instead of day shifts.

(iii) Nature of Production : Idle time, setting time, cycle time etc. all vary greatly with the nature of production and, hence the manpower requirements also. In mass production and continuous production, automatic machines are used. Because of automation, less manpower will be required, as compared to job order and batch production system industries.

(iv) Product Mix : Product mix means a production programme based on optimum productive capacity and sales forecast. This is based on optimum utilization of human and material resources and also for balancing the production line.

(v) Performance Rate : The performance rate depends on the working conditions, bonus schemes, suitable incentive plans, training programmes, motivation etc. If the employees are motivated to do their best, their performance rate will be more and less number of workers will be needed.

(vi) Hours Lost : If the productive man hours lost are less, their available productive hours will be more and less man power will be needed.

3.3 ADVANTAGES OF MANPOWAR PLANNING

1. Basis for Recruitment and Selection of Employees : Manpower planning provides a basis for recruiting new employees, considering the future manpower needs. As a result, the production or any other related work does not stop for lack of employees of desired skills and abilities.

2. To Plan the Development of the Employees : The present employees can be trained for some higher positions. This gives encouragement to the existing employees and in turn creates favourable psychological climate for their motivation.

3. Thorough Performance Appraisal : Manpower planning enables thorough performance appraisals, identification of gaps in the existing manpower, so that corrective training could be imparted. Thus, the training programme becomes more effective.

4. Reduction in Personnel Costs : It reduces personnel costs, because of management's ability to anticipate shortages or surpluses of manpower and correct these imbalances before they become unmanageable and expensive.

5. Manpower Inventory : Personnel or manpower inventory can provide information to management for the internal succession of managerial personnel, if there is a turnover which is not anticipated.

6. Greater Awareness Among Employees : Greater awareness among employees is the importance of sound manpower management throughout, at all levels of the organisation.

7. Better Industrial Relations : Information on surplus manpower would facilitate the introduction of an exit plan or scheme for surplus labour. A systematic approach to deal with surplus manpower, would check the problems of industrial relations.

8. Improvement in Business Planning Process : It leads to the improvement of business planning process.

9. Employment opportunities : It provides better employment opportunities and identifies the specific development or training programme, needed today to make specific skills available tomorrow.

3.4 STEPS IN MANPOWER PLANNING

Manpower planning involves the following steps:

1. Understanding the Business Objectives: Manpower planning should start with the study of the basic company objectives and strategies, such as, growth through diversification/expansion/merger/takeover etc. This would indicate:

(i) The new activities required to be undertaken.

(ii) The existing activities required to be deleted.

(iii) Changes/modifications in the existing activities in view of technological and other changes.

2. Identification of Tasks: Once the activities are ascertained, the specific tasks required to be performed at each organisational level should be identified. Identification of tasks would indicate the type of knowledge and skills required.

3. Manpower Forecast: Manpower demand forecasting at micro-level, could be done in either of the two ways, i.e. by ascertaining the total number and kind of people needed for the entire enterprise for a given period and then estimating requirements of each unit, division or department, or alternatively, first determine the manpower requirement of each department and subsequently make a total projection. While estimating manpower requirements, it is necessary to consider the vacancies on account of retirements, resignations, deaths, dismissal etc.

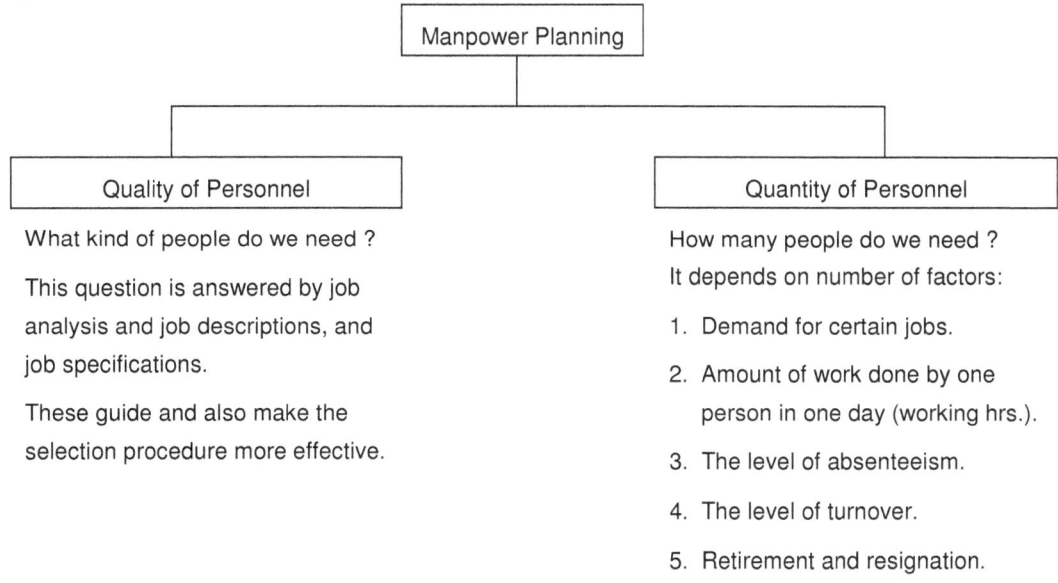

Fig. 3.2

4. Job Analysis: To decide the quality (kind of personnel needed it is necessary to carry out detailed analysis of various skills required to do the jobs and to spell out the duties and responsibilities associated with job i.e. job description and job specification). This will enable to determine the education, professional qualifications and the work experience required on the part of the personnel for specific jobs.

5. Reviewing the Existing Manpower (Manpower Inventory): A catalogue of present manpower incorporating their educational and professional qualifications, work experience, personal background, assignment handled, training received etc. should be maintained by the personnel department. The purpose of such manpower inventory is to know the number and quality of personnel available from within the organisation to fill up vacancies in various positions. The vacancies which cannot be filled through internal sources, indicate the shortfall.

6. Anticipating the Availability of Manpower from External Sources: The vacancies may be filled, partly by promotion from within, (internal sources) and partly by recruiting from outside sources. Assessment of labour market situation tells us the availability of the required manpower to be employed, through advertisement, recruitment and selection.

7. Manpower Management: Planning scientific recruitment, selection, training, development, utilisation, transfer, promotion, motivation, compensation etc. to ensure that future manpower needs are met. Thus, manpower planning covers forecasting future manpower needs and developing manpower plans for implementation.

3.5 RECRUITMENT AND SELECTION OF MANPOWER

Modern industries are in greater need of skilled workers, administrative, technical, supervisory and managerial personnel than in the past. Once the manpower requirements are estimated, the next step is to attract interested, competent applicants and then choosing the best of these for the available jobs.

According to *Edwin B. Flippo*, "Recruitment is the process of searching for prospective employees and stimulating them to apply for jobs in the organisation".

According to *Dales S. Beach*, "Recruitment is the development and maintenance of adequate manpower resources. It involves the creation of a pool of available labour upon whom the organisation can depend, when it needs additional employees".

Recruitment enables the management to select suitable employees for different jobs.

3.5.1 Sources of Recruitment

The sources of manpower supply for different categories of workers (unskilled, semi-skilled and highly skilled) can be broadly classified as:

(i) Internal i.e. recruitment from within the industry.

(ii) External i.e. recruitment from outside.

(i) Internal Sources of Recruitment

Many a time, just the right kind of employees are available in the organisation itself, either by promotion or from company's training schemes. Usually, announcements are made within the organisation about a vacancy and applications are invited for recruitment.

The employees may be transferred from one job to another. At the time of transfer, it should be ensured that the employee to be transferred to the new job, is capable of performing it. In fact, transfer does not involve any drastic change in the responsibilities and status of the employee.

The employees may be promoted to higher position carrying higher responsibilities, status and pay. This method is very much favourable with workers, because it provides them chance to develop financially and socially.

Advantages of Recruitment from Internal Sources:

1. This method creates a goodwill of the employees towards the industry. This helps to built up loyalty among employees to the organisation.
2. The employees promoted are fully aware of existing environments and can rapidly adjust themselves in their new positions as compared to those employed from outside. This reduces the period of induction training.
3. This method is less time-consuming.
4. Reliable information on the candidate's past work experience and background.
5. Reduces labour turnover and creates a sense of security amongst the workers.

Disadvantages of Recruitment from Internal Sources:

1. Pre-conceived ideas and prejudices may hinder the performance on the job.
2. Some of the employees who are not promoted are likely to be unhappy and employees at large may consider recruitment decision as unfair.
3. Inflow of new blood for new ideas may not be possible.
4. There is a limited choice for promotion to higher posts.
5. It may not be possible to find required talent, skill from within the organisation.

(ii) External Sources of Recruitment

1. Former Employees: Sometimes, certain persons leave the industry on their own accord or are retrenched. These persons, if ready to return, may be employed on the basis of the former record of their service.

2. Recommendations: Applicants introduced by friends and relatives may prove to be a good source of recruitment. Many employers prefer to take such persons because when the present employer recommends a person, a type of preliminary screening takes place. (Something about their background is known). But, in case the recommended applicants are rejected it may hurt the employee's feeling. Secondly, this method may lead to favourtism, whereby the advantage is largely offset.

3. Employment Exchange: Employment exchanges run by the government are regarded as a good source of recruitment for skilled, semi-skilled and unskilled employees. In this source, the prospective applicants for employment get themselves registered with the employment exchanges. The demand regarding the number, skill, educational qualification, experience etc. required for employment is sent by the employer to these agencies. In some cases, compulsory notification of vacancies to the employment exchange is required by law.

4. Advertisement: Advertisement in newspapers, employment news, trade and professional journals, radios, television etc. usually help to get prospective employees having suitable skills and qualifications. A well thought and nicely prepared advertisement reduces the possibility of receiving applications from those persons who do not possess the qualification, experience etc. necessary for the job. Most of the senior positions in industry and commerce are filled by this method. Advertisement also gives a wider choice.

5. Applications at the Gate: Even if vacancies do not exist in the organisation, the candidates who come to the factory gate for employment are allowed to fill up applications. These applications are kept in a file for future use. These are scruitinized whenever vacancies arise.

6. Educational and Academic Institutions: This method is being used by many industries. These companies send their selected teams in Industrial Training Institutions, Polytechnics, Engineering Colleges, Management and other professional institutions etc., to interview the candidates, who are nearing the completion of their studies and make selection. In fact, these professional institutions have provided an excellent recruitment source to the firms, who are capable of offering an attractive salary and future to these talents.

7. Labour Unions: The labour unions also supply the workers to the factory for employment. This source is not reliable and sometimes not sufficiently fit for the specific job. Now-a-days this system of recruitment is losing popularity.

3.5.2 Scientific Selection (Talent Aquisition)

Selection process is a tool in the hands of management to differentiate the qualified and unqualified applicants by applying various techniques, such as, interviews, tests etc. It is a decision-making process, where the management decides certain norms and principles to adhere to standards, on the basis of which, a discrimination between qualified and unqualified candidates may be made. A scientific selection procedure ensures the selection of suitable candidate for a particular job. The object of scientific selection is to place on each job, a worker who can maintain a given output with minimum expenditure of energy and who will be best fitted to the job, "right person for the right job".

The major factors in individual fitness for a job are:

1. **Physical Characteristics:** Sound body, limbs, height, weight, eye sight etc.
2. **Personal Characteristics:** Age, sex, marital status, previous experience, place of birth, number of children etc.

3. **Proficiency or Skill and Ability:** This is the basic characteristic in fitting worker to a job.

4. **Competency:** Potentiality of an individual for learning and becoming proficient in a job. It points out the capacity to acquire knowledge and skill for success on the job.

5. **Temperament and Character:** Emotional, moral and social qualities, honesty, loyalty etc. It is important to know about individual's character, his habits, his way of reacting in particular situation, his driving forces in determining his fitness for the job.

6. **Interest in Vocational Fitness:** Interest makes the work meaningful and worthwhile to the individual and with interest, abilities are developed as well as accomplishments are realised. Even if a person has skill, competency, efficiency, but he has no interest in the job, he may not be able to carry out the work effectively and may be found misfit for the job.

3.5.3 Selection Procedure (Method of Selection)

It is essential to devise a suitable selection procedure because, if the right type of persons are not selected, it will lead to huge loss to the organisation in terms of time, effort and money. Each step in action process should provide more and more information about the applicant to facilitate decision making in proper selection. However, the steps in recruitment and selection may vary from organisation to organisation.

The important steps followed by the modern organisations to select right type of persons, are shown in the Fig. 3.3.

1. Receipt of Applications: The job has to be carefully studied and analysed to determine the kind of requirements of knowledge, experience and skill necessary to do it effectively. The applications received, gives details of family background, education, age, training experience, interest in extra curricular activities, hobbies, previous employment, salaries drawn, salary expected etc. The detailed information contained in the application gives a fair idea about the applicant.

2. Scrutiny of Applications (Preliminary Screening): In order to ensure that no time, money and energy is wasted in interviewing unsuitable candidates, the applications received are scrutinised and manageable number of suitable candidates are called for preliminary interview. The applications received could be classified under the following categories:

(i) Must be interviewed

(ii) Should be interviewed

(iii) Need not be interviewed.

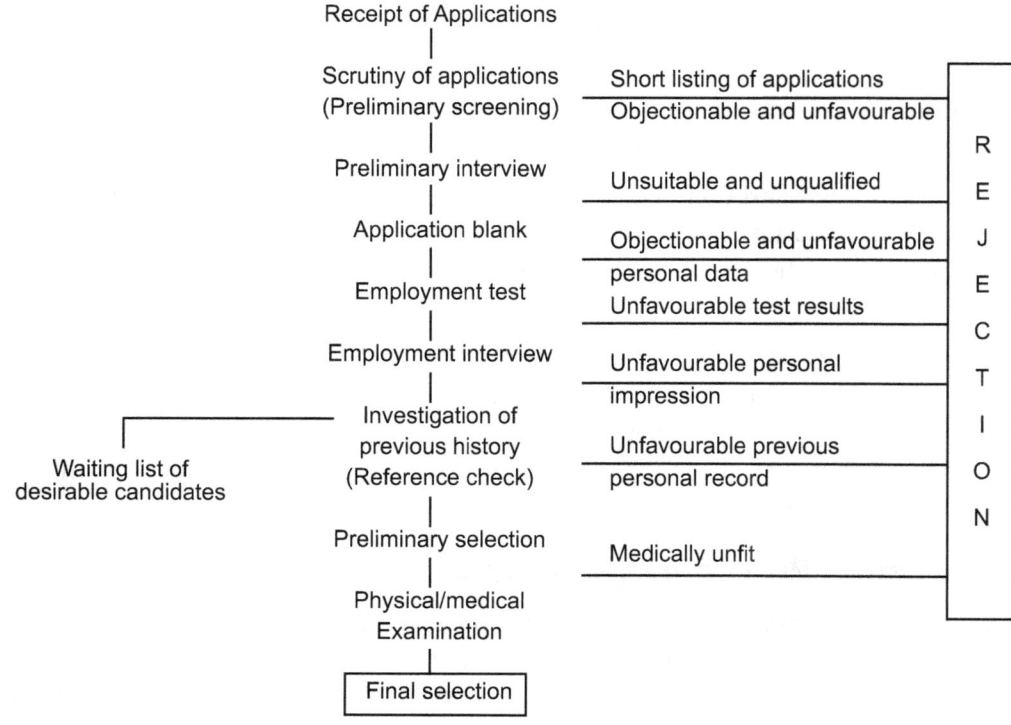

Fig. 3.3: Selection procedure

If there are adequate candidates in 'must be interviewed' category then candidates in the 'should be interviewed' are deleted at this stage.

3. Preliminary Interview: The purpose of preliminary interview is to eliminate unfit, unqualified or less qualified applicants. It is also a sort of screening test. It provides additional information about the candidates to judge their suitability for the job. It should be brief to have an idea of general education, experience, appearance, personality and salary requirements of the candidates.

4. Application Bank: The successful candidates in the preliminary interview are given printed standardized application form. Application blank is used to obtain information in the applicant's own handwriting. These forms can provide more factual information about the applicant. The application blank should incorporate questions having bearing on the fitness of the applicant for the job. Application blank gives a written record of identification (family background, date and place of birth, age, sex, citizenship, marital status, height, weight etc.), education, experience, references, salary expected etc.

5. Employment Test: Many large firms use employment tests in conjunction with interviews, for selecting, placing and training personnel. Employment test enables to know the level of ability, knowledge, the pattern of interest and aptitude of the candidate in details. A properly developed and administered employment test programme can provide a more objective way of judging job applicant's and improving the accuracy of the selection process.

Some of the commonly used employment tests are as follows:

(i) Intelligence Tests: These tests measure the individual's capacity or learning ability to grasp or understand instructions and also ability to reason and make judgement. IQ tests can help to reduce misfits by identifying applicants who fall below minimum standards and those who have considerably more mental ability than is required for the job. These tests are very useful for certain high level jobs.

(ii) Trade Tests: Technical jobs require 'trade tests'. The purpose of a trade test is to judge the candidate with respect to his proficiency and skilfulness in a particular trade. For example, for recruitment of a stenographer, a test can be conducted to check his speed at dictation and typing. A turner may be asked to produce a job on a lathe with desired accuracy and speed or asked questions related to construction and operation of a centre lathe.

(iii) Psychological Tests: Psychological tests are designed to measure emotional stability introversion, extroversion, interest etc. These tests are generally expensive to design and administer for a specific job.

(v) Aptitude Tests: Aptitude tests are used to determine whether an individual has certain minimum natural abilities or talents that can be developed through proper training. These tests measure ability to learn specific jobs. Special aptitude tests measure specific patterns of abilities necessary to perform certain jobs, for example, mechanical aptitude tests are useful in selecting apprentices for skilled mechanical trades.

(v) Interest Tests: Interest tests identify patterns of interest, that is, areas in which the individual shows special concern, fascination and involvement. These tests will indicate what type of jobs may be satisfying to the employees. These tests also help the individuals in selecting occupation of their interest.

(vi) Personality Tests: These tests are used to judge personality traits of the candidate such as emotional balance, attempt to determine the ability of an individual to meet interpersonal and situational stress.

6. Employment Interview: It is the most important and widely used tool in the selection process. This type of interview must be conducted in a friendly atmosphere. The questions should pertain to job specifications. A verification of the information finished by the candidate in application blank may be made. The candidate should be given a chance to ask questions to satisfy himself regarding the history of the concern, future prospects, salary offered and nature of job etc. The interview should be conducted in a room free from any disturbance, noise and interruption, so that interview may be held confidentially and in a quiet environment.

The following principles should be followed to improve the quality of interviewing:

(i) Formulate the objective of the interview and the questions to be asked before seeing the applicant.

(ii) Conduct the interview in private and put the applicant at ease with some general remarks about the business and the job.

(iii) Encourage the applicant to talk by asking pertinent questions and listening attentively to the answers.

(iv) Avoid any suggestion of discrimination.

(v) Retain control of interview and keep the interview headed towards the objective without dominating.

(vi) Allow plenty of time without wasting it.

(vii) Record the facts obtained in an interview while they are fresh.

7. Reference Check: This is generally the last step before the candidate is offered a job in the organisation. An investigation is made on the reference supplied by the applicant regarding his past employment, education, character, personal reputation etc. Reports of the referees may be either open or confidential. Referees may be contacted on telephones, through mail or personal visit. It is a good practice to call the confidential reports in a standard form to ensure that the requisite information is furnished. Reports of the previous employer which are specific are given a lot of weightage by the potential employers.

8. Medical Examination: This is the final step in the selection process. It is essential to ensure that the candidate is physically fit and is able to handle the job efficiently. It screens out the applicants who are physically unfit to meet the requirements of the specific job for which they are being considered.

Physical fitness requirements vary from job to job. Ability to cope with the stress is a critical factor in selection of individuals for stress prone jobs.

Medical examination is done with the following purposes:

(i) It serves to ascertain the applicant's physical fitness to meet the job requirements.

(ii) It serves to protect the organisation against unwanted claims under Worker's Compensation Act.

(iii) It helps to prevent communicable diseases entering the organisation.

(iv) It helps in selecting individuals with sound health, and in reducing the rates of accident, labour turnover and absenteeism.

9. Final Selection: The successful candidates are ranked in order of preference. Appointment letters are issued to the candidates depending upon the number of vacancies to be filled in. The appointment letter must indicate the post for which the candidate is selected, the terms and conditions of appointment, pay scale etc. The appointment letter must also indicate the date by which the acceptance of offer shall be communicated or the date of joining. If the offer of appointment is not accepted within the stipulated time, then other selected candidates should be considered in order of their ranks. Normally, in the initial stage, the candidates are appointed on probation basis, because it is considered better to try them for a few months on the job itself.

3.5.4 Introduction and Follow Up

Induction is the introduction of an employee to the job and the organisation. A planned induction properly welcomes a new employee, creates a good attitude, and reduces labour turnover. The information about the organisation history, its products, policies, rules, mission, philosophies etc. is given to the candidate. The candidate is introduced to his fellow workers, subordinates and other concerned, in a friendly atmosphere. It is the foreman's responsibility to help orient the worker, making him feel at home and part of the working team.

A good induction programme should cover:

1. Information about the company, its products, manufacturing processes and major tasks in his job.
2. Intricacies about the job including its hazards.
3. Organisational structure and functions of various departments.
4. Employee's own position in the organisation and department.
5. Personnel policy of the organisation.
6. Service conditions, amenities and welfare facilities.
7. Policies, objectives and rules and regulations of the company.
8. Grievance and discipline handling procedures.
9. Promotion, transfers, suggestion schemes etc.

Placement:

If the persons are not selected for specific positions, as in case of trainees, they are required to undergo training or work in different departments/sections for some time. Based on their performance and aptitude, they are finally assigned to specific jobs. This process of putting a person on the specific job is known as placement.

3.6 EDUCATION AND TRAINING METHODS OF MANPOWER

Building an efficient labour force requires not only proper selection, but also effective training of employees. Therefore, after the selection of an employee in an organisation, the next step is to train him for better performance.

Training is a process which improves individual's ability through imparting knowledge, developing skills and changing attitudes, to perform their jobs more efficiently and effectively.

Training may be defined as "a well thought and well planned processes of conscious learning of new knowledge and skills for improving the learner's ability to perform certain tasks and activities, more efficiently and effectively, in immediate/near future, with active support of some other individuals".

Training can also be defined as "a short-term process utilising a systematic and organised procedure by which people acquire technical knowledge and skills for a definite purpose".

Training and Development

Training is the act of increasing the knowledge and skill for doing a particular job, the development means growth of individual in all respects. Development is a long term educational process utilising a systematic and organised procedure by which managerial personnel get conceptual and theoretical knowledge. An executive development programme aims at increasing the capabilities of the individuals to achieve the desired objectives.

The personnel department determines the training needs of various units and different individuals and schedule them. The type of training, the method of training, the duration of training and all such matters should be taken care of, by the personnel department.

3.6.1 Need for Training

(i) The need for a systematic training programme has been increased by rapid changes in the business:
   - job changes.
   - changes in processes, methods and procedures - rapid changes in technology.
   - change in volume of business
   - changes in products etc.

   The changes are constantly taking place. They are also rapid. They demand modification and changes in skills, knowledge, attitudes and understanding on the part of workers and executives.

(ii) Training is necessary to impart knowledge to new recruits, to acquint them with the job to be done by them. Industry is frequently compelled, particularly during periods of business expansion, to employ unskilled labour and to train them for specific operations or tasks.

(iii) Many jobs in business consist of tasks which are unique and peculiar to the company and require systematic training.

(iv) Training is necessary to develop better behaviour patterns which are appropriate to their jobs and responsibilities.

(v) To achieve flexibility in the labour force versatility or multiskill training is necessary.

(vi) To provide remedial instructions to old employees to improve their workmanship.

(vii) Training helps to promote individuals for higher positions.

Training and development of personnel is therefore an ongoing and continuous process to meet and adopt changes effectively and quickly. In developing countries like India, there is a great demand for trained personnel at all levels.

3.6.2 Objectives of Training and Development

When any company undertakes training and development, it aims at fulfilling certain objectives. There are three broad objectives of training:

1. Disseminating of knowledge.
2. Development of skills.
3. Change of attitudes.

Normally, an organisation can have one or more objectives such as:

- better performance of employee.
- development of more economic working methods.
- greater job satisfaction or morale.
- harmonious team work.
- To familiarise the new employees with company rules, regulations, introduce him to his fellow workers and give him an idea of where his job fits into the total operation of the company. (Orientation cum induction training).
- Learning new techniques (refresher training).

Specific types of training programmes are conducted to carry out some particular objectives.

3.6.3 Benefits/Advantages of Training

The importance of training in an organisation is quite obvious from the following benefits resulting from properly trained personnel of the organisation. In fact, trained labour is an invaluable asset to the organisation.

1. Increased Productivity: A systematic training programme causes an increase in skill and efficiency of an employee. A trained worker gives better performance. Training of labour results in increase in quality, quantity and output. Machines and materials are carefully handled and they are more economically used.

2. Higher Employee Morale: Training helps the employee to acquire necessary skill and efficiency. This provides him job satisfaction and confidence, thus resulting in higher employee morale.

3. Reduced Accidents: Training develops safety attitudes in the workers and they can take necessary precautions to avoid accident. Machines and equipment are carefully handled and maintained properly.

4. Reduction in Spoilage, Wastage and Optimum Utilization of Resources: Training in improved method results in better utilization of materials, equipments and reduction in defective work, damage and spoilage and substantial reduction in the manufacturing cost.

5. Reduced Supervision: A trained employee shows a high degree of self-discipline and self supervision. He takes intelligent interest in his work. Proper training may enable him to contribute a lot to the solution of managerial problems through participation. When labour is trained, management can be democratic or participative. Management can concentrate on planning and encourage expert workers through motivation.

6. Increased Organisational Stability and Flexibility: Stability means the ability of the organisation to sustain its effectiveness, inspite of the loss of key personnel. This is because of the availability of a reservoir of trained replacement.

Flexibility means the ability of the organisation to adjust itself to the short term changes in the volume of work. Training helps to achieve this ability by developing multiple skills in employees so that they can be transferred to other jobs when the need arises. Job rotation enables the development of versatile employees for necessary adjustment in the personnel due to change in the volume of work.

7. Self-development Versatility and Adaptability: Automation, rapid changes in technology and increasing use of computerization, requires the employees to adopt themselves to changed situations (new work methods). Systematic training provides them an opportunity for self development, versatility and adopting to new work situations. Similarly, better security and greater opportunity for self-development within or without the present organisation are possible only for trained employees. Management has to take up the responsibility for continuous training and re-training of employees to update their knowledge, skills to meet the changed situations.

8. Reduced Turnover and Absenteeism: Training develops confidence and provides job satisfaction to employees associated with a sense of achievement. This results in lower complaints, reduced turnover and absenteeism.

9. Reduction in Machine Breakdown and Maintenance Cost: Training in preventive maintenance, improved methods, result in better care and handling of machines, minimizes the breakdown and maintenance cost of machines.

10. Increase in Earning of the Employees: In short, a systematic training programme improves the quality and quantity of work, safeguards machinery, reduces costs, raises employee's earning and morale, and provides an effective means for improving company policies and regulations.

3.6.4 Guidelines for Training Workers (NQN-Managerial Employees)

There are number of guidelines which must be borne in mind, while designing or imparting training to workers. A few of them are given below:

Craftsmen (Workers Training)

This is also called workers' training to achieve skill in their work. Up-to-date training is required for those who actually work on machines to increase their skill and also for new employees. A learned skill is an asset which cannot be taken away. It is, therefore, valuable to the employee in terms of better job security and greater opportunity for promotion within the organisation and if necessary in the outside world.

Guidelines for Training Workers

There are number of guidelines which must be considered, while designing or imparting training to workers. A few of them are given below:

1. Motivation is the main factor in training employees. It is very important to decide which incentive will motivate the employee - money, status, recognition etc. Motivating a new employee is always easier than motivating the old employees. The training sessions should be planned to meet the need of trainees, and factors motivating different employees should also be considered by the trainer.

2. A job should be broken down in requirements of the skill necessary to perform it successfully. Training should be planned and provided for each skill (physical, sensory and mental). Carefully spaced practice periods, are essential for effective learning.

3. Individual differences should always be remembered. Individuals vary in intelligence, interest and skills or capability.

4. The trainee should also gain personal benefit from training. Management should see that successful trainees are rewarded.

5. The trainee should be provided with the report of his progress. [Methods of training for (operative workers) personnel].

3.7 METHODS OF TRAINING WORKERS

The various methods of training workers are:

1. Demonstration.
2. On-the job training.
3. Vestibule training.
4. Apprenticeship.

1. Demonstration: This method is especially applicable where some physical process is to be learnt, particularly one that involves use of machinery or equipment. In this method, the supervisor/instructor actually demonstrates how to do a certain task. For example, the instructor actually shows how to perform a certain job on a centre lathe.

This type of training can be seen in very small concerns e.g. workshops, auto repair shops etc. where there is no established training programme.

2. On-the-Job Training: This method provides training to new employees by experienced, skilled workers or foreman/supervisor, while the trainee works at a specific job in the plant or office. In this method, the supervisor gives instructions to a new worker, explains the nature of work, the use of machine and tools, safety precautions etc. and shows, how it is being done by an experienced worker.

The new worker is then put on the job on a separate machine near the experienced and skilled worker. During working, whenever the new worker feels any difficulty, he can take the help and guidance of the skilled worker near him and acquire proficiency in course of time.

Advantages

1. This method of training is widely employed, because of its economy and convenience, no special training facilities and instructional staff are required.
2. The worker learns while doing. He gets introduced to the actual work situation.
3. The suitability of the worker for the specific job can be readily ascertained by the competent instructor/supervisor.

This method is particularly suitable, when the training period is short, because of the simplicity of the job and when the number of trainees is limited.

Limitations

1. It takes long time for a worker to acquire mastery in his work.
2. A new worker is likely to pick up some of the defective method of his colleagues.
3. Every experienced worker may not have the ability to impart his knowledge.
4. Working of a trainee on the production floor, may increase chances of spoilage of material, damage to equipment, accident etc.
5. If the workers are paid on piece wage, the experienced worker may be reluctant to spend much time to guide the new worker.
6. The worker may not be able to learn efficiently, because of noise on the shop floor.

3. Vestibule School Training: It is a special training school for training the employees. An attempt is made to duplicate as nearly as possible, the actual equipment, material and conditions found in a real work situation.

The vestibule training is desirable, when the demand for training is large and when on-the job training, is not practicable.

Advantages

1. The emphasis is on training, rather than on production. Hence, the training is properly planned and controlled.
2. A large number of trainees can be trained in similar skills, quickly and uniformly.
3. There is no disruption of production.
4. Wastage and spoilage of raw material, and damage to production machinery is eliminated.
5. The school atmosphere is calm, peaceful and conducive to efficient learning.
6. Specially trained and professional instructors can be employed for imparting instructions to trainees.
7. Full time instructors are able to apply good teaching techniques under controlled conditions and can increase confidence of the trainees.

Limitations

1. Its major limitation is the expense of both, of providing costly equipment and of maintaining a teaching staff, and every industry cannot afford it.
2. If the demand of workers to be trained is uneven, usually a part of vestibule school is idle or trainees are rushed through it, without proper training.

3. Moreover, since the actual shop conditions cannot be reproduced, the completion of training often finds the trainee, still in need of adjustment to plant conditions.

Many big industries have their own special training schools on permanent basis for training the newly selected employees.

4. Apprenticeship: Apprenticeship is one of the oldest methods of training. It is used to develop all round skilled craftsmen (machinists, tool makers, mill wrights, fitters, welders). It is generally best suited to the large firm with a steady demand for skilled labour. In this scheme, young boys of 16 to 18 years of age are trained for 2 to 4 years.

The training course usually consists of a predetermined schedule of factory work assignments (which generally contributes to production) and some related classroom instruction in the underlying principles of trade. Under the agreement, the trainee candidate is required to give a bond of service, e.g. 5 years' service in the organisation, after completion of training. An apprenticeship agreement, drawn up between the firm and the trainee stipulates the training period, wage rate (stipend), bonus and other conditions.

In order to provide training to the unskilled workers in the industries and workshops, an Apprentices Act was passed in 1961. The apprenticeship training programmes now adopted in different concerns, both private and government, include classroom instructions in blueprint reading, study of machine tools, shop mathematics, trade theory etc. in addition to the practical training in the related trade.

All big concerns like Hindustan Machine Tools, Heavy Electricals, Oil and Natural Gas Commission, Fertilizer Corporation of India, Bhilai Steel Plant, Tata Iron and Steel Company, Indian Railways, Godrej, Escorts etc. have their own training schools for imparting training to their new employees and apprentices.

Apprentice training aims to provide broad training to enable the trainee to take up a wide variety of tasks within his field of specialization.

3.7.1 Foreman Or Supervisory Training (Lower Level Management Training)

Lower level management consists of Foremen, Supervisors, Inspectors etc. They are just above the operational staff and their function is to get the work done from the operational staff.

The foreman/supervisor is in close contact with the workers and interprets the firm's plans to them and conveys the workers' views to the management. He is a key man in the organisation. He is in direct charge of labour and controls the activities of his section. The training of foremen is therefore of paramount importance and should be a continual process, especially in expanding industry.

The aims of foreman training can be listed as:

(i) Bring his impact to the standard, where he can handle interactions with others effectively.

(ii) Develop in him the necessary skill to impart instructions to the workers under him.

(iii) To develop in him the qualities of leadership.

(iv) To impart adequate knowledge of management methods to deal with other people.

(v) Impart to him deep knowledge about the work, so that workers should feel that he is superior to them.

(vi) Develop in him the skill to improve upon the existing method of work.

(vii) To provide him the knowledge of labour problems and legislation.

(viii) Make him qualify for advancement to positions of greater responsibility.

(ix) Develop the ability to plan, co-ordinate, control and build up efficient team in order to obtain best result.

(x) Train him about safety rules and practices to be followed in the shops.

Foremen are best trained through planned conferences, (or discussions) which may be supplemented by lectures and carefully selected text books. A homogeneous group of twelve to fifteen men from the plant constitutes an ideal conference group.

Foremanship training should first deal with the immediate problems of supervision and then cover such topics, such as, the techniques and responsibilities of shop management, company policies, production planning, methods of training workers, terms of union contract, job evaluation, merit rating, safety and work study and other methods of cost reduction.

Methods of Training Supervisors

1. Induction and Orientation: Induction and orientation training involves familiarizing the new employee about the following:

(i) The enterprise which he has joined, its history, organisation structure, products being manufactured.

(ii) Information about the authorities and responsibilities assigned to him.

(iii) Safety and proper use of tools and equipments.

(iv) Conditions of employment, disciplinary rules and other aspects of personnel policy.

2. Lecture (Classroom) Methods: Under this method, lectures are delivered by experts within or outside the company. The lectures may cover such topics as the techniques and responsibilities of shop management, company policies, production planning methods, methods of training workmen, job evaluation, merit rating, safety, time and motion study etc. The usefulness of this method can be enhanced by using audio-visual aids such as OHP, slides, technical films and other aids.

3. Conference: A homogeneous group of twelve to fifteen men from one plant constitutes an ideal conference group. People attending a conference, discuss the subject-matter of their interest, e.g. how to control absenteeism, how to reduce scrap etc. A conference helps in exchanging ideas and experiences of different persons and puts them open for discussion to arrive at a feasible solution of the problem in hand. A conference can uproot fixed ideas, change attitudes and develop analytical and questioning ability.

4. Written Instructional Method: This method is used to give to trainees the important information in permanent form for immediate or future use, e.g. standard practice instructions on how to perform various jobs.

5. Training within the Industry (T.W.I.): This was developed basically, as a supervisory training programme to make up for the shortage of civilian supervisory skills during World War II. In our country, the organisation like National Productivity Council, Small Industries Service Institute, Government of India and the Institution of Industrial Engineers, are running T.W.I. Scheme. T.W.I. courses are based upon group conference method, and supervisors attend on a part time basis. In this scheme for imparting training, 10 supervisors (trainees) and one instructor is the usual ratio. In this scheme the supervisors meet informally in the session and they apply the basic principles to their own jobs and thus they learn by doing.

T.W.I. Scheme Imparts Training in

(a) Job Instructions: The supervisor develops the ability to impart clear instructions to the workers, regarding the work to be done and the procedure to be followed.

(b) Job Relation: The programme helps to develop the following qualities in a supervisor - Leadership qualities, Ability to analyse and handle labour problems, Ability to develop good labour relations.

(c) Job Method: The programme increases the supervisor's skill to improve methods of doing work to make optimum utilization of human and material resources.

(d) Job Safety: Supervisor can anticipate the possible hazards and learns how to prevent accident, create safety awareness in employees etc.

3.7.2 Executive (Managerial) Training and Development

Training and development is a continuing process and it has to do at all levels of employees including executives. Executive development can be defined as "an attempt to improve managerial effectiveness, through a planned and deliberate learning process". It seeks to develop certain attitudes, skills and knowledge.

In a broader sense, executive development is one of the tools of organisational development and is aimed at increasing the effectiveness of the organisation.

The efficiency of any organisation depends directly on how well its managers are trained to plan and execute the plans effectively. An effective team of managers is of paramount importance for the survival of the organisation. Because, the managers have to bear the responsibility of running the organisation profitability and effectively. The executives must keep themselves up-to-date with latest development in their field of business activity.

Rapid industrial expansion after the Second World War and separation of management from ownership (as in corporate form of business) resulted in the necessity of evolving a system of executive training and development.

The vitality of business enterprise is largely dependent on the men who manage it. The generation of dynamic leadership, which can build great enterprises, is the need of the hour.

The first necessity of executive development is right thinking and develop their capacity to face challenge, assume responsibility and acquaint them with general business background.

Principles of Executive Development

1. The first principle upon which a management development programme should be based is given primary emphasis on self-development. There is no substitute for personal drive, initiative, inner motivation and basic abilities of an individual.
2. Individuals differ in their aptitude. The individual differences in aptitude and ability should form the basis of executive development.
3. It is more of an education rather than imparting a particular skill; because aim of executive training and development programme is to broaden the outlook of the people and their capacity of judgement and decision making ability.
4. An effective organisational climate should be provided.
5. The aim should be to ensure effective utilization of human resources by exploiting fully, their talents and potentials.
6. To provide an opportunity to the employees to prepare themselves for higher assignments.

Method of Training Executives

The methods of training and development of executives can be broadly classified into two categories:

1. On-the-job training.
2. Off-the-job training.

1. On-the-job Training Methods

(i) Understudies (Appointment as an assistant to): This method is used for training of young managers for general management positions. In this method, the trainee is appointed as an assistant to some senior manager. The trainee, while working as an assistant, learns the ways of working of his superior under whom he is appointed.

(ii) Membership of the Committee: Under this method, the trainee is appointed on some committee consisting of executives (managers) of different departments. The trainee develops the necessary skill of solving problems in a group situation. He also learns from the experience of senior persons. Committee assignments improve understanding and very well imparts the necessary general background.

(iii) Job Rotation: The major objective of job rotation is to broaden the employee's exposure, as well as experience in the organisation. In this method, the trainee is rotated periodically from one job to another.

The advantages of planned rotation are:

- It stimulates a more co-operative attitudes by exposing a man to the other fellow's problems and viewpoints.
- It provides a general background of the organisation to the executive and broadens his outlook.
- It makes the executive (trainee) versatile.

(iv) Job Enlargement, Job Enrichment: Job enlargement means adding some related tasks to the existing job, without increasing level of responsibility. It is a horizontal expansion of the job.

Job enrichment means, increase in level of the responsibility of the executive. This is vertical expansion of the job.

(v) Management by Objectives (MBO): MBO is a process of joint setting of objectives by superior and subordinate. The joint setting of objectives facilitates learning through interaction with the senior.

2. Off-the-job Training Methods

(i) Lecture Method (Refer supervisory training).

(ii) Case Study Method: A case is real life illustration for studying a problem. In this method of training, a real life or hypothetical problem is given to a small group of trainees for analysis and finding out the solution. This method was developed in Harvard Business School and is one of the first deviations from the standard teaching method. In this method, learning occurs through participation, discussion and problem analysis.

This method is best suited to small groups of twenty or less. The trainer, in this method plays a relatively passive role and the trainees learn from their own discussion. They learn to look objectively at the facts, analyse them, find out various alternative solutions and support the best solution. Great care is taken in the preparation of case study material and in case writing. The trainer assists the participants of the group through the use of questions, to draw out, guide or direct the thinking of the group. He helps in sharpening their analytical ability to enlarge their capacity, to take a broader look at the situations.

The **advantages of case study method** are:

- It develops analytical thinking.
- It gives problem-solving ability.
- It broadens their outlook to look at the problems from different angles.
- It develops decision-making skills, verbal communication skills and inter-personal relation skills.

Business Games

In this method, groups of participants are formed. The participants from each group may be from different departments within an organisation or from different organisations. The participants discuss and arrive at certain decisions concerning subjects, such as, production, planning, research and development, cost control, inventory control, sales forecasting etc. In management games, each group would be given data, relevant to the subject assigned to the particular group. The trainer also provides them with simulated data regarding results arising out of decisions made by them which in turn, lead to fresh decisions. At the end of the game, each group of participants is in a position to evaluate the performance of the group.

The advantages of this method are, that it develops decision-making abilities, a team work and an awareness on the effects of interaction between different groups. The participants would, as a result, develop talents to deal with their environment in the real life situations. The most important advantage is that, it gives opportunity to learn from experience, without paying the price that would result from wrong decisions made in real life. These games are powerful educational tools with numerous applications in problem-solving, anticipating the problems in advance, managerial decision-making and executive testing and selection.

Role Playing

Role playing is widely used for human relations and leadership training. It is a supplementary training method, usually combined with the lecture or the conference. The trainees are provided with either written or oral descriptions of a situation and the role they are to play. Two or more trainees are given parts to play, before other participants. They play their parts spontaneously, before the group. The role players and the other participants in the group watching the behaviour, analyse and criticize the behaviour of the role players. The situation is described as fish-bowl exercise, where the participants in the centre of the arena, become the object of observation for the rest of the participants.

Typical examples of role playing are: Manager conducting interview, a salesman presenting sales talk on a product to customers, a superior discussing a grievance with an employee, method study engineer stressing the importance of new method of doing the work etc.

The **advantages of role playing method** are:
- It generates tremendous enthusiasm and interaction among the participants.
- The trainee gets a chance to observe different patterns of behaviour.

They get a chance to act out behaviours, different from their own and develop insight into interpersonal problems.

The participants get a fair idea about the kind of behaviour, which is likely to be a success or failure in real life.

It helps to develop human relation skill and brings about attitudinal change.

Conference:

Refer methods of supervisory training.

3.8 LABOUR WELFARE

The Concept of Labour Welfare

According to *Arthur James Todd*, "Labour welfare means anything done for the comfort and improvement, intellectual or social, of the employees over and above the wages paid."

According to a *publication of ILO*, "Workers' welfare should be understood as meaning with services, facilities and amenities which may be established in or in the vicinity of undertakings to enable the persons employed in them to perform their work in healthy and peaceful surroundings and to avail of facilities which improve their health and bring high morale".

Labour welfare includes provisions of various facilities and amenities in and around the work-place for the better life of the workers. It is a part and parcel of social welfare. The term 'social welfare' means the welfare of the entire society whereas 'labour welfare' is a narrow concept concerned with the welfare of workers. Labour welfare facilities include medical, sports, education, cultural and other facilities. In India, some welfare facilities are compulsory as per labour laws while others are purely voluntary in character.

It should be noted that expenditure on labour welfare is a profitable investment in the long run as it motivates the workers for higher productivity.

Objectives /Advantages of Labour Welfare

1. The primary objective of labour welfare scheme is to provide better life and health and improve standard of life of the employees.

2. It keeps the workers satisfied, loyal and reduces chances of conflict between workers and management.

3. Welfare services are not a charity, they are essential to get higher productivity from the workers by satsifying their needs.

4. It creates a sense of responsibility and dignity among workers.

5. Motivates the workers to apply themselves fully to their work.

6. It relieves workers from industrial fatigue.

7. Employees secure benefits of higher efficiency, more wages, cordial industrial relations and low labour absenteeism and turn over.

8. An employer is able to attract talented workers from the labour market by providing attractive welfare facilities.

9. The social evils prevalent in the labour force such as gampling, drinking etc. are reduced and welfare activities keep them cheerful.

10. The service facilities such as housing scheme, medical benefits, education and recreation facilities for the workers' families help create contended workers' families. This helps them to devote greater attention towards their work.

Agencies of Labour Welfare

In India, the main agencies engaged in labour welfare include – (a) Central Government, (b) State Governments, (c) Employers and (d) Workers' Organisations (Trade Unions), (e) Charitable Organisations.

(a) Central Government: The Central Government has passed a number of Acts for the welfare of different types of workers. The important Acts which provide measures for the welfare of the workers are : Factories Act, the payment of wage Act, Workermen's Compensation Act, Maternity Benefit Act, Apprentices Act, Mines Act etc. Under these acts, employer has to provide welfare facilities for the workers. The government also provides housing, medical facilites, canteens, educational aid etc. to the workers employed in public sector.

(b) State Government: The State Government run health centres, educational centres etc. for the welfare of the workers. They also keep a watch on employers that they are operating the welfare schemes made obligatory by the central or state government. The state government have been empowered to prescribe rules for the welfare of the workers and appoint appropriate authorities for the enforcement of welfare provisions under various laws.

(c) Employers: Employers have to play a major role in providing welfare facilities to industrial workers. Many employers provide voluntarily facilities alongwith the statutory welfare facilities. These include residential accomodation to employees, medical and transport facilities, reading rooms, scholarships to children of workers, patronoise teams of employees for hockey, football etc.

(d) Trade Unions: Trade unions try to safeguard the interest of the employees in the organisations. They force the employers to provide various welfare facilities if not provided, and fix adequate wages to the employees. Unions can also provide educational, cultural and other facilities to their members. Some unions provide sports and educational faciliites. Co-operative stores are also run by some unions. Some trade unions like Rashtriya Mill Mazdoor Sangh, Textile Labour Association etc. are doing a good work in the field of labour welfare.

(e) Charitable Organisations: Charitable Organisations also conduct social welfare activities which are useful to all sections of the society including industrial workers. However, the contribution of such organisaitons in labour welfare is not so significant.

Labour Welfare Schemes (Measures)

Welfare measures relate to physical and social well-being of the employees both within and outside the organisation. They may be classified into three categories.

(1) Economic (2) Recreational (3) Facilitative.

1. Economic:
    - Pension facilities
    - Credit facilities
    - Health and accident services
    - Paid holidays
    - Insurance
    - Profit sharing
2. Recreational
    - Sports
    - Social get-together
    - Special interest groups such as dramatics, athletic programmes, flying and particular hobbies
    - T.V.

    Recreational services are essential because the employees are in need of occasional diversion. Their attitude improves when the routine of everyday living is broken.
3. Facilitative
    - Housing
    - Transport
    - Educational facilities
    - Medical services (including first-aid, hospitalization, sick leave etc.)
    - Fair price shops – Leave travel concession.
    - Canteens, Cafeterias and lunch rooms – Washing facilities.
    - Creches for children and nutrition facilities – Rest rooms etc.

3.9 COMMUNICATING IN INDUSTRY

Communicating is a process by which instructions, ideas, thoughts or information are transmitted, received and understood, by the persons working in organisation.

Components of Communication

The basic components of communication are:

(sender)
↓
(message) + Feedback = Communication
↓
(receiver)

The sender must appropriately prepare the message to be transmitted to the receiver. The receiver must understand the message clearly. Communication is never complete, until the sender knows that the message has been received and understood, either through feedback or observation of the receiver's behaviour.

The purpose of communication is to supply the information necessary to those to whom it is conveyed for better job performance and active co-operation; i.e. to develop the skill and the will to work. If the messages, decisions etc. are effectively and efficiently communicated, the management function also be executed effectively and efficiently.

Definition

The term communication is derived from the Latin word 'communis' that means 'common' and thus, if a person effects communication, he establishes a common ground of understanding. Literally, communication means to inform, to tell, to show or to spread information.

Thus, communication may be interpreted as an interchange of thought or information to bring about understanding and confidence for good industrial relations. It brings about unity of purpose, interest and efforts in an organisation.

As already defined, communication is a process by which instructions, ideas, thoughts or informations are transmitted, received and understood and acted upon by the persons working in the organisation.

Wibur Schramn has said that "the essence of communication is getting the receiver and the sender 'tuned' together for a particular message".

According to *Louis A. Allen*, "Communication is the sum of all the things one person does when he wants to create understanding in the mind of another. It involves a systematic and continuous process of telling, listening and understanding.

According to *Keith Davis* – "It is the process of passing information and understanding from one person to another. It is essentially a bridge of meaning between people. By using this bridge of meaning, a person can safely cross the river of misunderstanding that separate all the people".

To conclude from the above definitions, communication does not merely mean sending or receiving message. It is much more than that. It includes proper understanding of the message, its acceptance and action on it. It is the sum total of direct or indirect, consciously or unconsciously transmitted words, attitudes, feelings, actions, gestures and tones. Even silence is an effective form of communication. A twist in the face is often more expressive than a 100 words put together.

Process or Machinery of Effective Communication

For every communication, at least two persons are required i.e. a sender and a receiver. The various steps involved in communication are as given in the communication model as shown in Fig. 3.4.

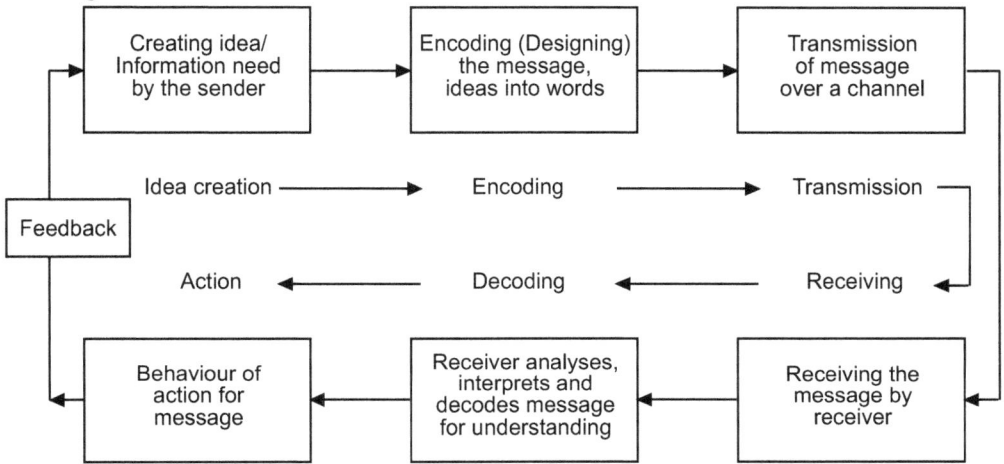

Fig. 3.4: Process of effective communication (Communication model)

These steps have been described as below:

1. **Idea Creation:** It is the preliminary step in communication, where the sender creates an idea to communicate. In other words, he thinks about the message or information required to be sent.

2. **Encoding:** Under this step, while encoding message, the sender assesses whether the receiver is literate, illiterate, educated to know written words or spoken words, whether he is accustomed to the data due to the context of his employment, whether he has actual experience of work. This information helps the sender to choose proper codes printed, sounds, gestures, pictures, real objects and events to encode his message for the receiver.

3. **Transmission:** The sender also selects certain channel or path for communication through which a message travels to the receiver. Selection of the proper channel in accordance with the message is necessary. Written report, letter, lecture, speech, illustrations, pictures, photographs, telegrams etc. serve as a vehicle or carrier for message. Channel selected should be free from barriers. The sender has to view the information needs, background knowledge, experience of the receiver while selecting a channel. Channel functions as a hardware, while the message, as a software.

4. **Receiving:** The receiver has to pay the necessary attention in receiving the message. Any neglect on the part of the receiver may make the communication ineffective or it means the message is lost. In case of oral message, the receiver should be a good listener and willing to understand the message.

5. **Decoding:** Decoding means the act of translating the message by the receiver in his own words and experience.

   Decoding means translation of the message received into ideas for understanding. Understanding the message by the receiver is the key to the decoding process. If the receiver does not understand the message or misunderstands it or pretends to misunderstand it, even though he has understood it correctly, the communication is ineffective. Encoding is done by the sender, while decoding is done by the receiver.

6. **Action:** It is the response of the communication received from the sender. The receiver may like to ignore the message or to store the information received, or to perform the task assigned by the sender through the message delivered.

7. **Feedback:** The receiver, after receiving the message from the sender, analyses, interprets it in accordance with his knowledge and experience. On perceiving and understanding the message and taking action, if necessary, he sends response to the sender. This response to the sender is nothing but feedback given by the receiver. It enables the sender to find out how far his message is followed by the receiver. It helps him to detect shortcomings and faults in the selection of the modes of communication, selection of channel etc. On evaluating the feedback, the sender restructures, modifies his message, if necessary and sends it to the receiver for his full understanding. Without feedback the process of interaction will not be complete.

Methods of Communication

1. Verbal or Written communication
2. Formal or Informal communication
3. Downward, Upward or Horizontal communication

1. Verbal Communication: In the case of verbal communication, everything is oral. The examples of verbal communication are orders and face to face discussions, telephonic talk, lectures, social gatherings, conference, interviews audio-visual aids etc. Verbal communication is quick, simple and comparatively more effective. It is the only way out during periods of emergency, when every activity is to be quickened.

Written Communication: They are always in writing. Written communication is the only way out, when both the communicator and the recipient are far off. It also provides a permanent record and whenever necessary, it can be referred as evidence.

2. Formal Communication: Formal communications are mostly written. Formal communications are generally associated with the particular position of the communicator and the recipient in future, e.g. when the general manager instructs his subordinates by virtue of his superior position, it is formal communication.

Informal Communication: Informal communication on the other hand are free from all sorts of formalities. Informal communications may be conveyed by a simple glance; gesture, smile and or silence. Example, conversation between and among workers about feeling, facts, rumors etc.

3. Downward Communication: It is the transmission of instructions and information from top executive to the lower grade employee.

Upward Communication: It is the flow of information from subordinates to the supervisors e.g. reports.

Horizontal Communication: It is the transmission of information between persons having the same level of authority in the organisation. For example, production manager informing maintenance manager, regarding a breakdown of a machine.

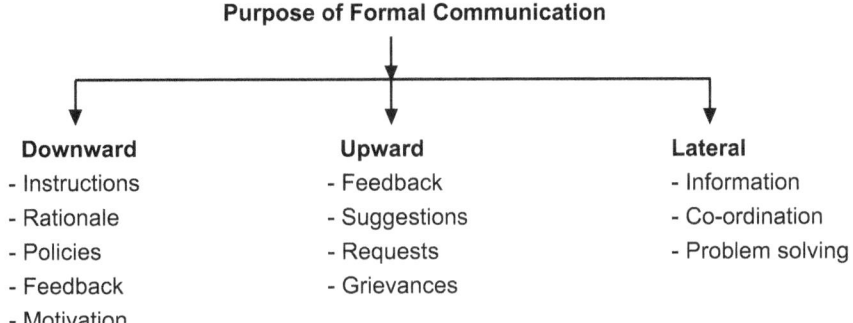

Fig. 3.5: Purposes of formation communication

Essentials of Communications

For effective communication the following points are important:

1. **It must be clear in purpose and intention:** For good communication, the ideas to be transmitted must be absolutely clear in the mind of communicator. The academic level of the workers, their power of grasping things etc. should also be taken into account, otherwise the communication is likely to go in waste.
2. **Participation:** Communicator should help the communicates (recipient) to listen, to participate and co-operate.

3. **Transmission:** In this connection, the communicator must plan carefully what to communicate and how to communicate.
4. It must be simple, and language must be understandable and specific.
5. Attach importance to action rather than words.
6. **Cordial Employer-employee relations:** Effective communication requires a quality of leadership between people immediately connected with each other. It requires sound industrial relation, policies and practices, an all-round atmosphere of friendly co-operation and a feeling of trust and confidence throughout the organisation, right from the top management to the workers.

Characteristics of Communication
1. Communication is a two way process because orders, instructions, directions, guidelines etc. are directed or communicated downwards while suggestions, complaints, grievances etc. are communicated upward.
2. No business can exist without communication because it is necessary to have a congenial relationship between the different employees working at different levels and that is why it is a continuous process.
3. It may be formal or informal and through different mediums.
4. The communication process continues to the extent that ideas and messages are communicated and received.
5. The communication should always be consistent with the plans, objectives, policies and programmes of the organisation and not conflicting.
6. The information should be adequate and complete in all respects.

Importance of Communication in Management

"Communication is the flow of accurate information which people want, need and are entitled to have for successful completion of the job". It is an established fact that one of the foundation stones upon which organisation rests is a system of communication. Co-ordination is achieved largely through communications. No organisation exists without communication network.

The importance of effective communication in management is described below:

1. **Smooth and un-restricted running of the enterprise:** In the manufacturing concerns, instructions and information is being passed on continuously from one end to the other from a superior to his subordinates, from the managing director to his executives. Therefore, the smooth and unrestricted running of an enterprise depends on effective system of communication.
2. **Quick decisions and implementation:** Communication helps the administration in arriving at vital decisions. Without communication it may not be possible for the top

administrators to come in closer contact with each other and discuss the important problems pertaining to the organisation. Through communication, the management conveys targets, issues instructions, allocates jobs and responsibilities and looks after the efficient performance of all activities.

3. **Proper planning and co-ordination:** Good communications are essential to co-ordination. They are necessarily upward, downward and sideways though all the levels of authority and advice for the transmission, interpretation and adoption of policies for the sharing of knowledge and information and for the more suitable needs of good morale and mutual understanding.

4. **Maximum productivity with minimum cost:** Through communication the employees can be instructed, clearly what exactly to do and the way in which it is to be done efficiently and economically. The management can sell their ideas, motivate the workers to work with a will and build up a high moral in the company. This helps to increase productivity.

5. **Morale building and democratic management:** Under effective system of communication it is quite convenient for the employees to express their difficulties, grievances if any, bring all their problems to the notice of management. Therefore, it helps to build-up a morale and democratic management.

3.10 SUGGESTION SYSTEM

Employees working in the organisation can point out inefficiency or drawbacks of the system through their experience. They can also think about improvement in method of doing the work, use of alternative materials, procedures and such other new ideas. Some of the employees volunteer their ideas because they derive satisfaction by making suggestions.

Objectives of Suggestion System

1. Suggestion system is necessary because talented and experienced employees may give suggestion regarding new ideas, concepts, procedures, reduction in wastage of materials, improvement in working conditions, their difficulties, grievances, workplace layout, preventing safety hazards etc.

2. To encourage the employees for their development through their participation in improving the efficiency of the organisation. It increases the employees feeling of accomplishment and satisfaction. Many organisations make a cash reward for a valuable and useful suggestion.

3. To raise employees moral by giving them a chance to express their ideas for the benefit of the organisation. The employees take pride in seeing that their suggestions are accepted.

A suggestion committee is usually formed in order to study, analyse and evaluate all suggestions made by the employees. The committee recommends valuable and useful suggestions for their implementation to the management.

For this purpose, suggestion boxes are placed at convenient places throughout the organisation. Employees write their suggestions, work difficulties, grievance etc. on the suggestion forms provided and drop the same in the box. The suggestions are periodically collected and put before the suggestion committee for evaluation and recommendation.

Suggestion System Problems

A number of problems may arise in the establishment and administration of suggestion system, some of them may be as under.

(i) Supervisors may oppose the suggestion system, they feel that they are bypassed if the workers' suggestions are accepted and implemented.

(ii) Supervisors feel that if worker's suggestions are adopted, they may be criticized by their superiors for not having thoughts of the suggestions presented by the workers.

(iii) Suggestions rewarded on an individual basis may hurt the other employees.

(iv) A good suggestion may result in doing the job with less effort, e.g. with less number of workers. Thus, workers jobs are threatened. Hence workers generally hesitate to submit suggestions. There may be opposition from trade unions for the same reason.

Another important source of suggestion is the 'Quality Circles'. Quality circles are presently becoming popular among industrial organisations throughout the world.

Quality circles are small groups of people doing similar work who together with their supervisors (circle leaders) volunteer to meet for an hour a week to study and solve work related problems which affect them. They identify problems, set priorities, discover causes and propose solutions. These may concern quality, productivity, safety, job structure, process flow, control mechanism, work environment etc. They prepare the plan of action for making the solution reality. Then they present the solution and action plan to the management for approval and implementation.

3.11 DISCIPLINE IN INDUSTRY

Definitions of Discipline

Discipline in industry may be defined as "willingness, co-operation and observance of the rules and regulations of the organisation".

Simply stated, discipline means orderliness.

It implies the absence of chaos, irregularity and confusion in the behaviour of employees.

Disciplines may be defined as "a force that prompts individuals or groups to observe the rules, regulations and procedures which are deemed to be necessary for the effective functioning of an organisation".

Discipline is said to be good when employees willingly follow company's rules and is said to be bad when employees follow rules unwillingly or actually disobey them.

Necessity of Discipline

Discipline in industry is necessary for the following reasons.

1. Maintenance of harmonious human relations in an organisation depends upon the promotion and maintenance of discipline. No organisation can prosper without discipline.
2. Discipline is the very essence of life. Absence of discipline means chaos and disorder. Smooth and efficient functioning demands a high degree of co-ordination among the various elements which form integral parts of an organisation. This is possible only through discipline.
3. Manpower can be used efficiently if there is a discipline in the industry.
4. Maintenance of discipline is a prerequisite for the attainment of maximum productivity, not only for the workers and organisation but also for the entire nation.

Forms of Discipline

1. Positive or Constructive discipline:

In this form of discipline, employees believe in and support discipline and adhere to the rules, regulations and desired standard of behaviour. Discipline takes the form of positive support and reinforcement for approval actions of the company. This type of approach is called positive discipline, constructive discipline or self-discipline.

Positive discipline usually takes place in the following circumstances.

- Adequate wages, bonus, incentives are paid to the employees.
- Chances of career advancement, promotion.
- Appreciation of good performance.
- Good labour relations etc.

which all motivates the employees to adhere to organisational rules and regulations or exercise self-control.

2. Negative discipline:

Negative discipline forces the employees to adhere the rules, regulations and desired standards of behaviour through warnings, penalties and other forms of punishment.

Managers should adopt positive approach to deal with indiscipline in the organisation. Attempts should be made to educate the workers' regarding the value of discipline. It changes the attitude of the workers towards their work and workplace. Discipline is to be developed from within, it should be reformative and not punishitive. The workers should be taught self-discipline because it is the highest form of discipline in any group activity.

Principles of Industrial Discipline (Pre-requisite to Improve Discipline)

The basic pre-requisite of discipline in industrial units are:

1. The goals or objectives of industrial discipline should be clearly stated.
2. Specific and clear rules and regulations should be laid down to serve as a code of conduct for the employees.
3. The code of conduct or rules and regulations should be communicated to all in the organisation.
4. The rules of conduct must contain provision for investigation and settlement of grievances arised during the course of employment.
5. The enforcement authority should be specified.
6. The punishment associated with breaking the rules should be specified.
7. The workers should be motivated and taught self-discipline through education.
8. The discipline policy should give more stress on the prevention of the break of discipline than on the administration of penalties.
9. Create within the employee a 'sense of belonging to industry' by introducing fair wages, fringe benefits, performance appraisal and their participation in management and other activities.

Effects of Indiscipline

Indiscipline increases:

(i) Absenteeism
(ii) Wastage of materials
(iii) Damage or breakdown of machines
(iv) Accidents
(v) Labour turnover
(vi) Sick leaves
(vii) Grievances and frustrations amongst employees.
(viii) Reduction in productivity and quality of work etc.

3.12 E-Business (Electronic Business)

E-Business means using the internet to operate the business. It represents only a fraction of worldwide business, but it is fastest growing sector. E-business can be as simple as using the internet to send e-mails between staff or communicate with suppliers. A business can be considered as an e-business even if it does not buy and sell products over the internet directly, but only create a website to promote their business.

Advantages of E-business

E-business has provided entrepreneurs and consumers with many new advantages and opportunities.

i) It provides the entrepreneurs with excellent opportunitieis to enter the worldwide market. The internet has created a business environment in which time and distance are less important.

ii) The initial investment of starting up an E-business is generally lower than the costs associated with starting an equivalent business using a traditional model.

iii) Low start-up cost enables more people to enter the market with their business ideas.

iv) Many barriers to opening own business have been reduced or removed, with many people able to operate an e-business whilst remaining employed in their regular day job.

v) People who lacked the confidence to start a full scale business are now able to test their abilities and ideas on-line for a relatively small initial investment.

vi) E-business makes it easier, faster and cheaper for business to communicate with their suppliers and their customers. Transactions can occur almost instantly between organisations situated anywhere in the world.

vii) The consumers has increasing amount of ways to interact with business. They have wide access to a diverse range of sellers and broader range of products and services. It also helps them to save money as they can search, shop around and compare price quickly and easily.

viii) The internet is accessible twenty-four hours a day, seven days a week. This means buyers and sellers can conduct transactions at any time as opposed to regular trading hours of transitional business.

ix) E-business can provide cost saving advantages for both buyers and sellers. On-line sellers are able to reduce their overheads as they do not need expensive shop fronts, as many employees or need to hold much inventory in hand. In turn, this allows them to reduce their prices and pass on the savings on to their customers, who save time and money by shopping from their own homes.

x) The business people can track and analyse the buying patterns of their customers easily through E-business and in turn tailor the business to suit the needs and expectations of the customers.

3.13 E-Governance (Electronic Governance)

E-Governance or electronic governance is the technology–driven government system which enables citizens to access government information and services by visiting the appropriate websites on the internet.

E-Governance is the use of ICTs for delivering relevant government information and services efficiently and transparently to citizens, businesses and other arms of government for a wider participation in a representative democracy.

E-Governance service delivery models are government-to-citizen, (G2C), government-to-employees (G2E) and government-to-government (G2G).

The Government of India has launched the National e-Governance Plan (NeGP) with the intent to support the growth of e-governance within the country. The plan intends to create the right environment in order to:

- Implement G2G, G2B, G2E and G2C services.
- Improve internal efficiency.
- Restructure and improve administrative processes.
- Improve accessibility and delivery of public services.
- Reduce government expenditure.
- Increase revenue.

The three main target groups that can be distinguished in e-governance concepts are, government, citizens and business/internet groups. In e-governance there are no disstinct boundaries.

Advantages of E-governance

1) Convenience and user-friendliness : It is more convenient to pay or apply for certain benefits etc. using a computer instead of going to the relevant office and wait in line. The ability of citizens to access E-government service from anywhere in the country is potentially the biggest benefit of an e-governance.

2) Speed and efficiency: Technologies (such as the internet and mobile phones) have made communications faster, and facilitate better communication between government and businesses. Digital information can move instantly from one office to another, without the need to wait for paper documents.

3) Cost saving: Moving away from a heavily paper based system saves the costs of stationary, maintenance of paper documents, man power, time etc. Use of ICT makes communication cheaper.

4) Transparency: Online posting of all official policies, legislation, information and statistics guarantees a high level of transparency and eliminates all bureaucratic tendency to cancel information.

5) Accountability: Transparency in all government processes automatically makes the bureaucracy more accountable, which is the main demand towards better governance.

Thus, E-governance is a wonderful tool to bring transparency, accountability and whistle blowing in India.

Disadvantages of E-governance

1) Source of corruption: E-governance has its own share of challenges that include, administrative, legal and technological challenges. There may be instances where E-governance can itself be a souce of corruption.

2) Requires efficient mechanism and huge resources: Moving countrywide paper documented data (both old and new) into electronic media is itself an uphill task, especially in a vast country like ours. Government retention and retrieval of transaction history will also require huge resources.

3) Huge investment: In a developing country like India, establishing efficient E-governance system involves huge investment in costly infrastructure. All public sector agencies at all levels will need Internet enabled computer system and servers to cope with vast amounts of information and cyber threats.

4) Prone to technical problems: E-governance, like many technology based services, is prone to technical problems from hardware failure, power shortage, slow or no connectivity etc.

5) Prone to attack from hackers and malwares: They endanger the citizens personal data such as name, age, address, bank details etc.

6) Literacy of the user and their ability to use the computer: can limit the implementation of e-governance.

7) No person to person interaction: The system looses the person to person interaction which is valued by many people.

EXERCISE

1. Define manpower planning state the factors affecting manpower planning.
2. (a) Describe various steps in manpower planning.
   (b) State the advantages of manpower planning.
3. Define recruitment. Describe the various sources of recruitment briefly.
4. State and describe the steps involved in recruitment and selection of employees (in brief.).
5. Define training. What are objectives of training and development function.
6. Describe the need of training. Name the various methods of training workers.
7. Describe "On the Job" training with its advantages and limitations.
8. Name the various methods of training workers and describe any two of them.
9. Describe the various methods of training supervisors.
10. Describe the following methods of training. (Any two)
    (i) On-the Job training   (ii) T.W.I.
    (iii) Case study method   (iv) Role playing
11. Describe the concept of 'Labour Welfare'. State its objectives.
12. Name and describe in brief the various agencies of labour welfare.
13. Define communication. Describe the machinery of effective communication.
14. Describe in brief (any two)
    (i) Methods of communication
    (ii) Essentials of sound communication
    (iii) Importance of communication in management
15. Describe in brief.
    (i) Suggestion system   (ii) Discipline in Industry
16. (a) What is discipline in industry? State its necessity.
    (b) Describe the forms of discipline.
17. What is E-business? State its advantages.
18. What is E-governance? State its advantages.
19. Define E-governance and state advantages and disadvantages.

FINANCIAL MANAGEMENT

4.1 INTRODUCTION

Every business enterprise irrespective of its nature and scale of business needs finance (funds) to carry out its activities and accomplish certain business objectives. No business venture can succeed unless it has enough money to take advantage of any opportunities that may arise. Finance is the life-blood of any business.

The management of finance therefore plays a key role in the anticipation of financial needs, acquiring financial resources and allocating funds in the business. In fact, it determines the success or failure of any business activity. The economic objectives of a business organisation are profitability, growth and survival. The attainment of these objectives largely depends upon the efficient management of finance.

Financial management basically deals with procurement of funds needed by the enterprise on the most favourable terms in the light of its objectives. It is not only concerned with effective procurement of funds, but also on the efficient utilization of funds.

Definitions

The finance function is concerned with the process of acquiring and efficiently utilizing the funds of a business system, with the objective of maximising the value of the firm. Financial management involves the application of general management principles to the finance function.

According to *Hoagland*, "Financial management deals with how the corporation obtains the funds and how it uses them".

According to *Mock, Schultz* and *Shuckectat* – "The financial management refers to the application of skills in the manipulation, use and control of funds".

Financial management may also be defined as that part of management, which is concerned mainly with raising the funds for the enterprise in the most economical manner, utilising those funds as profitably as possible for a given risk level, planning future investments and controlling current performance and future developments through financial accounting, cost accounting, budgeting, financial statistics and other means.

Functions of Financial Management

The financial management being a strategic and key area of management involves variety of functions. From the viewpoint of effective management of finance, the finance functions can be categorised as:

[I] Executive finance functions.

[II] Routine finance functions.

[I] Executive Finance Function

1. Determining Financial Needs: The anticipation of the total financial needs of the organisation is also called as 'Capitalisation decision'. It means determining the total financial requirements of an organisation in terms of long-term and short-term requirements. This is a key decision which decides the size of the organisation and the scale of operations. Sometimes the top management prescribes the maximum limit on the total funds to be raised from various sources. The total financial requirements (capitalization) should be anticipated very carefully, otherwise it is likely that the organisation may face a situation of over-capitalization (i.e. availability of more funds with little chances of their profitable investment) or under-capitalizsation (i.e. sacrifice of profitable channels of investments due to inadequate funds).

2. Determining Capital Structure and Sources of Funds: The capital structure decides the blending of the owned and borrowed funds in the total financial requirements. It also implies determination of the sources, timing and procedure to obtain funds which an enterprise needs for its long-term and short-term operations. The terms and conditions of the different financial resources vary significantly depending upon the financial image of the enterprise. The financial management should have full knowledge of the different sources of funds along with their advantages and limitations to make use of them in the best interest of the enterprise. The funds may be raised by different types of securities and debentures, or they could be borrowed from financial institutions or banks.

3. Investment Decision (Allocating Funds): Allocating funds in a business means investing them between the different components of fixed and current assets. The investment in fixed and current assets must yield reasonable returns. The returns from the business operations using fixed and current assets must be sufficiently high to meet the cost of raising funds. Assets are balanced by weighing their profitability against their liquidity. Profitability depends upon factors such as cost control, pricing, forecasting future profits, and measuring the cost of capital. Liquidity means convertibility to cash.

4. Management of Fixed Assets: The investment in fixed assets like land, building, machinery, equipment, furniture, fixture etc. constitutes 60% to 80% of total investments. It involves long-term commitment of funds for their purchase/replacement. This needs careful decisions after evaluating their utility and productive capacity. The investment in fixed asset is governed by the top level policies like owning the asset, to hire or to get it on lease, to make or buy the components etc. It also formulates the appropriate depreciation policies for the replacement of fixed assets.

5. Working Capital Management: Working capital is required for the day-to-day business activities of the enterprise. It is the life-blood of an enterprise which ensures smooth functioning. The important components of the working capital are inventories, receivables and cash balances, which keeps on circulating in an enterprise. The decision on inventory levels of raw-materials/components and finished goods ensures that production and sales do not suffer for want of raw materials/finished products and at the same time excessive stock may not result in increased capital cost for carrying the excessive inventory. Similarly, the levels of receivables is dictated by the credit policy followed by the management. The maintenance of the cash balance is the result of the preference of management towards the profitability or maintenance of liquidity.

6. Control Over Financial Activities: Controlling as a management function brings effectiveness in the operational performance, and it presupposes planning and budgeting. Generally, the following tools are employed in controlling the financial activities:

- **(a) Standard Costing:** The actual cost is compared with the standard cost to locate inefficiencies and trace out the reasons for it.
- **(b) Budgetory Control:** It is exercised through preparing various types of budgets like capital budgeting, cash budgeting and various types of operating budgets.
- **(c) Financial Analysis:** Financial analysis has to be carried out by making use of financial ratios to analyse the financial status and activities of the enterprise. Financial ratios help in measuring the liquidity, profitability, solvency, turnover of assets etc. of the business.
- **(d) Break Even Analysis (Cost-volume-profit Analysis):** This analysis is used to study the effect of changes in selling price, volume of production, variable and fixed costs or a combination of these factors on the profits for selecting these factors such that profit is maximised.

7. Management of Earning: Out of the total earnings available for the equity shareholders, how much should be retained in the business for reinvestment is an important executive decision. It is popularly known as dividend policies. The dividend decision also affects the market price of the equity shares in the stock market. The dividend policies should be formulated in such a manner so as to maximize the value of the firm by due considerating profitability and other financial considerations such as shareholders' reactions, requirement of additional capital, cost of capital, investment opportunities, accumulated surplus etc.

[II] Routine Finance Functions:

There are certain routine functions which are falling within the jurisdiction of the financial management. Generally, these functions are delegated to the subordinate staff in the finance department.

Some of the important routine functions are:

(a) Control on cash,

(b) Custody and safeguard of documents,

(c) Record keeping

(d) Management reporting etc.

Objectives of Financial Management:

The objectives of financial management may be such that they should be beneficial to the owners, management, employees and the customers. These objectives can be achieved by maximising the value of the firm. Elements involved in the maximisation of the value of the firm are:

1. **Allocation of financial resources profitability:** Financial management evaluates the alternative uses of funds and allocates the financial resources after considering marketing and production interrelationships.

2. **Increase in profit:** A firm should increase its revenues in order to maximise its value.

3. **Wealth maximisation:** Wealth maximisation is another important objective of financial management. It relates to maximising the present worth of the firm.

4. **Reduction in cost:** A firm should make efforts to reduce the cost of capital and to launch economy drive in its operation.

5. **Minimize risks:** The financial management should carefully evaluate the financial risks involved before making an investment decision when achieving the goal of maximisation of the value of the firm.

6. **Long run value:** Financial management should not only maintain the business in sound financial health but also strive to produce a rate of earnings which will reward the owners adequately for their investment and keep the business in sufficient liquidity for the confidence of its creditors and investors.

4.2 CAPITAL STRUCTURE

In order to start and run a business i.e. to produce and sell the goods or services, money has to be invested. The money invested in the business in order to yield an income is known as capital.

Capital is needed for the following purposes:

1. Purchasing fixed assets (building, equipment, machinery, tools, furniture etc.).
2. Purchase of raw materials and other supplies.
3. To meet the day to day expenditure such as wages of workers, selling and distribution expenses, equipment and plant maintenance costs etc.

Importance and Scope of Capital

Capital plays a vital role in the modern productive system. Capital is the life blood of any business. Production without capital is not possible. Nature cannot furnish goods and materials to man unless he has the tools and machinery, for mining, farming, foresting, fishing etc. With the growth of technology and specialisation, capital has to play a vital role. Productivity of the modern economy is mainly due to the extensive use of capital, i.e., machinery, tools or implements in the productive system.

Capital is one of the important factors of production. It plays a strategic role in raising productivity. Economic development is not possible without the making and using of machinery, construction of irrigation works, the production of agricultural tools and implements, building of dams, bridges and factories, railways, air ports, ships, harbours etc. which are all capital.

Another important economic role of capital formation is the creation of employment opportunities in the country. Capital formation creates employment at two stages. *First*, when the capital is produced some workers have to be employed to make capital like machinery, factories, equipments, irrigation works etc. *Secondly*, more men have to be employed when capital has to be used for producing further goods. Thus, we see that the employment opportunities will increase with the increase in capital formation. If the population grows faster than the increase in the stock of capital then it will result in unemployment. The rate of capital formation must be kept sufficiently high so that the employment opportunities are enlarged. In India, the stock of capital has not been growing at a fast enough rate so as to keep pace with the growth of population. That is why there is huge unemployment and under employment in both the urban and rural areas. It is thus very much essential to speed up the rate of capital formation.

4.2.1 Types of Capital

Capital may be classified as:
1. Fixed capital or Block capital, and
2. Working capital

1. Fixed Capital:

The funds required for acquisition of the fixed assets, such as land, building, equipment etc. that are to be used over and over again for a long period is known as fixed capital. It cannot be disposed off without breaking the business.

Fixed capital is required for the following items:
1. Land
2. Building and other installation
3. Power and electric supply installation
4. Water supply and drainage fittings
5. Machinery, material handling equipment
6. Tools, jigs, fixtures
7. Administrative office and equipment
8. Furniture
9. Patents etc.

Firms engaged in commerce, trade agency and banking etc. need very little fixed investment. But manufacturers of heavy and capital goods need major part of their capital in fixed assets.

2. Working Capital:

Working capital is required to meet the expenditure for day to day working of the business. It includes:
1. The cost of raw materials, purchased parts, supplies, material in process and finished goods.
2. Wages and salary bills (cost of direct labour, indirect labour).
3. Cost of maintenance and service activities, utilities and fuel, property taxes and insurance.
4. Cost of sales activities such as advertising promotion, shipping services and credit extension to customers.

Components of Working Capital

The components of working capital are:

1. Inventories including,
    (a) Raw material
    (b) Work in process
    (c) Finished goods
    (d) Stores and spares
2. Debtors which include,
    (a) Bills receivable
    (b) Sundry debtors
3. Cash and bank balances, and
4. Advances to suppliers of raw materials.

These components in aggregate, represent gross working capital and the net working capital is equal to;

Gross working capital – (Sundry creditors + Advances from customers + Outstanding expenses).

Thus, net working capital refers to the difference between - current assets and current liabilities.

The current assets are the assets which can be converted into cash within an accounting year and include cash, short term securities, debtors, bills, receivables and stock (inventories). Net working capital can be positive or negative. A positive net working capital results when current assets exceed current liabilities. A negative net working capital occurs when current liabilities are in excess of current assets.

The gross and net working capital concepts are the two important facets of the working capital management. The gross working capital concept focuses attention on two aspects of current asset management (a) Optimum investment in current assets and (b) Financing of current assets. The net working capital indicates; (a) Liquidity position of the firm and (b) The extent to which working capital needs may be financed by permanent sources of funds.

4.2.2 Need for Working Capital

Working capital is that capital which is required to ensure smooth and efficient business operations, without interruptions. It is required to meet day-to-day business activities of an enterprise. The object of any business is to earn profit. The main factor affecting the profit is the magnitude of sales of the business. However, the sales cannot be converted into cash immediately. There is a time lag between the sales of goods and realisation of cash. Therefore, working capital is needed in the form of current assets to fill up this time lag. The working capital is constantly circulating and is being turned over continuously. It is therefore also known as circulating capital. The working capital cycle converting the sales into cash is shown in Fig. 4.1.

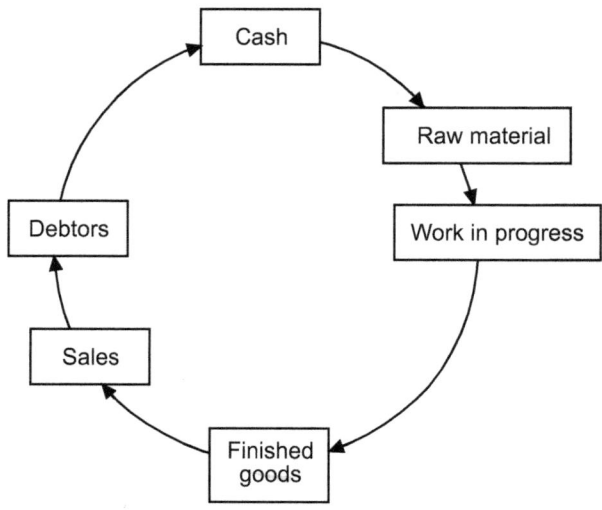

Fig. 4.1: Working capital cycle

If the organisation has certain amount of cash, it will be required for purchasing the raw materials. Then the organisation has to spend some amount on labour and factory overheads to convert the raw-materials into work in progress and ultimately finished goods. The finished goods, when sold on credit basis, get converted in the form of sundry debtors. Sundry debtors are converted to cash only after the expiry of credit period. The cycle repeats itself again and again, thus, there is a cycle in which the originally available cash is converted in the form of cash again, but only after following the stages of raw material, work in progress, finished goods and sundry debtors. Thus, there is a time gap for the original cash to get converted in the form of cash again. Working capital is needed to fulfill the requirements of funds during this time gap, and the quantum of working capital needs varies as per the length of this time gap. Thus, some amount of fund is blocked in raw materials, work in progress, finished goods, sundry debtors and day-to-day cash requirements. However, some part of these current assets may be financed by the current liabilities.

4.2.3 Assessment of Working Capital

The assessment of correct amount of working capital is extremely important to run the business successfully, with reasonable amount of profit. Both, overestimation as well as underestimation of working capital, is harmful to the business. Overestimation of the requirements will result in blockage of scarce funds in idle assets and reduction of profitability of the firm.

Similarly, underestimation of working capital will result in shortage of funds and will deprive the firm from many profitable opportunities. Because it may cause interruption in production.

Shortage of funds may also affect the reputation of the firm due to its inability to meet the demand of the customers in time.

Disadvantages of Excessive Working Capital

1. There is an unnecessary accumulation of inventories resulting in inventory mishandling, wastage, obsolescence, theft and other losses.
2. It results in lower return on investments because the capital is not being used efficiently for the operations.
3. It results in lowering the efficiency of management.
4. It results in losing control over inventory turnover ratios which are used in conducting an efficient business.
5. It results defective credit policy and slack collection period resulting in higher incidence of bad debts, thus adversely affecting profits.

Disadvantages of Inadequate Working Capital

1. Because of non-availability of working capital some profitable projects cannot be undertaken.
2. It becomes difficult to implement operating plans and achieve the profit objectives of the business.
3. The man and machines may remain idle due to lack of working capital, thus there is inefficient utilization of available fixed assets, resulting reduction in productivity.
4. Operating inefficiencies may result due to difficulties in meeting day to day commitments.
5. The organisation loses its reputation as it is not in a position to honour its short term obligation (meeting delivery promises).
6. It cannot avail savings resulting from bulk purchasing of raw materials.

4.2.4 Aspects and Factors to be Considered while Estimation of Working Capital

The following aspects should be considered, while estimating the working capital required to run the business profitability.

(i) Raw Material and Stores/Spares etc.: The need to stock raw material is affected by:

    (a) Nature of raw material

    (b) Storage facilities available

    (c) Lead time

    (d) Expectations of changes in price levels

    (e) System of procurement i.e. inventory ordering system used by the firm

    (f) Seasonality in availability and

    (g) Adoption of new technology.

In the case of the already existing units, the past record serves as guide for estimating the working capital requirement for the next year.

(ii) Cycle Time: The cycle time i.e. the average time required to produce one unit remains more or less constant for a particular industry, unless there is a change in technology or the method of production. During this period, certain amount of material is blocked at various stages. Industries having less cycle time will need less amount of working capital as compared to those with more cycle time.

(iii) Finished Goods: The need to stock finished goods arises, because of factors like nature of market, availability of transport facilities, type of demand for goods, quantity and regularity of orders received etc.

(iv) Receivables: When the products are sold to the customers on credit, the period of credit will extend the operating cycle of the firm. The period of credit allowed to the customers is determined by factors like terms and usage of trade, nature of marketability of the products, method of payments etc.

(v) Expenses: It is good to treat one month's manufacturing and administrative expenses as payable in advance (reserve funds). This will serve as a cushion against any uncertainties and such provision will further strengthen the liquidity position of the firm.

The physical quantities representing consumption/sale of the component during the period are then converted into monetary values for assessment of working capital requirements.

Factors Affecting Working Capital

The working capital requirement of industries vary from one unit to another. The important factors which should be considered while determining the working capital are:

1. Length of period of manufacture.
2. Turnover of inventories.
3. Terms of purchase and sales.
4. Size (volume) of the business.
5. Seasonal variations.
6. Importance of labour.
7. Business cycle.
8. Banking facilities.
9. Nature of business.

1. **Length of Period of Manufacture:** A factory using simple short period process of production requires a small amount of working capital. Whereas, a factory which needs a long period of manufacture, will need large amount of working capital for the large amount of raw material, wage payments and other incidental expenses. Moreover, it has to wait for a long period till the finished product is ready for sale. Thus, large amount of capital is tied up in the process of manufacture. Example, ship building industry.

2. **Turnover of Inventories:** Turnover is the ratio of annual gross sale to the average inventories. If the inventories are small and their turn-over is quick, (products are sold quickly) the unit will require a smaller amount of capital. For example, a retail store deals with a product which has a large demand and which can be sold as quickly as they are stocked, will need a less working capital. On the other hand, a firm having large inventory and slow turnover will need more amount of working capital. For example, a firm dealing with products having irregular and slow demand, will need more working capital.

3. **Terms of Purchase and Sales:** The amount of working capital varies directly with the use of credit. A firm which purchases its requirements on credit will need less working capital than the firm which purchases on cash. Similarly, a firm which sells its products on cash will need less working capital than that selling the products on credit.

4. **Size of the Business:** The amount of working capital depends directly upon the volume of business. The bigger the size of the firm, the large the amount of working capital required and vice versa.

5. **Seasonal Variations:** Industries producing seasonal goods such as coolers, umbrellas, rain coats, fans etc. require large amount of working capital during the off season when the goods are produced. During the season, the goods are sold and less amount of working capital is required.

6. **Importance of Labour:** Small scale and cottage industries are labour-intensive units and therefore require large amount of working capital.

7. **Business Cycle:** At the peak of the business cycle, the turnover is quick, the products are sold quickly as they are produced and hence, smaller amount of working capital is necessary.

8. **Banking Facilities:** If the firm has good banking connections, it may have minimum margin of regular working capital over current liabilities.

9. **Nature of Business:** Working capital also depends upon the nature of business. There are certain businesses which require large amount of fixed capital, than the working capital e.g. railways, state transport etc. whereas trading companies need more amount of working capital than the fixed capital.

4.3 ROLE OF SEBI

SEBI was established by the Government of India in the year 1988 and given statutory powers in 1992. The office of SEBI is situated at SEBI Bhavan, Bandra Kurla Complex, Bandra East, Mumbai, with its regional offices at Kolkata, Delhi, Chennai, Ahmadabad, Jaipur and Banglurue.

The SEBI is managed by its members which consists of :

(a) A chairman nominated by Union Government of India.

(b) Two members, i.e. officers from Union Finance Ministry.

(c) One member from the Reserve Bank of India.

(d) Remaining five members nominated by Union Government of India out of which three shall be whole time members.

Role and Responsibilities

SEBI is the regulator of the securities (capital) market in India. The basic functions of the Securities and Exchange Board of India is to protect the interests of investors in securities and to promote the development of, and to regulate the securities market and for matters connected therewith or incidental there to.

SEBI has to be responsive to the needs of three groups, which constitute the market.

- the issuers of securities.
- the investors
- the market intermediaries.

SEBI has three functions rolled into one body : quasi-legislative, quasi-judicial and quasi-executive.

- It drafts regulations in its legislative capacity.
- It conducts investigations and enforcement action in its executive function, and
- It passes ruling and orders in its judicial capacity.

SEBI has achieved success as a regulator of securities by pushing systematic reforms aggressively and successively. SEBI is credited for quick movement towards making the markets electronic and paperless by introducing T+5, T+3 and then T+2 rolling cycles. The rolling cycle of T+2 means, settlement is done in two days after Trade date. SEBI has been active in setting up the regulations as required under law. SEBI did away with the physical certificates that were prone to postal delays, theft and forgery, apart from making the settlement process slow and cumbersome by passing Depositors Act, 1996.

SEBI has also been instrumental in taking quick and effective steps in light of the global meltdown and the satyam fiasco in October 2011, it increased the extent and quality of disclosures to be made by Indian corporate promoters. In light of global meltdown, it liberalised the take over code to facilitate investments by removing regulatory structures.

Powers

For the discharge of its functions effeciently, SEBI has been vested with the following powers.

1. To approve by laws of stock exchanges.
2. To require the stock exchange to command their by-laws.
3. Inspect the books of accounts and call for periodical returns from recognised stock exchanges.

4. Inspect the books of accounts of a financial intermediatories.
5. Compel certain companies to list their shares in one or more stock exchanges.
6. Registration brokers.

There are two types of brokers:
1. Circuit borker
2. Merchant broker

SEBI Committees

1. Technical advisory committee.
2. Committee for review of structure of market infrastructure institutions.
3. Member of the advisory committee for the SEBI. Investor protection and education fund.
4. Primary Market Advisory Committee (PMAC).
5. Takeover Regulations Advisory Committee.
6. Secondary Market Advisory Committee (SMAC).
7. Mutual Fund Advisory Committee.
8. Corporate Bonds and Securilization Advisory Committee.

4.4 SOURCES OF FINANCE

Business enterprises raise the funds from various sources and invest them in various types of fixed and current assets for the purpose of conducting business operations and earn profits out of them. Each source possesses different types of characteristics in terms of cost and contractual conditions. The fundamental consideration in the financial decision is the 'cost of capital' and that in the investment decision is the 'rate of return on investments'. The profitability of the business operations can be maximized through widening the gap between the cost of capital and the rate of return i.e. the cost of capital should be minimized and the rate of return should be maximised.

Features of Short Term, Medium Term and Long Term Finance

On the basis of periodicity i.e., the time limit within which the funds can be used in the business; the sources of finance can be classified as:

1. Long term finance/funds,
2. Short term finance, and
3. Medium term finance.

1. Long Term Funds: The funds which are raised for more than ten years are called as long term funds. They are required to finance the fixed assets like land, building, machinery, equipments etc.

The important characteristics of long term funds are:

(i) The investments of these funds are more or less of a permanent nature.

(ii) These funds consist of owner's contribution in the form of equity shares and supplemented by the long term borrowings in the form of debentures or long term loans.

(iii) The industries employing sophisticated technology would need more long term funds, while trading business would require less amount of long term funds.

(iv) The degree of business risk tends to be higher in the investment of long term funds.

2. Short Term Funds: Short term funds are required to meet the working capital needs like investment in inventories, debtors, bank balance, cash on hand, marketable securities etc. The financial needs which are required upto one year are treated as short term funds.

Characteristics of Short Term Funds are:

(i) These are required for short term period i.e. upto one year.

(ii) Short term funds are required to meet the day-to-day requirements of the business.

(iii) They are required to finance the working capital needs.

(iv) Short term funds enjoy greater degree of liquidity as compared to long term funds.

(v) The relative proportion of short term funds varies from industry to industry and from time to time. In trading companies, the need of short-term funds will be greater as compared to manufacturing industries.

3. Medium Term Funds: The funds which are raised for more than one year and employed in the business for ten years, are usually treated as medium term finance. However, there is no perfect line of demarcation between various categories of funds.

Raising of Finance

The small scale industries have little problems of finance as compared to large scale industries. The individual investment is the main source of finances for small scale industries (individual ownerships and partnership enterprises). The large scale industries are mainly run by joint stock companies and they feel large problems of financing.

The main sources of finance are as follows:

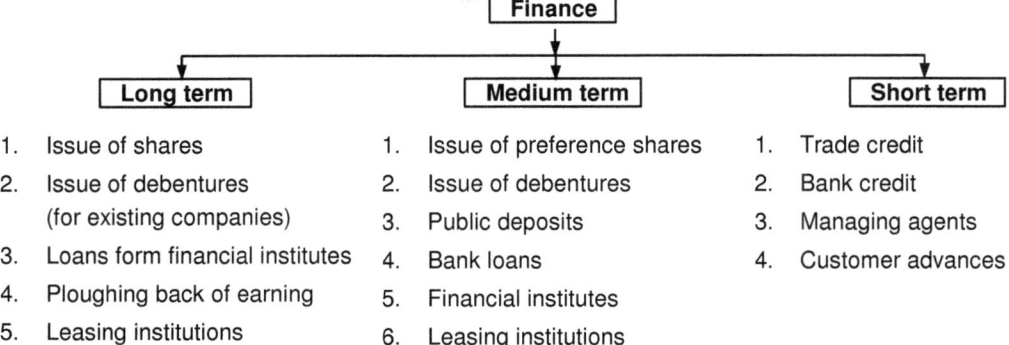

Fig. 4.2: Short term, medium term and long term sources of finance

Source of Finance for Fixed Capital

1. Shares
2. Debentures
3. Public Deposits
4. Loans from Financial Institutions
5. Managing Agents etc.

Source of Finance for Working Capital

Working capital is financed for:

A. Regular works, through
   1. Shares
   2. Debentures
   3. Ploughing back of earning

B. Seasonal works, through
   4. Loans from Banks
   5. Trade Credit
   6. Public deposits
   7. Managing Agents
   8. Financial Institutions

1. Shares

A big amount of funds can be collected by selling shares to the public. Shares are issued for raising funds either when starting a business or when it is decided to expand or improve the existing business. The shareholders are paid dividend every year depending upon the performance of the industry.

Share is a basic form in which a company can raise finance from own sources. A share in a company is one of the units into which the total requirement of capital is divided. If the requirement of the capital is ₹ 10,00,000, and it is divided into 10,000 units, each unit of ₹ 100 is called a 'share'. Shares can be classified into the following types:

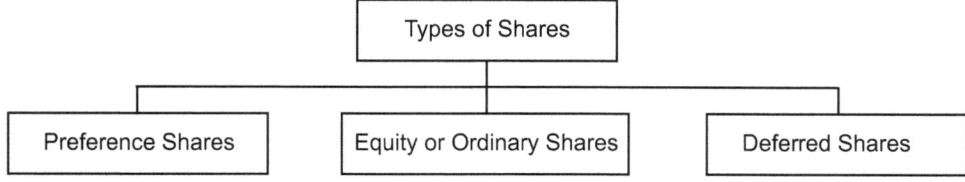

1. Cumulative preference shares
2. Non-cumulative
3. Participating
4. Redeemable
5. Convertible

Fig. 4.3: Types of shares

(a) Preference Shares:

Preference shares are those which carry a preference in regard to:

(i) Payment of dividend, so long as the company is in existence, and

(ii) Return of capital in case of winding up of the business.

The preference shares as the name implies, have the right to be paid first before paying any dividend on other shares. The rate of dividend on preference shares is fixed.

Characteristics of Preference Shares

(i) They are the part of ownership funds and so they do not put any restrictions on the use of funds like debentures or term loans.

(ii) They enjoy preference in getting dividends.

(iii) The rate of dividend is fixed at the time of issue.

(iv) Generally, the preference shareholders do not enjoy voice in the management of the company, except in matters affecting their interest.

(v) The dividends on preference shares is paid only out of the profits of the company.

Types of Preference Shares

1. Cumulative Preference Shares: In case of these shares, the shareholders are entitled to receive fixed dividend even for the years when there is no profit. The dividend on these shares gets accumulated for the years in which they have not been paid. The accumulated arrears of the dividends are paid in the subsequent years when the company gets enough profit to pay them before the dividends are paid to equity shareholders.

2. Non-cumulative Shares: In this case, the shareholders will get dividend only for the years when the company has made enough profit to pay them. In case of these shares the arrears of dividend do not accumulate. The dividends are lapsed in lean years.

3. Participating Preference Shares: In case of participating preference shares, they get the dividend at the fixed prescribed rate. But in addition to the same, they have a right to participate in the excess profit of the company as well with the equity shareholders. These types of preference shareholders can also participate in the excess assets of the company in case of winding up. In case of non-participating preference shares, they cannot have a claim in the excess profits or excess assets of the company. It should be noted that according to the control of capital issues, the participating preference shares are not permitted to be issued in India.

4. Convertible Preference Shares: The convertible preference shareholders are granted an option to convert their preference shares into equity shares according to the terms of the issue. In case of non-convertible preference shareholders, they do not enjoy a right to convert their preference shares into equity shares.

5. Redeemable Preference Shares: In case of redeemable preference shares, these shares can be repaid by the company during its lifetime, as per the terms of issue, either after a specified period is over or whenever the company so chooses after giving proper notice. In case of non-redeemable preference shares, these shares can be repaid only on the winding up of the company.

It should be noted that preference shares have never remained a popular form of security in Indian capital market. The main reasons are that they possess the income weakness of creditorship securities without the safety of returns and the risk of ownership securities without sharing the fortune in case of large earnings.

(b) Equity Shares (Ordinary Shares):

The equity share capital represents the backbone of company's financial structure. The word equity means the ownership interest of shareholders as measured by capital and reserves. An equity shareholder is the absolute owner of the company. He can share in the profit earned by the company (in the form of dividend) and also in the residual assets of the company.

The dividend on equity shares is paid only after the payment of fixed dividend on preference shares. There is no limit of dividend in case of ordinary shares. They may get very high dividend in prosperous years of the company. If there is a loss then equity shareholders do not get any dividend. The fortune of the equity shareholders is tied up with the success or failure of the company. If the company fails, they are greatest losers in the deal.

Conversely, if it succeeds, they are sharing windfall profits. They provide the permanent funds in the business. They are not permitted to withdraw their equity capital during the existence of the company. They participate in the management of the company through their voting rights.

Characteristics of Equity Shares:

1. **Permanent Capital:** Equity shares provide the permanent capital to the company. It is not repayable during the lifetime of the company, but only on winding up. However, statutory right has been given to the equity shareholders to transfer the shares to another person.

2. **Dividend:** The equity shareholders get dividend only after the payment of dividend is made to preference shareholders. Even though the company has sufficient income, it is not obligatory for it to pay the dividend to the equity shareholders.

3. **Claims on Assets:** Equity shareholders can have the claim on the assets of the company in the event of winding up, but only after the claims of all the creditors and preference shareholders are settled.

4. **Control:** Equity shareholder enjoys supreme control on the operations of the company through voting powers. The voting right of the shareholder is in proportion to his share in the capital of the company.

5. **Pre-emptive Rights:** Equity shareholders cannot compel the company to pay the dividend, but they enjoy the right to maintain proportionate interest in profits, assets and control of the company. As such, if the company wants to offer new equity shares, it is under legal obligation to offer these shares to the existing shareholders first, before going to the open market. This right of the equity shareholders is called 'Pre-emptive Right'.

6. **Value of Shares:** The value of equity share changes according to the present and prospective earning of the company. The value of the equity share is reflected in the prevailing market price of the equity shares at the stock exchange.

(c) Deferred Share:

As the name suggests, these shares have their claim to get dividend last of all. They are few in numbers. These shares are issued to founders or promoters of the company.

First of all dividend on preference shares is paid, then ordinary shares are paid the dividend. Whatever is left of the total profit after preference shareholders and ordinary shareholders have been paid, is distributed among the deferred shareholders. Generally, these shareholders may get lion's share of the profits.

2. Debentures

A debenture is a loan to the company at fixed rate of interest. Like shares, the company invites the members of the public to buy debentures. The terms and conditions of issue of debentures are written on the back of the document, unlike shareholders the debenture holders do not take any risk. Profit or no-profit, they must get their interest. They are the creditors of the company. Debenture holders cannot claim the ownership and they are to be paid interest only. The debentures are redeemable after a fixed time, which may be five years or more.

Debenture financing is cheap as compared to equity and preference shares. However, they cannot be raised indiscriminately. They can be issued within the prescribed limits of debt-equity ratio. The interest is paid to the debenture holders at a fixed rate and at fixed intervals and that too before any dividend is paid to shareholders. At the time of winding up of the company, the claims of debenture holders are paid in full, before any amount is paid to shareholders.

Kinds of Debentures

The various kinds of debentures which a company can issue, are as follows:

(a) Registered Vs. Bearer Debentures: The names of registered debenture holders are registered with the company. The interest is paid to the registered debenture holders. Such debentures can be transferred to another person only through the company.

The names of the bearer debenture holders are not registered with the company. They can be freely transferred to any body. Generally, the interest coupons are attached to the debenture certificates, which are lodged with the company for the claim of debenture interest.

(b) Secured Vs. Unsecured: Secured debentures are also called as mortgage debentures. Secured debentures are those which are secured by some charge on the assets of the company. They are empowered to sell such assets for the recovery of their claims in case any default is made by the issuing company.

The unsecured or simple debentures are not secured by any charge on the assets of company. However, their claim is settled before any payments are made to preference and equity shareholders.

(c) Redeemable Vs. Non-redeemable: Redeemable debentures are redeemed at the end of certain stipulated period, say 10 or 12 years. The non-redeemable debentures are not redeemable during the existence of the company. Thus, like equity shares, they provide the permanent finance. As per the controls on capital issue, such debentures are not issued in India.

(d) Convertible Vs. Non-convertible Debentures: As the name suggests, convertible debentures can be converted into equity shares at the option of the debenture-holder as per the conditions of the issue. The time of conversion, conversion price and the proportion of the conversion are stipulated at the time of issue.

Nowadays convertible debentures and convertible bonds have become a popular security in India. Non-convertible debenture holders do not enjoy the right to convert their debentures into equity shares.

Characteristics of Debentures

(i) The debenture holders receive interest at a fixed rate. They hold a priority of claim over that of shareholders.

(ii) Profit or no-profit the debenture holders must receive their interest. In case of non-payment of the interest due to them, they can take legal action as the company is under contractual obligation to pay the same.

(iii) The debenture holders are the creditors and in case of winding up of the company, they hold priority of claim to assets over that of shareholders.

(iv) They do not enjoy the control over the affairs of the company. They do not have voting power. However, in the event of non-payment of interest or principle amount, they can interfere in the working of the company by taking a legal action.

(v) The face value of debenture is higher as compared to equity shares.

(vi) It is a cheaper source of fund, as compared to other sources.

(vii) The interest paid on debenture is considered as the deductable business expense for tax purposes.

Difference between Preference Shares and Equity Shares

Preference Shares	Equity Shares
1. Preference shares have first claim to get dividend.	1. Equity shares have second claim to receive dividend.
2. They get fixed dividend per annum.	2. The dividend paid on equity shares is variable, depending upon profit earned.
3. Preference shareholders do not have voting right.	3. They enjoy voting right.
4. The face value of each share is relatively high, say ₹ 100.	4. The face value is relatively low say ₹ 10.00.

Contd...

5. Redeemable, after fixed period.	5. Ir-redeemable, represents permanent capital.
6. Small risk of investing.	6. Relatively high risk of investing.

Difference between Debentures and Shares

Debentures	Shares
1. A debenture holder is a creditor only and has no control over the affairs of the company.	1. A shareholder is an owner of the company i.e. he has ownership interest in the company.
2. A fixed rate of interest is paid on debentures.	2. Dividend is paid on shares out of the profit.
3. Interest is paid on the basis of whether the company runs in profit or loss.	3. It is based upon the type of share whether the annual dividend is paid or not (depending upon profit/loss incurred by the company).
4. A debenture holder gets his money back after the stated number of years.	4. Money of the shareholder is not refunded to him by the company.
5. A debenture holder does not enjoy any right of voting.	5. While equity shareholders are allowed to vote and attend company's meeting.
6. Debentures can be issued at a discount without any legal restriction.	6. While shares can be so issued only subject to certain conditions as laid down in section 79 of the Companies Act.
7. In the event of liquidation of the company, a debenture holder will get his money before the share holder gets something.	

3. Ploughing back of Earning (Internal Financing)

'Ploughing back of earning' refers to the reinvestment of the internally generated funds of the business. It is also called as 'retained earnings'. It is the important source of finance for extensions or improvements in business activities. The internal financing consists of two components:

(i) Retained earnings, and
(ii) Depreciation.

(i) Retained Earnings: It refers to that part of earnings (profits) which remains in the business after the distribution of the dividend. The equity shareholders, as the owners of the business, are entitled to the residual profits. The entire residual profit is not distributed to the equity shareholders, a part of it is retained in the business. The reserve of capital thus built up during the prosperous period can be used as a working capital. This helps the depression period, in addition to that for expansion and improvements of the organisation.

(ii) Depreciation: Depreciation on fixed assets also represents an important segment of internal finance. It is an accounting adjustment which does not involve any outflow of cash from the business.

Internal financing has proved an important source of finance, not only in India, but also in other parts of the world.

Advantages of Internal Financing

(i) It is convenient source of funds as it arises spontaneously, rather than any type of negotiations.

(ii) It enables the company to stabilize the rate of dividend.

(iii) It enables the replacement of fixed assets.

(iv) It strengthens the equity base of the company and thus enhances the potential borrowing power of the company.

(v) It facilitates the redemption of long-term liabilities.

Limitations of Internal Financing

(i) It can be tapped effectively only by the profitable companies.

(ii) Re-investment of profits in the same company, results into monopolies and concentration of economic powers.

(iii) The shareholders are deprived of their rights to invest their funds elsewhere etc. more profitability.

4. **Loans from the Banks**

Commercial banks are the important sources of working capital. Usually, the working capital is supplied for the period not exceeding one year. They also provide loans for the periods of 3 to 7 years. Commercial banks charge 16 to 18% interest on the loan. and advances.

Form of Assistance

The commercial banks provide the financial assistance as under:

(1) Bank Overdraft: It is a special type of facility provided to business community who operate current account with the bank. Under this facility, the clients are allowed to overdraw the money from the bank within the prescribed limits. Interest is charged on the overdrawn amount.

(2) **Cash Credit:** Under this arrangement, cash credit limit for each client is sanctioned for one year. However, it can be renewed from year to year. Separate cash credit is opened for each client and he is allowed to draw cheques within the agreed cash credit limit. The client can also deposit his cash surpluses in his cash credit account and thus can reduce the interest liabilities.

(3) **Bank Loan:** The bank loan is usually provided for one year. The term loans are provided for 3 to 7 years. The loan amount and periodicity is negotiated with the bank.

(4) **Bill Discounting:** Under the discounting facility, the business sector is allowed to discount the time bills before their maturity. The bank deducts interests on the basis of time lag between the discounting date and the maturity date.

(5) **Export Finance:** The commercial banks also provide assistance in the field of export financing. This facility helps purchasers of materials and other items.

(6) **Working Capital Term Loans:** To meet the working capital needs of the company, bank may grant the working capital term loans for a period of 3 to 7 years, payable in yearly or half yearly instalments.

(7) **Packing Credit:** This type of assistance may be considered by the bank to take care of specific needs of the company when it receives some export order. Packing credit is a facility given by the bank to enable the company to buy/manufacture the goods to be exported. If the company holds a confirmed export order placed by the overseas buyer, it can approach the bank for packing credit facility. Basically, packing credit facility may be:
   (a) Pre-shipment packing credit.
   (b) Post-shipment packing credit.

Security for Assistance

The bank may provide the assistance in any of the above forms, but normally the bank provides the assistance against some security. The security offered for loan may be in one of the following forms:

Hypothecation: Under this form of security, the bank provides assistance to the company against the security of movable property, usually inventories, under hypothecation neither the property nor the possession of goods hypothecated, is transferred to the bank. But the bank has the right to sell the goods hypothecated to realise the outstanding amount of assistance granted by it to the company.

Pledge: Under this type of security, the bank advances the assistance to the company against the security of movable property, usually inventories. But unlike in case of hypothecation, possession of the goods is with the bank. As such, it is the responsibility of the bank to take care of the goods in its custody. In case of default on by company to repay the amount of assistance, the bank has the right to recover the outstanding amount by selling the goods.

Mortgage: Mortgage pertains to immovable properties like land, buildings, machineries attached to earth etc., as security for providing assistance. Under this form of security, the possession of the property as security remains with the borrower while the bank gets full legal authority to acquire the same if the borrower is unable to repay the debt. The party who transfers the interest (i.e. the borrowing company) is called the mortgagor while the party in whose favour the interest is so transferred (i.e. the bank) is called mortgagee.

Lien: Under this mode of security, the bank has a right to retain the goods belonging to the company untill the debt due to the bank is paid. Lien may be of two types (1) Particular lien (2) General lien.

Particular lien is valid till the claim; pertaining to specific goods are fully paid. And General lien is valid till all the dues payable to the bank are paid. Normally, banks enjoy general lien.

5. Trade Credit

Trade Credit is often described as the self-generating source of short term finance. The firms enjoying reputation in the market are found purchasing their requirements of raw materials, tools etc. on credit as a matter of routine.

Willingness of the supplier to permit a delay in payment and buyer's need for it largely determines the extent to which trade credit is to be used to finance short term requirements of the firm.

Trade credit agreements usually carry a stipulation of allowing cash discount for prompt payments.

Importance of trade credit in short term financing of a firm is largely determined by the following factors:

(a) Terms and conditions at which trade credit in short term is available.

(b) Payment record of the borrowing firm.

(c) Financial position of the supplier.

(d) Volume of purchases to be made by the borrowing firm.

6. Public Deposits

A company may invite the general public to deposit their savings for certain period at a certain rate of interest. Fixed capital is generally raised through long-term deposits, while working capital is generally raised by short period deposit. The deposits accepted may be withdrawable at the option of the depositor or on expiry of the specified period.

This method is being employed by cotton textile industries of Mumbai, Ahmedabad and Sholapur. The deposits are taken for 6 months in the purchasing season when cotton has to be purchased and are repaid after 6 months when the clothes are sold.

This method enables the company to keep its share capital low and to borrow at cheap rates. But it cannot be relied upon, specially during the period of depression, when the industry is on the downgrade. During such period, industry requires more money but the depositors withdraw their funds, which creates difficult position for a concern.

The advertisement inviting the public deposits must contain the detailed information, such as, name of the company, date of registration, details regarding head office, particulars about the profit and dividends for the last three years, the condensed balance sheet, the object of raising deposits etc.

Advantages of Public Deposits

Public deposits has the following advantages as a source of finance:

(i) The rate of interest payable on public deposits is usually less than that payable on bank borrowings.

(ii) It is unsecured loan which does not require any pledge or hypothecation.

(iii) There is no need to submit the periodical financial statements, as required in case of bank borrowings.

(iv) The companies can raise public deposits for any purpose. The end use of public deposits is never questioned.

(v) In case of credit squeeze introduced by banks, public deposits may play a very important role.

Disadvantages of Public Deposits

(i) The public deposits are most unreliable source, specially during the period of depression, as already explained.

(ii) According to Income-Tax Act, 1961, only 85% of the interest on public deposits is allowed as deductable business expenses. This increases the effective cost of borrowing.

(iii) The companies are required to deposit 10% of the amount of the public deposits, becoming due on the next 31st March, latest by 30th April of the previous year to that, in bank or specified securities.

(iv) Public deposits are costlier as compared to debentures and preference shares.

7. Managing Agents

This source has played a very important role in early days of industrial development in India for setting up and development of industries. Managing agents have provided fixed and working capital themselves and also arranged through other sources like inducing their friends and relatives to purchase the shares and debentures, arranging loans from banks and public deposits.

The financing of Indian industries has become less dependent on managing agents, because of the malpractices done by some of the managing agents.

8. Financial Institutions

Financial Institutions and their Financial Procedures:

The financial institutions provide the industrial finance for the economic development of the country.

These financial institutions are known as "Developing banks" because of the following reasons:

(1) Unlike commercial banks they sacrifice their commercial motive in favour of the national development.

(2) They lend their funds at concessional rates of interest.

(3) They assist nationally desired projects with low and uncertain returns.

(4) They provide finance to encourage the development of backward areas and small scale sectors.

(5) They provide financial help in assisting the basic, export-oriented industries.

(6) They also provide financial assistance for modernisation and for supporting the sick units in restoring their health etc.

The following specialized financial institutions have been established in Indian Constitution immediately after independence:

- Industrial Development Bank of India (IDBI)
- Industrial Finance Corporation of India (IFCI)
- State Financial Corporation (SFC)
- Unit Trust of India (UTI)
- Life Insurance Corporation (LIC)
- Industrial Credit and Investment Corporation of India (ICICI)

4.5 WANTS, UTILITY, DEMAND

4.5.1 Wants

Want is that desire which can be fulfilled and which is backed by the ability and willingness to fulfill (or satisfy) it. Human wants are infinite in variety and number. Some of his wants are organic and natural. The first fundamental thing is that a man wants to exist and survive, and for this, he needs basic necessities of life. He must have some food to live, some clothing to cover his body and some sort of shelter to protect himself from environment, and also against danger; without these things man's life would be impossible.

As man becomes more civilized his wants multiply. He wants better food, fashionable clothing, comfortable lodging and so on. Basically people are motivated to put sincere efforts to fulfill their wants and derive satisfaction.

1. **Wants in General are Endless and Ever-growing :**

   Human wants are unlimited and continuous. As soon as one want is satisfied, another appears in its place. The process is un-ending. It continues from birth to death. It keeps man to work (or struggle) continuously. Man's mind is so made, that he is never completely satisfied. There is no limit to his wants, so long as he breathes.

2. **Particular Wants are Capable of being Satisfied :**

   Although, wants are unlimited, yet it is possible to satisfy a particular want provided, one has the means or struggles to achieve the means. For example, if a man is thirsty, he drinks water and his want is satisfied.

3. **Wants vary from Individual to Individual :**

   All people do not have the same wants. Wants vary from person to person. They are relative to man's social and economic position. They are also outcome of one's education, taste and temperament.

4. **Wants Multiply with Civilization / Modernization :**

   As man become more civilized, his wants multiply. He is not satisfied with bare necessities of life. He wants to live in comfort and enjoy life. That is why people living in urban areas have more wants than people living in rural areas.

5. **Wants are Complementary :**

   A single article out of a group, cannot satisfy our wants by itself. It needs other things to complete its use. Thus, a motor car needs petrol and mobil oil for its working.

6. **Wants are Alternative :**

   There are number of ways to satisfy a particular want. If we feel thirsty, we can have sharbat, lassi or cold water in summer and tea, coffee or hot milk in winter. The final choice among these alternatives, depends on their relative prices, the money at our disposal and our liking.

7. Wants are Recurrent :

Most of the human wants are of a recurring nature. These wants may be felt again and again after some time. For example, wants to satisfy hunger or thirst.

8. Wants are Influenced by Income, Salesmanship and Advertisement :

A poor man is unable to satisfy even the bare necessities of life, however, a rich person can enjoy comforts and luxuries. Secondly, clever salesmanship and advertisement may induce a person to buy a particular brand even though better alternatives may be available.

9. Wants vary with Time, Place and Person :

Different people want different things and the same person wants different things at different times and at different places. People may prefer to drink coffee, sharbat, lassi or simply cold water in summer depending on their liking. We use umbrellas or raincoats in rainy season and sweater or warm clothes in winter.

10. Wants vary in Urgency and Intensity :

Some wants are more urgent and intense than others. They are generally satisfied first, while others are postponed.

11. Present Wants are more Important than Future Wants :

Future is uncertain and unpredictable. Man is therefore, more concerned with the satisfaction of his present wants, rather than being worried about his future wants.

12. Wants are the Result of Custom or Convention :

Many of our wants are conventional. They are dictated to us by society.

Classification of Wants :

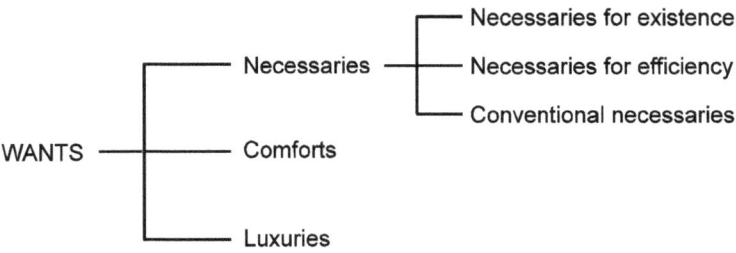

Fig. 4.4 : Classification of wants

The commodities and services that we want are generally classified into three categories:

[I]   Necessaries   [II] Comforts   [III] Luxuries

[I] Necessaries

Necessaries are further classified as :

(a) Necessaries for Existence : These are the basic wants in life. These are as food, shelter, clothes, water and air.

(b) Necessaries for Efficiency : These are necessary for maintaining the efficiency of an individual, e.g. education, medical facilities, balanced diet etc. A table and a chair are necessaries of efficiency for a student. Having these, he will be able to study better.

(c) Conventional Necessaries : These are the needs that arise either by social custom or because the people around us expect us to do so. Offering tea, snacks or biscuits to guest is one of the conventional necessaries. Another example is that, we cannot dress in a strange fashion. We must dress according to our status and in a manner acceptable by the society.

[II] Comforts

Comforts are those wants which add to comfort, efficiency and pleasure of an individual. Having satisfied with necessaries of life, we desire to have some comforts too. The examples are, cushioned chair, fan, air conditioned office, well decorated houses etc.

[III] Luxuries

As soon as the needs for comfort are satisfied, the need for luxuries may arise. Luxury is a superfluous want, which, is satisfied, gives great pleasure, but if not satisfied, it does not cause pain or inefficiency, or something we could easily do without, like costly furniture, air conditioning, luxurious car, shower baths, jewellery, cosmetics, washing machines, cushioned beds etc.

It should be remembered that there is no perfect line of demarcation between necessaries, comforts and luxuries. The same thing may be necessary under one set of conditions and a luxury under others. The luxuries of yesterday, have become the conventional necessaries of today. This is due to the rising standard of living and growing economy.

4.5.2 Utility

Utility is the capacity of a commodity to satisfy human desire and depends upon the intensity of desire to be satisfied.

Marginal Utility : Utility of the last unit of commodity consumed at any particular time, is said to be marginal utility.

Total Utility : The sum of the utilities of all the units consumed at a particular time is known as total utility.

Law of Diminishing Marginal Utility

Other things being equal, as we go on consuming a commodity, the satisfaction derived from its successive units goes on decreasing. The more we have of a commodity, the less we want to have more of it.

Dr. Marshall State the law thus : "Other things being equal, the additional benefit which a person derives from a given increase of his stock of anything, diminishes with the growth of the stock that he has".

In this statement of the law, the word "additional" is very important. It is only additional (marginal) benefit which decreases, and not the total benefit, as explained in the following Table 4.1.

Suppose a man who is hungry requires six chapatties to satisfy his hunger. As he goes on eating chapatties, the additional or marginal utility goes on decreasing. The utility of the first chapatti is higher, as it saves him from starvation. The second chapatti is necessary, but not so as the first one. Similarly, utility of the third chapatti further reduces and so on. The utility of the seventh chapatti falls to zero. The 8th and 9th chapatti will have a negative utility. Their consumption, instead of giving satisfaction or pleasure, causes dissatisfaction.

Table 4.1 indicates as to how the utility of each successive unit goes on reducing till zero and then falls to negative.

Table 4.1

No. of Chapatties	Marginal utility	Total utility
1	20	20
2	18	38
3	15	53
4	10	63
5	8	71
6	4	75
7	0	75
8	−10	65
9	−15	50

The words 'other things being equal' implies that :

1. Each unit of commodity must be similar in quantity.
2. The period of consumption must be the same.

3. Mental outlook of the consumer should remain the same.
4. The price of commodity should remain the same.
5. If the period is long; the fashion, habit and income of the consumer should remain the same.

Zero Utility : The consumption of a unit of commodity makes no addition to the total utility. The total utility is maximum, when the marginal utility is zero.

Negative Utility : If the consumption of a commodity is carried to excess, then instead of giving any satisfaction, it may cause dissatisfaction. The utility in such cases is negative. In the table given above the marginal utility of 7th unit is zero and that of 8th and 9th units is negative.

4.5.3 Demand

Ordinarily, the word demand is often confused with desire. Mere desire for an article does not mean the demand for that article. Desire is the wish to have something or to enjoy a service. But demand implies that the person is willing and able to pay for the article he desires. A beggers desire to have a car has no significance, as he cannot pay for it. On the other hand, a businessman's desire to have a car is a demand, as he is able to pay for it and is willing to do so. Demand thus, means desire backed by willingness and ability to pay.

In order to change desire into demand, it is essential that the person should be both, willing and able to pay. If a man is willing to pay but he is unable to pay his desire will not become demand. Similarly, if he is able to pay but is not willing to pay, his desire will not become demand.

Besides, demand also signifies a price and a period of time in which demand is to be fulfilled. Therefore, demand means the quantity of commodity, which people are willing to purchase at the given price and at a given time.

Demand is composed of the following elements :
1. Desire to posses an article.
2. Ability to pay (purchasing capacity).
3. Willingness to pay.
4. Relation between demand quantity and price.
5. The period of time in which demand is to be fulfilled.

Demand Schedule

A demand schedule is a table or a chart which shows the quantities of a commodity demanded by an individual or a group of individuals at different prices in a given period of time.

Table 4.2 shows the demand schedule of an imaginary consumer of sugar.

Table 4.2 : Demand Schedule

Price per Kilogram (₹)	Quantity Demand / Month
20 per kg	0.5 kg
16 per kg	0.7 kg
12 per kg	1 kg
10 per kg	1.2 kg
8 per kg	1.5 kg

Market Demand Schedule

It is composed of demand schedules of all the individuals in the market and is defined as "the quantities of a given commodity, which all consumers will purchase at all possible rates at a given time".

Table 4.3 : Market Demand Schedule

Price per kg (₹)	Demand of class C (kg)	Demand of class B (kg)	Demand of class A (kg)	Total kg
20	5	6	8	19
16	6	8	10	24
12	8	10	12	30
10	10	12	15	37
8	12	15	16	43

For constructing the table above we have divided the consumer's in a particular area in to three classes A, B, and C depending upon their purchasing capacity.

Law of Demand

This law states that "demand varies inversely with price", i.e., if the price rises demand falls, and if the price falls, demand rises. In other words, demand increases with a falling price and decreases with a rising price.

The law of demand thus states that :

"At any given time, the demand for a commodity or service rises with decrease in price, and falls with increase in price".

The qualifying phrase at 'any given time' is very important, because the demand is different at different times and under different conditions (circumstances) even if the price does not change. The price of the commodity may not rise even if the demand falls due to change in fashion, season, custom. Sometimes, rise in price leads increase in demand, particularly when the people anticipate a further rise in price in the near future and they may rush to purchase larger quantities than routine.

It is clear from the above statements that, demand and price move inversely like two ends of see-saw, where one end goes down and other end goes up and vice-versa.

Law of demand is shown graphically in Fig. 4.5.

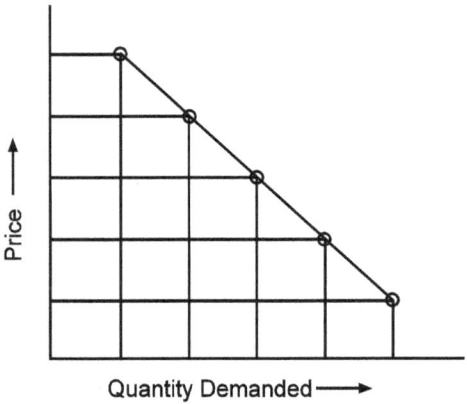

Fig. 4.5 : Law of demand

4.6 SUPPLY, ELASTICITY OF DEMAND AND SUPPLY

4.6.1 Supply

Supply is the quantity of commodity which is offered for sale at a particular rate and time. More precisely, supply means the quantities that a seller is willing and able to sell at different prices.

It is obvious that if the price goes up, he will offer more for sale. But if the price goes down, he will be reluctant to sell and will offer less quantities for sale. Like demand, supply is also relative to a person, place and time. It would be different in a different places, at different times and with a different persons.

Distinction between Supply and Stock

Supply means the quantity actually offered for sale at a certain price, but stock means the total quantity which can be offered for sale, if the conditions are favourable.

The stock will change into supply and vice-versa, accordingly as the market price rises or falls. Supply cannot exceed stock.

In case of perishable goods like fresh milk, vegetables etc., there is no difference between stock and supply. The entire stock is supply and has to be sold off. Otherwise, it will perish.

4.6.2 Elasticity of Demand

The quantity of demand by virtue of which it changes (increases or decreases) with the change in price (decrease or increase) is called Elasticity of Demand.

The demand is elastic when, with a small change in price there is a great change in demand, it is inelastic or less elastic, when even big change in price induces only a slight change in demand.

In the words of Dr. Marshall, "the elasticity of demand in a market is great or small according as the amount demanded increases much or little for a given rise in price."

Types of Elasticity

Price Elasticity : Price elasticity is the responsiveness of demand to change in price.

Income Elasticity : Income elasticity means a change in demand in response to a change in the consumer's income.

Cross Elasticity : Cross elasticity means a change in the demand for a commodity owing to change in the price of another commodity.

Degree of Elasticity of Demand

(a) Infinite or perfect Elasticity of Demand : Elasticity of demand is infinite when even a negligible fall in the price of the commodity leads to an infinite extension in the demand for it.

Fig. 4.6 shows infinite elasticity of demand. Even when the price remains the same, the demand goes on increasing. The horizontal line shows perfect elasticity of demand.

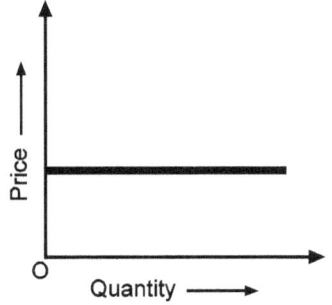

Fig. 4.6 : Infinite elasticity

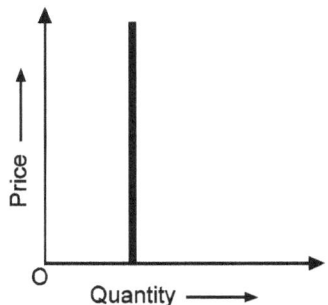

Fig. 4.7 : Zero elasticity

(b) Perfect Inelastic Demand : The demand is perfectly inelastic when, whatsoever great the rise or fall in the price of the commodity may be, its demand remains absolutely unchanged. In Fig. 4.7 the vertical line shows a perfectly inelastic demand. In this case elasticity of demand is zero.

In real life, the elasticity of demand of most of the goods and services lies between the two limits stated above, viz. infinity and zero. Some commodity may have highly elastic demand while others have less elastic demand.

(c) Very Elastic Demand : Demand is said to be very elastic when even a small change in the price of a commodity leads to a considerable extension / contraction of the amount demanded of it.

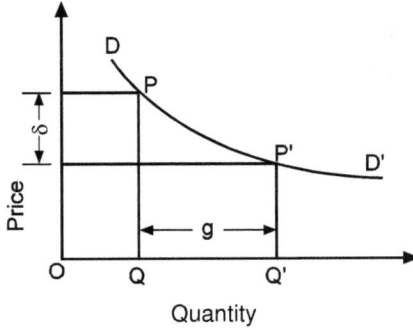

Fig. 4.8 : Very elastic demand

In Fig. 4.8, curve DD' illustrates that for a small change in price, there is a large change in demand.

(d) Less Elastic Demand : The demand is said to be less elastic when even a substantial change in price produces only a small change (extension / contraction) in demand.

Fig. 4.9 shows less elastic demand. A rise of P_1P_2 in price results fall in demand by Q_1Q_2 only which is very small.

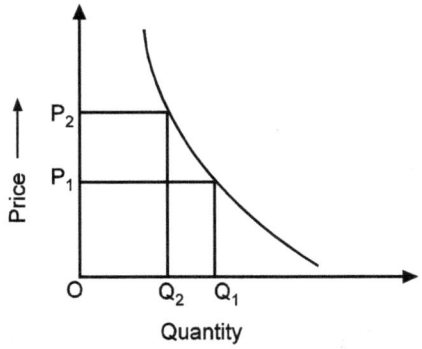

Fig. 4.9 : Less elastic demand

Determination of Elasticity

The elasticity of demand for a commodity depends on a number of factors. We cannot straight a way say, that the demand is elastic or inelastic. All these factors must be taken into consideration to conclude whether the demand is elastic or inelastic.

The following are some of the factors on which elasticity of demand for a commodity depends.

1. **For Necessaries :** The demand is less elastic or comparatively inelastic. The consumers have to purchase them whatever be the price. The demand remains practically unchanged.

2. **For Luxuries :** In case of luxuries, the demand is more elastic. Hence, in such cases, the demand extends and contracts considerably, when the price falls and rises respectively.

3. **Existence of Substitutes :** For commodities having substitutes there is, greater extension or contraction of demand. If the price rises, demand for it will contract, because people will buy its substitute.

4. **Several uses :** When the commodity has several uses, demand for it is elastic. When the price rises, the commodity tends to be put to use only for more urgent uses. The demand for the commodity may be elastic for one use and inelastic for another use.

5. **Possibility of Postponement :** When we can postpone the purchase of commodity, its demand is elastic. More is purchased when the price falls, and less when it rises.

6. **Range of Prices :** Elasticity of demand depends also on the level of prices. If the price is too high or too low, the demand will be comparatively inelastic. For moderate prices, it is elastic.

Thus, it can be concluded that there is no hard and fast rule to determine, whether the demand for any commodity is elastic or inelastic.

4.6.3 Elasticity of Supply

The law of supply states that "the supply varies directly with the price". If the price rises, the quantity offered will extend, and as it falls the quantity offered will contract. This characteristic of supply by virtue of which it extends or contracts with a rise or fall in prices, is known as *Elasticity of Supply*.

We can say that if a small change in price (rise or fall) leads to a big change in supply (extension or contractions), the supply is elastic; on the other hand, if a considerable change in price (rise or fall) lead to only a small change in supply (extension or contraction); it is inelastic or less elastic.

Diagrammatic Representation

Fig. 4.10 shows inelastic supply. When the price rises from PQ to P'Q' (which is a considerable rise) the quantity offered extends OQ to OQ' only which is not much. Hence, supply is less elastic.

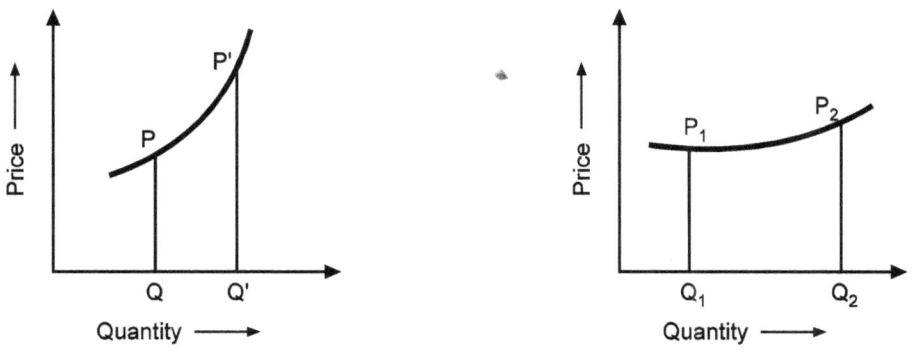

Fig. 4.10 : Less elastic or inelastic supply   **Fig. 4.11 : Elastic supply**

Fig. 4.11 shows that rise from P_1Q_1 to P_2Q_2 is not so large, but the extension of supply from OQ_1 to OQ_2 is quite considerable. Hence, the supply is elastic.

Measurement of Elasticity of Supply

A vertical straight line will represent absolutely inelastic supply (zero elasticity) and a horizontal straight line, an infinitely elastic supply. The following formula gives a general measure of elasticity.

$$\text{Elasticity of Supply} = \frac{\text{Increase/decrease in amount supplied}}{\text{Amount originally supplied}} \times \frac{\text{Original price}}{\text{Rise/fall in price}}$$

EXERCISE

1. Define 'Financial Management'. Describe the nature and scope of financial management.
2. Define capital. State its importance in business enterprises.
3. Differentiate between 'Fixed Capital and 'Working Capital' with suitable example.
4. 'Working capital is known as revolving or circulating capital'. Justify the statement.
5. Describe the factors affecting working capital.
6. Name the sources of finance for raising fixed capital and describe any two of them in brief.

7. Differentiate between :
   (i) Preference shares and equity shares.
   (ii) Shares and Debentures.
8. Describe the assistance provided by commercial banks for the enterprise.
9. Describe 'Public deposit' as a source of finance with its advantages and disadvantages.
10. Describe the internal finance with its advantages and limitations.
11. (a) Name the various financial institutions in India.
    (b) Financial institutions are known as "Developing Banks". Justify the statement.
12. State and describe various types of shares.
13. Describe the role of Securities and Exchange Board of India (SEBI).
14. Define the term 'wants'. Describe the main characteristics of human wants.
15. Explain the distinction between necessaries, comforts and luxuries giving two examples of each of them.
16. Will you regard the following articles as necessary, comfort or luxury ?
    (i) A motor car for a minister.
    (ii) A bicycle for a college student in a city.
    (iii) Air conditioner in a residential house
    (iv) Air conditioner in industrialists office.
17. "The luxuries of yesterday have become conventional necessaries of today." Justify the statement.
18. a) Define the terms : Utility, Marginal utility and Total utility.
    b) Explain the law of diminishing marginal utility with a suitable example.
19. What is utility ? Show that the 'Total utility is maximum when the marginal utility is zero'.
20. Explain the meaning of the word 'Demand'. State the law of Demand.
21. What is supply ? Distinguish between supply and stock.
22. Explain the term 'Elasticity of Demand'. Name four goods of daily use having comparatively elastic demand and four goods having comparatively inelastic demand.
23. What is elasticity of demand? How is it measured ?

24. Fill in the blanks by using one of the words given in bracket :
    (i) The demand for tea is (more elastic / less elastic).
    (ii) The demand for light is (more elastic / less elastic).
    (iii) The demand for salt is (more elastic / less elastic).
    (iv) The demand for motor car is (more elastic / less elastic).
    (v) The demand for wheat is (more elastic / less elastic).
25. Describe the factors on which the elasticity of demand depends.
26. What do you understand by 'supply'. State the law of supply.
27. What do you understand by Elasticity of supply ? Give three examples each of elastic and inelastic supply.
28. How is elasticity of supply measured ?
29. Write short notes on.
    (i) Characteristic of wants
    (ii) Law of diminishing marginal utility
    (iii) Degree of elasticity of demand
    (iv) Elasticity of supply

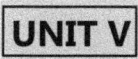

QUALITY MANAGEMENT AND INDUSTRIAL ACT

5.1 THE DEFINITIONS OF "QUALITY"

Quality is a relative term and it is generally used with reference to the end use of the product. For example, a gear used in a sugarcane juice extracting machine may not possess good surface finish, tolerance and accuracy as compared with the gear used in the head stock of a lathe, still it may be considered of good quality if it works satisfactorily in the juice extracting machine. Quality depends upon the perception of a person in a given situation. The situation may be user-oriented, cost-oriented or supplier oriented. Since the item is manufactured for the use of the customer, the requirements of the customer dictates the quality of the product.

The word "Quality" has variety of meanings :

1. **Fitness for purpose:** The component is said to possess good quality, if it works well in the equipment for which it is meant. Quality is thus defined as "the fitness for purpose".

2. **Grade:** Quality is a distinguishing feature or grade of the product in appearance, performance, life, reliability, taste, odour, maintainability etc. This is generally called as quality characteristics.

3. **Degree of preference:** Quality is the degree to which a specified product is preferred over competing products of equivalent grade, based on comparative test by customers normally called as customer's preference.

4. **Degree of excellence:** Quality is a measure of degree of general excellence of the product.

5. The quality of a product is a measure of fulfillment of the promises made to the customers".

6. In terms of product characteristics, the quality of the product can be defined as :

"The total composite product and service characteristics of Engineering, Manufacturing, Marketing and Maintenance through which the product and service in use meet the expectation of the customers".

The key point of this definition is that, 'Quality depends mainly on customer's perception' as described earlier. Hence, it is essential that all these features must be built in the design and maintained in manufacturing which the customer would like to have and is willing to pay for it.

For example, the product must perform its intended function repeatedly as called upon, over its stipulated life cycle under normal conditions of use. Many times it is required that the product must look attractive and be safe in handling. It should last for a longer period and be economical. It should be easy to operate or use.

Thus, we conclude that the product should have certain abilities to perform satisfactorily in a stated application. These abilities may be categorised into ten factors as under :

1. **Suitability:** For specific application
2. **Reliability:** It should give efficient and consistent performance.
3. **Durability:** It should have desired life.
4. **Safe and foolproof workability.**
5. **Affordability:** It should be economical.
6. **Maintainability:** It should be easy to maintain.
7. **Aesthetic look:** It should look attractive.
8. **Satisfaction to customers:** It should satisfy the customers' requirements.
9. **Economical:** It should have reasonable price.
10. **Versatility:** It should serve number of purposes.

A product can be said to possess good quality if all the above requirements are properly balanced while designing and manufacturing it.

Quality of Design

The quality of design of a product is concerned with the tightness of specifications for the manufacture of the product. For example, a part which has a drawing tolerance of ± 0.001 mm would be considered to have a better quality of design than another with a tolerance of ± 0.01 mm.

The factors controlling the quality of design are:

1. Type of customers in the market.
2. Intended life, environmental conditions, reliability, importance of continuity of service.
3. Profit considerations.
4. Special requirements of the product such as strength, fatigue resistance, life, interchangeability of manufacture of item etc.
5. Economic considerations and feasibility.

Quality of Conformance

The quality of conformance is concerned with how well the manufactured product conforms to the quality of design.

For good quality of conformance with the design the following factors are important:

1. The raw material, machines, tools, measuring instruments should be of adequate quality and should be maintained properly.
2. A proper process should be selected, and there should be adequate process control during manufacturing.
3. Operators should be well-trained and experienced.
4. Proper care should be taken in shipment and storage of finished goods.
5. Inspection programme should be planned properly.

Quality of Performance

The quality of performance is concerned with how well the manufactured product gives its performance. It depends upon

(a) Quality of Design.

(b) Quality of Conformance.

It can be a best design possible, but poor conformance control can cause poor performance, conversely the best conformance control cannot make the product function correctly, if the design itself is not right.

5.2 QUALITY CONTROL

The term quality control has variety of meanings:

1. Quality control is the process through which we measure the actual quality performance, compare it with the standards and take corrective action if there is a deviation.

2. It is a systematic control of various factors that affect the quality of the product. It depends on: Material, Tools, Machines, type of labour, working conditions, measuring instruments etc.

3. Quality control can be defined as 'the entire collection of activities which ensures that the operation will produce the optimum quality products at minimum cost'.

4. It can also be defined as 'the tools, devices or skills through which quality activities are carried out'.

5. It is the name of the department which devotes itself full time to quality functions.

6. The procedure for meeting the quality goals is termed as quality control.
7. It is a system, plan or method of approach to the solution of quality problems.
8. As per A. Y Feigorbaum, Total Quality Control is :

"An effective system for integrating the quality development, quality maintenance and quality improvement efforts of the various groups in an organization, so as to enable production and services at the most economical levels which allow full customer satisfaction."

Aims or Objectives of Quality Control

1. To improve the company's income by making the product more acceptable to the customers; by providing long life, greater usefulness (versatility), aesthetic aspects, maintainability etc.
2. To reduce company' cost through reduction of the losses due to defects. For example, to achieve lower scrap, less rework, less sorting, fewer customer returns etc.
3. To achieve interchangeability of manufacture in large scale production.
4. To produce optimum quality at minimum price.
5. To ensure satisfaction of customers with products or services of hig quality level, to build customers's goodwill, confidence and reputation of manufacturer.
6. To make inspection prompt to ensure quality control at proper stages to ensure production of non-defective products.
7. Judging the conformity of the process to the established standards and taking suitable action when there are deviations.
8. To improve quality and productivity by process control, experimentation and customers feedback.
9. Developing procedure for good vendor-vendee relations.
10. Developing quality consciousness in the organisation.
11. To determine the realistic tolerances required as engineering specifications.
12. To ensure production of non-defective parts and reduce wastage.

Functions of Quality Control

The following are the functions performed by the quality control department:

1. Formulation of quality control policy
2. Setting up inspection standards
3. Selection of inspection plan and inspection points.

4. Selection of inspection gauges, instruments and their maintenance.
5. Detect deviations from set standards or specifications.
6. Take corrective action through proper authority and make necessary changes to achieve standards.

Statistical Quality Control (S.Q.C.)

A quality control system performs inspection, testing and analysis to conclude whether the quality of each product is as per the laid quality standards or not. It is called statistical quality control when statistical techniques are employed to control quality or to solve quality control problems. "Statistics is based on the law of large numbers and the mathematical theory of probability". It is in this sense that, the adjective 'statistical' is accurately used in the expression statistical quality control.

Statistical quality control is systematic as compared to guess-work of haphazard process inspection, and the mathematical, statistical approach neutralizes personal bias and uncovers poor judgment. Statistical quality consists of three general activities.

1. Systematic collection and graphic recording of accurate data.
2. Analyzing the data.
3. Practical engineering or management action, if the information obtained indicates significant deviations from the specified limits.

Modern techniques of statistical quality control and acceptance sampling have an important part to play in the improvement of quality, enhancement of productivity, creation of consumer confidence and development of the industrial economy of the country.

Relying itself on the probability theory, S. Q. C. evaluates batch quality and controls the quality of process and products. S. Q. C. uses three scientific techniques, namely:

1. Sampling Inspection,
2. Analysis of the data, and
3. Control charts.

Statistical methods can be used in arriving at proper specification limits of product, in designing the product, in the purchase of raw material, semi-finished and finished products, manufacturing processes, inspection, packaging, sales and also after sales service.

Quality Control and Inspection Difference

Quality control, should not be confused with inspection. Inspection means checking of material, product or components of product at various stages, with reference to certain pre-determined factors and detecting and sorting out the faulty or defective items. In inspection activity, the emphasis is placed on the quality of the past production. To illustrate, if the production schedule calls for manufacturing 1,000 rods with a diameter of 25 ± 0.05 mm, the inspector will concern himself only with whether the rods produced meet this specification. Those that do not, will be rejected, and will continue until 1,000 good units have been produced.

Quality control is a broad term, it involves inspection at particular stage but mere inspection does not mean quality control. As opposed to the inspection, in quality control activity emphasis is placed on the quality of future production. There are various ways of doing this. For example, care may be taken to provide operating personnel with correct instructions prior to the production of an item. However, one of the more important ways is based on technique of statistical nature. For example, to return to our illustration, as the rods are being produced, periodic samples might be taken of the output and the rods in each sample inspected. If the quality of the items in a particular sample is satisfactory, production will be allowed to continue. But if it is not, corrective action will be taken immediately. This action might involve adjusting the machine, eliminating defects in the raw material, instructing or replacing the operator etc.

In brief, what is learned from inspection of a sample of the product is used as a basis to ascertain whether the quality of the products produced is according to the set norms or it is necessary to make changes in the production processes. Hence, in short, in inspection quality of past production is ascertained, and in quality control quality of future production is regulated. Secondly, inspection is merely an act of checking and sorting out the defective item, whereas quality control is a broad term which includes number of activities, (including inspection), in order to build up and regulate the quality of product.

5.3 PROCESS CONTROL

Causes of Variation in Manufacturing Process

In nature two extremely similar things are difficult to obtain. If at all we come across exactly similar things, it must be only by chance. This fact holds good for production process as well. No production process is good enough to produce all items of products exactly alike. Most industrial and administrative situations involve a combination of men, material and machines. Each of these elements of combination has some natural or inherent variability, the causes of which can not be isolated plus the unnatural variability or variability, due to assignable causes which can be isolated and therefore controlled or reduced to economic conditions.

There are two kinds of variations.

1. Variations due to assignable causes.
2. Variations due to chance causes.

1. Variations Due to Assignable Causes : These variations posses greater magnitude as compared to those due to change causes.

These variations may be due to following factors.

1. Differences among machines.
2. Differences among workers.
3. Differences among materials.
4. Differences in each of these factors over time.
5. Differences in their relationship to one another.
6. Change in working conditions.
7. Mistake on the part of operator.
8. Lack of quality mindness.

2. Variations Due to Chance Causes : Variations due to chance causes are inevitable in any process. They are difficult to trace and difficult to control even under best conations of production. Since these variations may be due to inherent characteristics of the process or a machine which function of random. The change factor affect each component in a seperate manner. It has been established that if the variations are due to chance factor alone, the observations will follow a 'normal' curve.

For determining the lack of control, control charts such as $\overline{X}$, R, P etc. are generally used. On these control charts, two limits i.e. upper control limit and lower control limit are drawn. Then actual dimensions of actual observations from a batch of products are plotted on this chart. Lack of control is indicated by points falling outside the control limits. It means that some assignable causes of variation are present. It is necessary to take corrective action to make the process under control.

When all the points fall inside the control limits, we say that the process is in control. It really means that for all practical purposes it acts as if no assignable causes of variations are present based on how many points fall outside the control limits, 1 out of 35 points or 2 out of 100 points can also be tolerated and the process is said to be under control.

From a batch of products manufactured by a certain production process, some of the products are selected at random. Their quality characteristics say (length, diameter, thickness etc.) are measured and classified according to actual dimensions. If we tabulate these dimensions in order of size (in ascending or descending order), and give the frequencies with which each size occurs, we have a frequency distribution.

If the distribution of observation follows a normal curve, then it is assumed that the variations are due to chance causes and no assignable causes of error are present. The conditions which produces these variations are said to be under control and it is concluded that the process is under statistical control. On the other hand, if the distribution does not follow a normal curve then it is concluded that one or more assignable causes of error are present and the process is not in statistical control.

5.4 TOTAL QUALITY CONCEPTS

5.4.1 Total Quality

Total quality is a people focussed concept that aims at continued increase in customer satisfaction at continually lower cost. In involves all employees, top to bottom and extends to include supply chain and customer chain.

The definition of Total Quality used by *Procter & Gamble* is

"Total quality is the unyielding and continually improving effort by everyone in an organisation to understand, meet and exceed the exceptions of customers".

Total Quality Control gives stress on prevention of defects rather than setting it right by rectification. The concept of total quality is different from product quality. It includes product quality and much more. Its approach towards quality is in all its forms in people and processes, in products and costs, in planning and management. All the operations of a company market research, the needs of the customer, the optimal use of raw materials and other inputs, product development and design, manufacturing processes, sales, service after sales, the whole of it comprise total quality.

Total quality can be achieved only through Total Employee Involvement. It starts with people. Total quality comes from employees' creativity, team work, participation, continuous improvement, leadership, motivation etc.

5.4.2 Concept of Total Quality Management (TQM)

Total Quality Management has been accepted throughout the world these days. Many organisations are trying to adopt TQM as a way of life. In fact, TQM is the need of all modern organisations, which was realized first in Japan. TQM is an organisation-wide quality focused culture. It is a system approach to quality management and a journey to achieve excellence in all aspects of organisation's activity. The quality standards do not remain the same for ever. They are to be modified or changed to meet the changing requirements of the customers and to make use of new technology. The launching of ISO : 9000 series standards is an attempt to help the industrial organisations in adopting TQM to improve their quality and productivity.

Definition

TQM has been defined in number of ways.

The following are some of the definitions of TQM.

1. Fig. 5.1 (model of foundation pillars of TQM) defines TQM clearly.

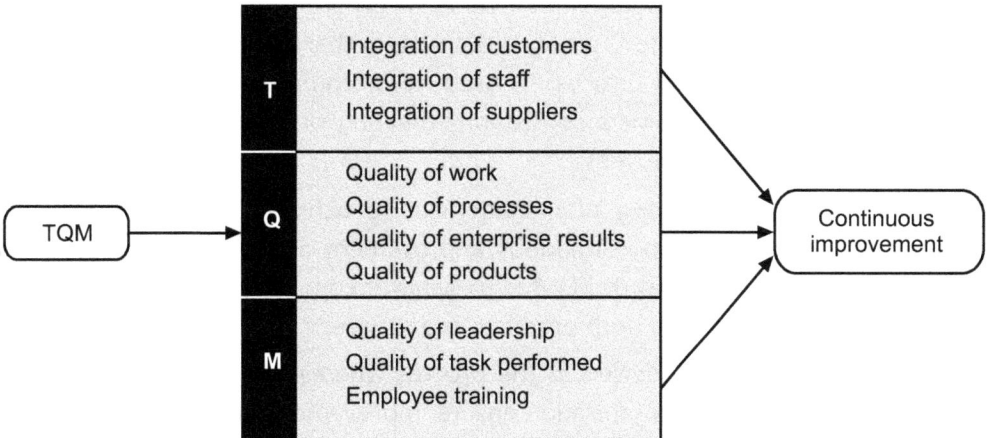

Fig. 5.1: TQM

2. TQM refers to the total involvement of staff in an organisation together, which includes suppliers, distributors and even customers in bringing about quality satisfaction by promoting quality cultures through quality circles, job enrichment and effective purchasing. Workers and supervisors have to be trained to solve the problems in product/process variations.

3. According to *Prof. Leopald S. Vasin*,

   "TQM is the control of all transformation processes of an organisation to best satisfy customer's needs in the most economical manner".

4. TQM is a management approach of organisation, centred on quality, based on the participation of all its members and aiming at long term success through customer satisfaction and benefits to the members of organisation and society (ISO : 8402/IS 13999).

5. According to *Sashkin and Kiser*,

   TQM may be defined as "creating an organisational culture committed to the continuous improvement of skills, teamwork, processes, product and service quality and customer satisfaction".

   Thus, TQM is a continuous customer-centred employee driven improvement.

6. "TQM is a combination of socio-technical process towards doing the right things (externally), everything right (internally), first time and all the times with economic viability considered at each stage of each process".

7. According to *Price and Chen* (1993),

   TQM is a management system, not a series of programmes. It is a system that puts customer satisfaction before profit. It is a system that comprises a set of integrated philosophies, tools and processes used to accomplish business objectives by creating delighted customers consistently meeting or exceeding their expectations and creating happy employees.

8. TQM is a style of working of management to achieve customer satisfaction by boosting quality through continuous improvement and by motivating employees towards quality. The goal of TQM is to achieve complete lack of defects i.e., zero defects. It is applicable to both products and services.

9. TQM therefore, can be viewed as the process wherein the top management along with the people in the organisation ensure improvement in the product quality and work environment continuously at all stages and levels, with the aim of improving customer's and employee's satisfaction. It is a process of examining every critical system in an organisation establishing base line measures of performance and then constantly working to improve them.

5.4.2.1 Elements of TQM

In order to adopt and initiate TQM within any organisation it is necessary to understand key elements. These elements which form the essential core of the TQM philosophy help to change the attitude and culture within the organisation so as to create well-defined process to achieve the continuous improvement of products and services.

Some of the important elements of TQM are described below:

1. Customer Orientation/Satisfaction (Internal and External): It is the ultimate goal in TQM and thus forms the focal element in TQM. The company should exceed the customer's expectations and make him delighted. This means, giving the customer more than he ever thought possible. TQM aims at satisfying customer's requirements which never remain constant, but keep on changing with the change in times, environment, circumstances, needs, fashion, standard of living etc.

Customer's satisfaction has several dimensions, such as:

- Suitability (Fitness for use).
- Reliability (It should give efficient and consistent performance).

- Durability, the life aspect of quality.
- Safe and foolproof workability.
- Maintainability.
- Aesthetic look.
- Good packaging.
- Versatility (It should serve number of purposes).
- Variety in products and services.
- After sales service and support to customer.
- Customer information and training/demonstration/consulting.
- Speed of service (quick response time).
- Civility of service at all levels.
- Affordability (Economical).
- Value for money spent by customer.
- Good image of the company and customer confidence in the organisation based on past experience.

Initially, the organisation must identify and define the customers in terms of internal, external, short term, long term, end users, intermediate users, products/service user and their categories as industrial or consumer their buying capabilities and locations. After identifying the customers, their needs and requirements should be established and defined. The organisation should then establish its quality policies, code of conduct, legislation etc. keeping in view the defined customer requirements.

2. Do it right first time: TQM adopts the policy of zero defect. There is no scope for rework and rejection. The right first time or zero defect is the result of an emphasis on prevention, and diligent use of SPC (Statistical process control), SQC and, data driven elimination of waste and error. Effort is made for rigorous application of EPDCA approach which means.

$$\text{Evaluate} \rightarrow \text{Plan} \rightarrow \text{Do} \rightarrow \text{Check} \rightarrow \text{Act}$$

3. Continuous improvement: The organisation has to cope up with the changing requirements of the customers. The various factors in improving the quality may be change in environment, development of new process, equipments, materials, innovations in a particular field, advancement in technology, change in fashion etc. TQM strives for ever better quality, cost reduction to face competition and for the survival of the organisation.

4. Employee involvement: All the persons working in the organisation (including managers and workers) should be involved in TQM operation, if it is to serve its purpose fully.

TQM is a strategic direction and such a direction can be triggered only by the top management. The commitment of the management to quality mission is of vital importance to promotion and movement of TQM culture within the organisation. Developing organisational vision, mission, philosophy, strategies, objectives and plan is the responsibility of the top management. Moreover, to ensure that TQM is smoothly implemented, necessary skills and resources must be invested in the organisation. It requires every member of the organisation to accept quality as his major area of responsibility. A positive attitude towards customer and constant enhancement of quality must be ingrained in the minds of the employees. Some of the practices which encourage teamwork and training employee involvement include suggestion system, quality circles, self-managed teams, participative leadership etc.

5. Empowering the staff: Empowering the staff assists to accomplish optimal business results through team work. Empowerment occurs when employees are adequately trained, provided with all relevant information and the best possible tools, fully involved in key decision and are fairly rewarded for best results. This involves training and focusses on communication skills, interactive skills and effective meeting skills. Such training enables people to think for themselves and to make decisions for themselves. This principle of empowerment may result in few mistakes but the risks of staff errors are outweighed by increase in creativity, productivity, motivation, commitment and customer service that results from empowerment.

6. Benchmarking: Benchmarking is the practice of identifying, studying and building upon the best practices in the industry or in the world. Dynamic companies are constantly monitoring information from the external environment to compare their process, products and services with the best industry practices. Such companies help establish quality targets which enhances the competitive strength of the organisation.

7. Feedback mechanism: The customer feedback and employee feedback mechanisms are the essential requirements to create customer-oriented quality culture. These feedback mechanisms provide an accurate evaluation of the operations of the company from both internal and external perspectives. This evaluation indicates how the operations affect internal and external customers and provide a measurement of customer satisfaction. The information can be gathered through questionnaire surveys, interviews, use of focus groups and field complaints, suggestion system etc.

Fig. 5.2 shows the framework for creating customer-oriented quality culture in the organisation.

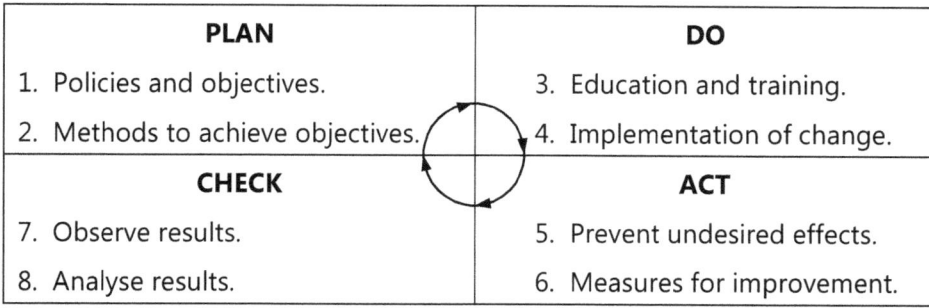

Fig. 5.2: Steps in TQM process

5.4.2.2 Implementation of TQM

Implementation of TQM is not an easy task as it requires a total change in organisational culture, shifting of responsibility to management and continuous participation of all in quality improvement process. W. E. Deming, father of TQM, has suggested Plan-Do-Check-Act cycle for the implementation of TQM in any organisation. The various steps in PDCA cycle, are as shown in Fig. 5.2.

Benefits of TQM

A. Advantages unique to TQM

1. It makes company a leader not follower.
2. TQM creates goal directed connection between customers, management, and workers. Everyone is motivated to contribute. It thus creates effective team work.
3. It makes the company more sensitive to customer needs.
4. It makes the company adopt more readily to change.

B. Benefits of customers

1. Fewer problems with the product or service.
2. Better customer care.
3. Greater satisfaction.

C. Benefits for the company

1. Better product quality.
2. Staff are more motivated and quality-conscious.
3. Productivity improvement.
4. Reduced quality costs.
5. Enhanced problem solving capacity.

6. Increased market.
7. Increased competitive position of the firm, improved profitability.
8. Good public image of the enterprise by helping it to provide goods and services of higher quality at lower cost to the society.
9. Improvement in human relations and work area morale.

D. Benefits to staff

1. Empowerment.
2. Enhancement of job interest and security.
3. More training and improvement in skills.
4. More recognition.
5. Reduced employee grievances.

5.5 ISO 9000 Series Standards in General

International Organisation for Standardisation has developed the following standards on quality systems. The corresponding Indian standards are given in the brackets in Fig. 5.3.

ISO : 84021 (IS : 13999)	Vocabulary

ISO : 90001 (IS : 14000)	Selection and use of quality system standards

NON-CONTRACTUAL SITUATIONS		CONTRACTUAL SITUATION	
ISO : 9004 (IS : 14004)	Quality Management System Standards	ISO : 9001 (IS : 14001)	Quality Assurance Model for design / development / production / installation and servicing
		ISO : 9002 (IS : 14002)	Quality Assurance Model for production and installation
		ISO : 9003 (IS : 14003)	Quality Assurance Model for final inspection and testing
		ISO : 10011-1 to ISO : 10011-3 (IS : 14011-1 to 14011-3)	Guidelines for auditing quality system

Fig. 5.3 : Structure of quality system standards

ISO : 9000 quality standards stipulate certain management practices as guidelines and minimum requirements for making quality of products and services, conforming to the needs of customers. These are developed for facilitating international exchange of goods and services. All these systems are essentially self-disciplined standards, based on the principles of harmonization of specification and continuous surveillance by third party.

ISO : 8402 : 1986 (IS 13999 : 1988) Vocabulary

This gives the definitions of various terms (for example, Quality, Inspection, Reliability, Specification etc.) used in the development of standards on quality systems. The definitions given in this standard, are for use in understanding the Quality Concepts, preparation of Quality Standards and for use in communication to avoid ambiguity in understanding the terms related to quality.

The definitions of few important terms, related to quality as given in ISO: 8402 standard, are given below :

Quality : Quality is the totality of features and characteristics of a product or service that bear on its ability to satisfy stated or implied needs.

Inspection : Inspection implies the activities, such as, measuring, examining, testing, grading one or more characteristics of a product or service and comparing these with specified requirements to determine conformity.

Reliability : It is the ability of an item to perform a required function, under stated conditions for a stated period of time.

Grade : Grade is an indicator of category or rank related to features or characteristics, that cover different sets of needs for products or services, intended for the same functional use.

Quality Policy : It is the overall quality intentions and direction of an organization as regards quality, as formally expressed by top management.

Quality Management : That aspect of the overall management function, that determines and implements the quality policy.

Quality Loop; Quality Spiral : It is the conceptual model of interacting activities that influence the quality of a product or service in the various stages, ranging from the identification needs to the assessment of whether these needs have been satisfied.

Quality Assurance : All those planned and systematic actions necessary to provide adequate confidence that a product or service will satisfy given requirements for quality.

Quality Control : The operational techniques and activities that are used to fulfill requirements for quality.

Quality System : The organisational structure, responsibilities, procedures, processes and resources for implementing quality management.

Quality Plan : A document setting out the specific quality practices, resources and sequence of activities relevant to a particular product, service, contract or project.

Quality Audit : A systematic and independent examination to determine whether quality activities and related results comply with planned arrangements and whether these arrangements are implemented effectively and are suitable to achieve objectives.

Quality Surveillance : The continuing monitoring and verification of the status of procedures, methods, conditions, processes, products and services and analysis of records in relation to stated references, to ensure that specified requirements for quality are being met.

Quality System Review : A formal evaluation by top management of the status and adequacy of the quality system, in relation to quality policy and new objectives resulting from changing circumstances.

Design Review : A formal documented, comprehensive and systematic examination of a design to evaluate the design requirements and the capability of the design to meet these requirements and to identify problems and propose solutions.

Traceability : Traceability implies the ability to trace the history, application or location of an item or activity, or similar items or activities, by means of recorded identification.

Concession Waiver : It implies written authorization to use or release a quantity of materials, components or stores already produced but which do not conform to the specified requirements.

Product Liability, Service Liability : It is a generic term used to describe the responsibility on a producer or others to make reinstitution for loss, related to personal injury, property damage or other harm caused by a product or service.

Non-Conformity : It implies the non-fulfillment of specified requirements.

Defect : It implies the non-fulfillment of intended usage requirements.

Production Permit, Deviation Permit : It implies the written authorization, prior to production or before provision of a service, to depart from specified requirements for a specified quantity or for a specified time.

Specification : It implies the document that prescribes the requirements with which the product or service has to conform.

ISO : 9000 (IS 14000) Quality Management and Quality Assurance Standard :

ISO Standard has given different models for adoption which relate to the stage of the product or service at which the quality of the later needs assurance. This standard gives guidelines for selection and use of appropriate model.

ISO 9001 : 1987 (IS 14001 : 1988) :

Model for Quality Assurance in Design/Development, Production, Installation and Servicing :

A product of a service has to pass through several stages after it is conceived and before it is supplied to the customer. Even after it is supplied to the user, a necessity may arise to keep a followup action; so that the user does not face any problem or difficulties in using the product. ISO : 9001 standard, gives a model for quality assurance at all stages starting from designing the product and continuing, even after the product is delivered to the customer.

ISO 9001 applies to industries who design, produce, install product and provide service after sales as per the requirements of the customer. Some specific examples are heat exchangers, coolers, filters, extraction columns for process industries etc.

In these cases, the customer states his application and the supplier works out the final design, makes changes, if required. A set of specification is then prepared, after the design requirement are mutually agreed. The manufacturer has to open his manufacturing stages to the customer, so as to enable the customer to judge the supplier's capability of manufacturing the product, as per his requirements.

After the product is manufactured and inspected for conformance with specifications, it should be installed by the supplier at the customer's premises and a trial run should be conducted. Even after installation, the supplier has to provide necessary service for maintenance of equipment for trouble-free performance.

ISO : 9002 : 1987 (IS : 14002 : 1988)

Model for Quality Assurance in Production and Installation

Some products require quality assurance only during production and till they are delivered to the customer or installed in his premises. ISO: 9002 gives a model quality assurance for such products. In such cases, the manufacturer gives his own design to meet the customers' requirements and has to only prove the production process is capable of producing the product / equipment as per the requirements of the customer; and that the supplier can install the product / equipment at the customer's premises satisfactorily. Civil structures, construction of bridge etc. are the examples. So, this model is applicable, where the assurance on quality is required only during production and upto satisfactory installation.

ISO : 9003 : 1987 (IS :14003 : 1988)

Model for Quality Assurance in Final Inspection and Test

Certain products require quality assurance, only after they are manufactured i.e. at the time of supply. The customer is not concerned with how they are manufactured. He is interested only in getting the product of desired quality as stated by the supplier or by him. ISO 9003 standard gives a model of quality assurance in such cases. Examples of such products are : domestic appliances, petroleum products, components used in the assembly of manufacture of bigger items such as automobiles etc. Most of the consumer items also fall in this category.

ISO : 9004 : 1987 (IS : 14004 : 1991)

Quality Management and Quality System Elements/Guidelines

ISO : 9001, 9002 and 9003 apply, where a contract between supplier and contractor exists. In non-contractual situations, companies may adopt ISO : 9004 which gives guidelines for quality management.

It is essential to build confidence in the customer that the organization supplies the desired quality of the products or service. The organization has to take several integrated steps in managing all matters, which have direct or indirect effect on its image to deliver the products of desired quality. These integrated efforts of the organization towards maintaining the quality culture, is Quality Management. All these elements of quality management, taken together, make the quality system. ISO : 9004 : 1987 gives guidelines comprising different elements of a quality management system.

ISO : 10011-1 : 1990 to 10011-3(1990) IS : 14011 Part 1; 1990 to IS : 14011   Part 3 : 1990

Guidelines for Auditing Quality Systems

The Quality System has to be checked from time to time for its proper functioning. It has to be updated or modified to meet the requirements of time. It is also necessary to show to the users, that the system is functioning well in its expected objectives.

ISO : 10011-1 describes the rule of auditors, their responsibilities, the elements of auditing, executing the audit, reporting etc.

ISO : 10011-2 deals with the qualification criteria for quality system auditors; their capabilities to perform the audit and their freedom from influence. It also gives guidelines for evaluating auditor candidates.

ISO : 10011-3 deals with establishment of audit function. It says that the management should establish a separate quality audit function. Outside the quality system implementation.

Benefits/Advantages by becoming an ISO : 9000 Company

1) ISO : 9000 series of standards enable to meet the requirements of an internationally uniform quality system. Countries affiliated to European Free Trade Association (EFTA) have reached an agreement that the post-1992 trade transactions would be dealt with only those companies, who have a registered ISO : 9000 quality system. ISO : 9000 is thus recognized internationally, as a benchmark for measuring quality.

2) If Indian Industry adopts the ISO : 9000 standards, it would enhance foreign exchange. So it is important for the Indian industry to adopt ISO : 9000 to compete in the international market.

3) It enables the company to build customer confidence that it is capable of delivering the products or services of desired quality.

4) It reduces the need for assessment by multiple buyers. It thus avoids time and money spent on multiple inspections of the products for conformance.

5) In our country, some concessions for import have been given, as per Export and Import Policy of 1992-97, to the companies adopting ISO : 9000 standard.

6) To adopt ISO : 9000 standards, it is necessary to establish and maintain sound quality assurance system. This results in improvement in efficiency and reduction in inspection, scrap and rework.

7) Adoption of ISO : 9000 helps to enhance the quality image of the company and gives a competitive edge over the other companies which do not have ISO : 9000 quality system.

8) Motivates the employees and develops pride in them for achieving excellence.

9) The suppliers, not having registered ISO : 9000 quality system, may be required to pay higher insurance premium or insurance coverage may be denied to them in some countries.

10) ISO : 9000 helps the company to:
    - Define clearly the need of the company.
    - Specify the right components, processes, tools and equipments for the job.
    - Distribute information to right people and at the right time.
    - Achieve a system of management and control.
    - It provides a framework for continuous improvement in quality.
    (i) Once ISO : 9000 has been adopted, it automatically enables the company control of its production quality and delivery schedules, cut waste and down-time, and boost productivity.

(ii) It enables the company to offer the very best service to its customers. It also gives a measure of product liability protection.

(iii) In business-to-business relationships the organisation that applies ISO: 9000 to itself can create confidence about their quality assurance system among its business partners.

Disadvantages by becoming an ISO-9000 Company

There are few disadvantages of ISO : 9000 series of standards. These are :

1. The implementation of ISO : 9000 series of standards is very much demanding on resources. The formulating and documenting of the system is time-consuming and may involve considerable clerical expenses.

2. Assessment and registration are also expensive.

3. Unless carefully interpreted and planned, the system can become burdensome and expensive, quite often impending normal operations.

4. The need to change attitudes and accept new working practice, may strain the management capability of the company, beyond its ability to cope.

Steps to Registration / Certification

ISO standards are adopted by National Standard Bodies of the individual countries. These bodies, if mutually recognized by the countries, are the certifying or registering bodies. In our country, Bureau of Indian Standards (BIS), is the National Certification Body. The Bureau of Indian Standards has introduced the Quality System Certification Scheme, according to IS : 14000 series of standards. These standards are identical to the internationally accepted ISO : 9000 series of standards of quality system.

The quality system certification scheme or BIS entails implementation in the day to day operating of the organisation, in conformity with the provisions of IS/ISO 9000 series of Standards. The quality system certification of BIS has been accredited by the *Raad Voor de Certificate* (RVC) of the Netherlands. It has also entered into mutual agreement with DQS, Germany, a leading ISO: 9000 certification agency for recognition of each other's certification.

The following steps may be followed for ISO: 9000/IS: 14000 registration.

1. Management commitment to start implementation of ISO : 9000 Standards.

2. Prepare the workmen for change (Make sure about the workmen participation)

3. Selection of appropriate model.

4. Set up steering (co-ordinating) Group and Subgroups.
5. Arrange training of leaders and co-ordinators.
6. Prepare check list.
7. Prepare corporate quality manual.
8. Prepare procedure manuals, operation manuals and work instructions.
9. Update all drawings and specifications.
10. Prepare schedule of training programme and educate employees.
11. Provide tooling, equipments, facilities etc. to meet standards.
12. Carry out internal audit.
13. Take corrective action.
14. Apply for Trial/External Audit to Bureau of Indian standards or any other certifying body and get their recommendation.
15. Implement recommendation.
16. Apply for registration.
17. Grant of license.

5.6 INDUSTRIAL LEGISLATION (ACT)

5.6.1 Introduction

Industrial legislations (Act) are the laws enacted by the Government to provide economic and social justice to the workers in industries. These laws provide guidelines to the industrialists in dealing with the matters of wages, incentives, facilities and other working conditions of the workers.

Mr. V. V. Giri explained industrial legislation as, "A provision for equitable distribution of profits and benefits occurring from industry, between industrialists and workers and affording protection to the workers against harmful effects of their health safety and morality."

Industrial legilsation may be classified into two categories:

(a) General legislation and (b) Specific legislation.

General legislation looks after the general labour problems like social welfare, insurance and industrial disputes, while specific legislation looks after the work of specific industries, transport, mines, electricity, waste disposal, boilers etc.

Necessity of Industrial Legislation

1. Improves industrial relations and minimises industrial disputes.
2. Protects workers' interest and avoids their exploitation by the employer.
3. Helps to pay fair wages to workers.
4. Minimises unrest among the workers.
5. Reduces conflicts, strikes etc.
6. Helps to protect the larger interests of society by aiding in the improvement of trade and industry.
7. Provides job security for the workers.
8. Promotes good environmental conditions in the industry.
9. Fixes hours of work, rest pauses etc.
10. Provides compensation to workers suffered from industrial accidents.

Principles of Industrial Legislation

Industrial/labour legislation is based upon the following principles:

1. Social justice.
2. Social equality.
3. National economy.
4. International uniformity and solidarity.

1. Social Justice: Industrial laws provide social justice to the employees by ensuring suitable distribution of profits and benefits between the employer and employees. It also ensures better working conditions in industry.

Industrial acts based on social justice are

- Factories Act
- Minimum Wage Act
- Workmen's Compensation Act etc.

2. Social Equality: Another objective of industrial legislation is to ensure social equality or social welfare of workers. These laws make the employers to improve social status i.e. material and morale conditions of the workers by ensuring adequate wages, working hours, health and safety of the workers.

3. National Economy: It ensures normal growth of industry for the development of nation. It satisfies the workers' need and increases their efficiency. Efficient industry finally contributes a lot to improve national economy and makes the country self-sufficient.

4. International Uniformity: International Labour Organisation (ILO) has been set up to safeguard the interest of labour. The main objective of ILO is to secure minimum standards on uniform basis in respect to all labour matters. Uniformity of standards can be maintained only by enforcing various industrial laws.

5.6.2 The Indian Factories Act, 1948

The Factories Act was passed by the Governor General of India on 23rd Sept. 1948 and it came into force on 1st April 1949. The Act was further amended in 1950, 1951, 1954 and 1976 which came into force on 26th November 1976. This act is applicable to any factory in India that employees 10 or more than 10 workers.

Aims and Objectives

The major objectives of the factories act are:

(i) The main object of the act is to provide protection to the workers employed in factories against industrial hazards and to ensure safe and better working conditions.

(ii) It regulates and properly maintains various safety health and welfare activities in the factories.

(iii) It also regulates and properly maintains working hours and rest hours of workers, employment of children and adolescents, employment of women, annual leave with wages etc.

Some Important Definitions

Factory: A working place under one management wherein 10 or more than 10 persons are normally working with power aid or 20 or more persons working without power aid.

Manufacturing process: A manufacturing process is a process for:

- Making, altering, repairing, ornamenting, finishing, packing, oiling, washing, cleaning, breaking up, demolishing, or otherwise treating or adopting any article or substance with a view to its use, sale, transport, delivery, disposal etc.
- Pumping oil, water or sewage or any other substance, or
- Generating, transforming or transmitting power, or
- Composing types or printing, printing by letter press, lithography, photography or other similar process or bookbinding, or
- Constructing, reconstructing, repairing, refitting, finishing or breaking up ships or vessels or
- Preserving or storing any article in cold storage.

Adult: A person who has completed 18th year of age is called adult.

Child: A person who has not completed 15th year of age.

Adolescent: A person who has completed 15th year, but has not completed 18th year of age.

Worker: Any person employed directly or through any agency for any manufacturing process or for cleaning any part of machinery, or premises, or other identical work connected with manufacturing process is called worker.

Machinery: Machinery means different appliances used in a factory like prime movers, plants, machines, transmission machinery or any other appliances whereby power is generated, transformed or transmitted.

Occupier: A person who has ultimate control over the affairs of factory.

Hazardous Process: Hazardous process means any process or activity in relation to an industry where, unless special care is taken, raw-materials therein or the intermediate or finished products, by products, wastes or effluents thereof would:

(a) cause material impairment to the health of the persons engaged in or connected therewith or

(b) result in the pollution of the general environment.

Approval, Licensing and Registration of Factories

The act specifies that before starting a factory:

(1) It is necessary to take permission of the state government or chief inspector for the site on which the factory is to be situated or for the construction or extension of the factory.

(2) The plans and specifications have to be approved by the factory inspector.

(3) The factory has to be registered and the license obtained after paying the necessary fees.

The application for permission should be sent to the Chief Inspector, it should contain name and address of occupier and factory, nature of manufacturing process, nature of power to be used, name of factory manager, number of workers required etc.

If after submitting the application to the State Government or the Chief Inspector, nothing is communicated to the applicant within 3 months, the permission is deemed to have been granted.

If a State Government or a Chief Inspector refuses to grant permission to use a particular site, the applicant may appeal to Central Government in this connection with 30 days from the date of refusal.

Inspection Staff

The act permits the State Government to appoint a Chief Inspector and other inspectors who

(a) may enter the factory and

(b) may make examination of premises, plant, machinery and any documents related to factory.

Certifying Surgeons

The act also permits the State Government to appoint qualified medical practioners as qualifying surgeons for

(a) the examination and certification of young workers and

(b) the examination of workers engaged in dangerous occupation or processes.

The factories act makes detailed provisions in respect of the following:

1. Health
2. Safety
3. Welfare
4. Working hours of adults
5. Employment of women
6. Employment of young persons
7. Leave with wages
8. Special provisions
    (a) Dangerous Operations
    (b) Accidents and Diseases
    (c) Penalties and Procedure.

[I] Health Provisions

The factories act makes the following provisions for maintaining the health of workers and for reducing the possibilities of injuries:

(1) Cleanliness:

(a) All dirt and refuse from floors, benches etc. should be removed daily.

(b) The floors of the work-room should be washed at least every week, using disinfectant.

(c) All inside walls, partitions, ceiling, sides and tops of passages and staircases should be whitewashed or varnished at least once in every 14 months. If they are painted, they should be repainted at least once in 5 years.

(d) Effective means of drainage should be provided to avoid collection of water etc. on the work floor.

(2) Disposal of Wastes and Effluents:

Effective and suitable arrangements should be made for the disposal of wastes and effluents due to manufacturing process.

(3) Ventilation and Temperature:

Effective and suitable provisions should be made for securing and maintaining in every workroom

(a) Adequate ventilation by fresh air circulation.

(b) Suitable temperature to provide conditions of comfort and prevent injury to the health of workers.

(4) Dust and Fumes:

Effective measures should be taken for the prevention of inhalation or accumulation of dust and fumes in the work-room.

(5) Artificial Humidification:

In factories (e.g. textile) where artificial humidification is used

(a) Prescribed method should be used for achieving humidification and the artificial humidification should be maintained within the prescribed limits.

(b) The water employed for humidification should be from a source of drinking water.

(6) Over-Crowding:

(a) No work-room should be over-crowded so as to be injurious to the health of the workers.

(b) The minimum space provided for a worker should be 14 m^3. To arrive at this figure, a height above 4.2672 metre from floor level should not be taken into consideration.

(7) Lighting:

(a) Light whether artificial or natural or both, should be sufficient and suitable in all work places.

(b) Sky lights and glazed windows for lighting the workplaces should be kept clean and unobstructed.

(c) Glares and shadows which may cause eye strain and increase the chances of accidents should be prevented.

(8) Drinking Water:

Drinking water should be made available at suitable points. All such points should be legibly marked "Drinking Water". No such points should be located within 3.5 metres from urinal or latrine.

(9) Latrines and Urinals:

(a) Sufficient latrine and urinal accommodation of the prescribed type should be provided.

(b) Separate enclosed accommodation should be provided for male and female workers.

(c) Latrines and urinals should be adequately lighted, ventilated and maintained clean at all the times.

(10) Spittoons:

Sufficient number of spittoons should be provided at convenient places. The spittoons should be maintained in clean hygienic condition.

[II] Safety Provisions

(1) Encasing and Fencing of Machinery:

Every prime mover like engine or motor, moving part of the machinery and every dangerous part of the machinery should be fenced properly.

(2) Work on OR Near Machinery in Motion:

(a) Examination of any part of the machinery in motion should be carried out only by a specially trained adult male worker, wearing tight fitting clothes.

(b) No woman or young worker should be permitted to clean, lubricate or adjust any part of a moving machinery which may involve a risk of injury.

(3) Employment of Young Persons on Dangerous Machines:

No young person should be allowed to work on a dangerous machine unless he is properly trained and carefully supervised.

(4) Hoists and Lifts:

(a) Every hoist and lift should be of good mechanical construction, adequate strength and must be protected by enclosures and fitted with gates.

(b) Every hoist and lift should be adequately maintained and periodically (at least once in six months) examined.

(5) Lifting Machine, Chains, Ropes and Lifting Tackles:

Lifting machines such as cranes, crab, winch, pulley block etc. should be of good construction, adequate strength. They should be properly maintained and thoroughly examined at least once in a year by a competent person.

(6) Pressure Plants:

It should be ensured that the working pressure of pressure vessels such as boilers does not exceed the safe limit.

(7) Floors, Stairs and Means of Access to different Places:

All floors, steps, stairs, passages and gangways should be of sound construction and free from obstructions.

(8) Pits, Sumps, Opening in Floors etc.:

Every pits, sumps, opening in floors, fixed vessels, tanks etc. should be securely covered or fenced.

(9) Excessive Weights:

No person should be asked to lift, carry or move any load so heavy that is likely to cause him injury.

(10) Protection of Eyes:

To protect the eyes of workers from the flying particles (such as in grinding, fitting, rivet cutting, chipping etc.) or from exposure to welding rays, each worker should be provided with effective screens or suitable goggles.

(11) Precautions against Dangerous Fumes:

(a) Adequate protection should be provided against dangerous fumes. No person should be allowed to enter confined space, chamber, tank pit etc. in which dangerous fumes are likely to be present.

(b) If a manufacturing process is producing dust, gas, fumes or vapour which can explode on ignition, the plant should be effectively enclosed; and such dust, gas, fumes etc. should not be allowed to accumulate.

(12) Precautions in case of Fire:

(a) Effective fire warning signal.

(b) Unlocked doors and opening towards outside the workroom as a means of escape in case of fire.

(c) A free passageway and easily openable windows.

[III] Welfare Provisions

(1) Washing Facilities:

In every factory, separate and adequate washing facilities must be provided and maintained for male and female workers.

(2) Facilities for Sitting:

Suitable sitting facilities should be provided for all workers obliged to work in standing position so that they may take rest if an opportunity occurs in the course of their work, without affecting the work.

(3) First Aid Appliances:

First aid boxes equipped with prescribed contents and not less than one in number for every 150 workers at any one time must be provided and maintained at accessible places.

(4) Canteen:

A canteen should be provided and maintained in every factory employing more than 250 workers.

(5) Shelters, Rest-rooms and Lunch-Rooms:

Every factory in which more than 150 workers are ordinarily employed, adequate, suitable, clean, sufficiently lighted and ventilated rest and lunch rooms should be provided.

(6) Creches:

In factory, wherein more than 50 women workers are employed, suitable rooms (creches) must be provided for the use of the children under the age of 6 years of such women.

(7) Welfare Officers:

Every factory employing 500 or more workers should employ prescribed number of welfare officers.

The State Government may prescribe the duties, qualifications and conditions of service of welfare officers employed.

[IV] Working Hours

Hours of Work for Adults: No adult worker should be required or allowed to work in a factory for more than 48 hours in any week ; or 9 hours in any day. Moreover, no worker should work for more than 5 hours before he had an interval of half-an hour.

Holidays: No adult worker should be required or allowed to work in a factory on the first day (i.e. Sunday) of the week, unless the factory manager substitutes Sunday by a holiday one or three days immediately before or after Sunday. If he is required to work on Sunday, he shall be entitled to the compensatory holiday for the same.

Extra Wages for Over-time: Where a worker is required to work for more than 9 hours in any day or for more than 48 hours in any week, he shall be entitled for an overtime at the rate of twice his ordinary rate of wages as specified in the act. The manager of every factory should maintain a register of adult workers to be available to the inspector at all times during the working hours.

Restriction on Double Employment: No adult worker should be allowed to work in a second factory on any day on which he has already been working in one factory.

[V] Employment of Women

No women should be allowed to clean, lubricate or adjust any part of the machinery while that is in motion. Every factory must provide for the creches wherein more than 30 women workers are ordinarily employed. No woman should be permitted to work in any factory except between the hours of 6 a.m. and 7 p.m.

[VI] Employment of Young Persons

A young person means a person who is either a child or an adolescent. A "Child" means a 'person who has not completed his 15th year of age. An "adolescent" means a person who has not completed his 18th year.

No child who has not completed 14th year should be required or allowed to work in a factory. But a child who has completed his 14th year or an adolescent may be allowed to work in a factory if:

(1) A certificate of fitness for such work granted by certifying surgeon is obtained by the manager of the factory.

(2) Such a child or adolescent carries a token giving a reference to such certificate while he is at work.

Working Hours of the Children

(1) No child should be employed or permitted to work in any factory for more than 45 hours in any week and during the night hours.

(2) The period of work for all children employed in a factory should be limited to two shifts which should not overlap or spread over more than 5 hours each. The manager of every factory in which children are employed should maintain a register of child workers, showing the details such as name ; nature of work the group in which he is situated, fitness certificate etc. of the child worker.

[VII] Annual Leave with Wages

Every worker who has worked for a period of 240 days or more in a factory during calendar year should be given leave with wages for a number of days calculated at the rate of;

(a) One day for every 20 days of work performed during the previous calendar year by an adult worker.

(b) One day for every 15 days of work performed by a child worker.

(c) If a worker does not in any one calendar year take the whole of the leave allowed to him, any leave not taken by him shall be accumulated and allowed to him in the succeeding calendar year subject to a maximum of 30 days in case of adult or 40 days in case of the child.

(d) A worker interested to take leave should apply 15 days in advance (30 days in case public utilities). A worker cannot take leave more than 3 times during a year.

[VIII] Special Provisions

(a) Dangerous Operations:

If any operation carried out in the factory is likely to cause bodily injury, poisoning or disease to the worker, the State Government, may declare such operations as dangerous and make the following rules:

(a) Stopping the employment of women and children in such operations.

(b) Provision of proper safeguards of all concerned with that operation.

(c) Periodical medical check-up of all concerned with such operation etc.

(b) Accident and Diseases:

(1) If an accident causes death or bodily injury due to which the worker cannot work for a period of 48 hours or more immediately after the accident, it should be reported to the factory inspector within the prescribed time.

(2) If a worker is suffering from any disease specified in the schedule, a report to that effect should be immediately send to the chief inspector. Such a report should include the particulars of the worker and the disease from which he is suffering.

Power to take Samples: Any inspector, during working hours, after informing the manager may take samples of any substance or materials being used in the factory.

(c) Penalties:

No court shall take cogniance of any offense made under this act except on complaint by or with the previous sanction in writing of an inspector.

If in any factory, there is any contravention of any of the provisions of the act or of any rules made there under, the occupier and the manager of the factory shall each be guilty of an offense and punishable with imprisonment for a period upto 3 months or with fine upto ₹ 2,000 or both. If the contravention is continued after conviction, they shall be punishable with further fine which may extend to ₹ 75 for each day on which the contravention is continued.

5.7 INDUSTRIAL ACCIDENTS AND INDUSTRIAL SAFETY

Introduction

Technological development is taking place at a very fast rate in all the fields like mechanical, metallurgical, chemical, electrical and civil. These days every man is surrounded by automobiles, trains, aeroplanes, explosives, noise and air-pollution etc. which may cause accidents. The danger of life of human being is increasing with the advancement of scientific developments in different fields. The importance of industrial safety was realised because every year millions of industrial accidents occur which result in either death or in temporary disablement or permanent disablement of the employees and involve large amount of loss resulting from damage to property and wasted man hours and machine hours. Now-a-days serious attention is being paid to reduce the rate and severity of accident. Safety rules have been devised for each and every field to safeguard the interest of society. Hazard control and accident prevention have been considered as a basic need. Health and safety are basic desire and instinct. We believe in concept of safety, human protection and protection of nature. The benefits of accident prevention have been well-understood and accepted by industries throughout the world.

Safety: Safety is the state of being safe.

- S – Spot the hazard
- A – Assess the risk
- F – Find a safe way
- E – Every body

Industrial Safety Management

Any method, technique or process which can minimize unwanted events (accidents) in industrial concern may be referred to as a method, technique or process of Industrial Safety.

Industrial Safety management is mainly concerned with minimizing hazards in the industries ; and safety of people's life and property. Hazard is a state, physical or chemical having potential to injure the person or impairment of health. Risk or danger arises out of hazards.

Industrial Safety Management is a branch of management which is concerned with identifying, evaluating, reducing, controlling and eliminating hazards from the industrial units. Safety management designs safety rules and makes the employees safety conscious.

Problem of Industrial Accidents

Accident may be defined as "an unforeseen, uncontrollable and sudden mishap which may result in minor injuries or death of the person involved, loss of property and interruptions in activities or functions in industry".

- As per Factory Act 1948, industrial accident has been defined as ; "An occurrence in an industrial establishment causing bodily injury to a person which makes him unfit to resume his duties in the next 48 hours".

- An unexpected, uncontrolled event which cannot be anticipated in advance.

5.7.1 Causes of Accidents

It is an established fact that accidents are caused, they do not just happen out of nothing. Whenever there occurs an accident, there must be some cause, which may be obvious or difficult to trace.

It is therefore necessary to investigate the causes and then take steps to prevent them in future.

The causes of accident may be classified as:

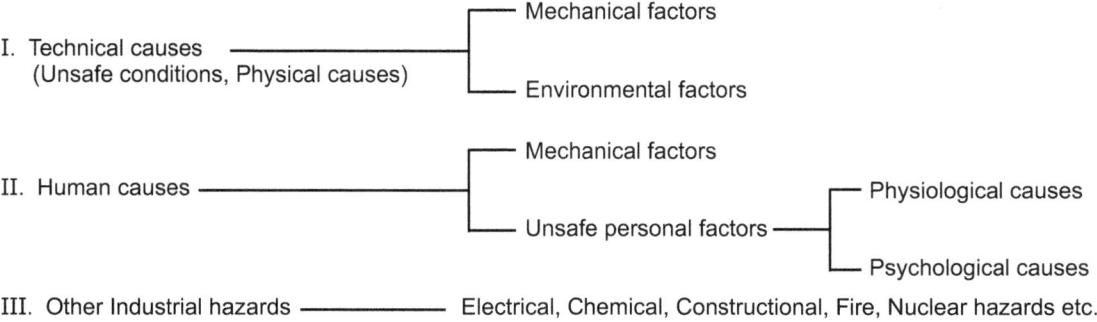

Fig. 5.4: Causes of accident

[I] Technical Causes

A. Mechanical Factors:

1. Continued use of old, poorly maintained or unsafe equipment. This is generally accompanied by failure to have regular plant safety preventive inspection of all production facilities in accordance with a properly designed time schedule.

For example:

(a) If crane elevator cables are not regularly inspected and promptly replaced when dangerously worm.

(b) Power lines may be poorly insulated and worn insulation may be repaired with adhesive tape.

2. Unguarded or improper guarded machines or equipment, guards of improper height, strength, mesh etc.

3. Unsafe process, mechanical, chemical, electrical, nuclear etc.

4. Unsafe design and construction of building structures etc.

5. Improper material handling system.

6. Improper plant layout.

7. Untested boilers or pressure vessels.

8. Violation of prescribed safety practices.

9. Unsafely clothed, no goggles, gloves or masks, smoking in non-smoking areas, wearing high heal shoes etc.

B. Environmental Factors:

1. **Temperature and humidity:** Low temperature cause shivering. Too high temperature cause headache and sweating, this also causes fatigue to the operator. Too high humidity (as in textile industry) may cause uncomfort, fatigue drowsiness especially when the atmosphere is too hot.

2. **Defective and inadequate illumination:** It causes glares, shadows, eye strain etc.

3. Presence of dust, fumes and smoke (e.g., in foundry or welding shops).

4. **Overly fatigued worker:** Excess fatigue may arise out of work assignment that may tax the worker's physical and mental powers (excessive overtime, inadequate rest pauses).

5. Unsafely arranged, poor house keeping, congestion, blocked exits, bad plant layout or arrangement of machines.

6. Harsh or dominating behaviour of management or supervisors towards worker.

7. The type of leadership style adopted by the management in the organisation.

8. Excessively long duration of work, shift duty.

9. Annoying outside noise and vibrations.

[II] Human Causes

A. Unsafe Acts:

Unsafe act may be defined as "the deviation from the normal and correct procedure or practice". It results in unnecessary exposure to hazards, or conduct minimizing the degree of safety. Any human action is manifestation of mental or psychological set up. Hence unsafe act is related to the psychological aspect of the workers.

The following are unsafe acts:

1. Operating without authority.
2. Operating or working at unsafe speed.
3. Making safety devices unoperative (removing, misadjusting, disconnecting etc.).
4. Using unsafe equipment or using equipment unsafely.
5. Taking unsafe position or posture (standing or working under suspended loads, lifting with back bent etc.).
6. Unsafe loading, placing, mixing, combining etc.
7. Working on moving or dangerous equipment.
8. Failure to use personal protective devices.
9. Improper use of tools.

B. The Unsafe Personal Factors:

The unsafe personal factors are the mental or bodily characteristics which promote unsafe act. These may be classified as (a) Physiological causes, and (b) Psychological causes.

(a) Physiological Causes: These causes of accidents are related to the bodily defects or health of the worker.

Following are some of the physiological causes:

(i) Reduced hearing capacity of the worker.
(ii) Poor eye sight.
(iii) Arms or legs or any other part of the body may be defective or damaged.
(iv) Sleepiness due to fatigue or over eating.
(v) Poor health in general.
(vi) Old age or to young age.
(vii) High blood pressure and other diseases.
(viii) Colour blindness.

(b) Psychological Causes: These causes are related to the mental processes of the workers. Some of the psychological causes are:

(i) Improper attitude (disregard of instructions, failure to understand instructions, nervousness, excitability, depression etc.).

(ii) Ignorance, forgetfulness, carelessness, day dreaming etc.

(iii) Lack of knowledge and skill (unaware of safe practices, unskilled).

(iv) Home environment.

(v) Mental worries.

(vi) Feeling of job insecurity among workers.

(vii) Over confidence.

(viii) Accident proneness etc.

[III] Other Industrial Hazards

Hazards may be defined as "a potential condition which might be converted into an accident". Hazards may be broadly grouped under the following head:

(i) Mechanical (ii) Electrical

(iii) Chemical (iv) Fire

(v) Nuclear (vi) Constructional.

A. Electrical Hazards may include:

(i) Ungrounded machine tools, casings and structures.

(ii) Uncovered switches and switch boards.

(iii) Poorly insulated powerlines which may cause fire and may give shocks.

(iv) Fuses of unsuitable capacity.

(v) Exposed resistances, rheostats etc.

(vi) Overconfidence in working on the live circuits etc.

B. Fire Hazards: The main sources of fire are:

(i) Matches and smoking.

(ii) Heating and cooking.

(iii) Poor house keeping.

(iv) Electrical wiring and apparatus.

(v) Open flames and sparks.

(vi) Flammable liquids, explosive materials.

(vii) Welding and cutting torches etc.

C. Constructional Hazards:

(i) Faulty structural design.

(ii) Improper repair and maintenance.

(iii) Substandard and defective material of construction which do not satisfy the relevant standards and specifications.

(iv) Improper planning or layout.

(v) Lack of supervision during construction.

(vi) Ignoring the norms of sound engineering practice etc.

D. Chemical Hazards:

Industrial processes involve use of chemicals and hazardous materials. The raw materials used in industries could be hazardous due to toxicity inherent to materials. The products both intermediate and finished as well as the bye-products (including industrial wastes can pose serious problems of chemical safety. Hence storage, handling, manufacture and use of chemicals call for strict surveillance on the part of managers, supervisors and workmen. Some of the toxic chemicals are Carbon Monoxide, Carbon disulphide, Chlorine, Chromium, Mercury, Lead, Naptha, Sulphur dioxide etc.

5.7.2 Effects of Accidents

The adverse effects of accident can be summarized as under:

Effect on the Industry or Owner:

An accident can be very costly to the industry as well as to the employees. The costs associated with accident can be classified as:

- Direct costs
- Indirect costs

Direct costs of an accident

1. Compensation has to be paid to the worker for temporary or permanent disability caused by accident.

2. Money paid for treatment and cure of workers disabled by on-job accident.

3. Money value of damaged equipment and materials, expenses towards repairs, replacement of damaged machines and equipment.

Indirect costs of an accident

4. Cost of lost time of injured worker.
5. Cost of time lost by other employees who stop work
   (a) Out of curiosity
   (b) Out of sympathy
   (c) To assist injured employee
   (d) For other reason.
6. Cost of time lost by foreman, supervisors, safety engineers or other executives as follows:
   (a) Assisting injured employees.
   (b) Investigating the cause of accident.
   (c) Arranging for the injured workers production to be continued by some other worker.
   (d) Selecting and training a new worker to replace the injured man.
   (e) Preparing the accident report.
7. Cost of interruptions and delays in production due to accident.
8. Cost of lowered production due to substitute worker.
9. Cost of subsequent injuries that occur in consequence of the excitement or weakened morale due to original accident.

Effect on Worker:

In addition to the industry, the injured worker suffers financially as under:

1. If the worker dies in the accident, the family loses the bread earner.
2. Injury compensation never equals his earnings.
3. Accident also affects the morale of employee.
4. If the worker gets injured, he loses his efficiency and the workmanship. His rating gets lowered due to handicapness and therefore loses the incentives due to not performing at higher level.
5. After the accident, the worker is psychologically hesitant to work at the same place and even reluctant to exert himself in the job.

Cost to Society

Work connected injuries also put a considerable burden on society as a whole, as under:

1. Even though a victim receives compensation, he may require additional helps from the society.
2. Obviously, for those who do not come under Compensation Act, the need for help from society is much greater.
3. Loss of production hours cause less products in market.
4. Employers necessarily include the costs of accident to the selling prices of their products. Therefore, the society has to pay more price for the products.
5. If the worker is involved in social activities, then his replacement is difficult to achieve.

5.7.3 Types of Industrial Accidents (Classification of Accidents)

There are several methods of classifying accidents. Some of them are as follow:

1. According to the nature of injuries
2. According to the event
3. According to place of accident
4. According to damage caused
5. According to length of recovery

1. Nature of Injury (based on seriousness of injuries caused)

(a) Fatal Accident: In which case a worker losses his life due to an injury by the machine, electric shock, inhalation of poisonous chemicals, fumes, fire and fall etc.

(b) Accident which Cause Permanent Disablement (total or partial): In these type of accident, the worker receives permanent injuries because of which he looses his earning capacity. The employee is not capable of earning that much money which he was capable to earn before the accident. He losses his efficiency and workmanship consequently, his earning gets reduced. The employee may cut his finger, arm or hand, damage his eyes etc. due to accident.

(c) Accident which cause Temporary Disablement: Less serious injuries are caused in this type of accidents and the worker becomes temporally unfit and looses his earning capacity for a short period of time. The worker starts work after receiving first aid in workshop or factory hospital when he suffers from minor injuries. Fracture of arm is an example of temporary disablement.

2. **According to the Event**

   This type of accidents are classified as
   - Machine Accidents
   - Non-Machine Accidents

   (a) Machine Accidents: These include
   - Accidents caused because of catching of tools, breaking of guides, metals chips flying from the machine.
   - Catching of fingers, arms, legs, clothing etc. in machine.

     These accidents are mainly caused by loose cloths or body parts of the worker being caught in the moving parts of the machine.

     These accidents are more serious because the work is suddenly stopped and it may cause damage to the machinery, body of the worker and material etc.

   (b) Non-Machine Accidents: Nearly 80 % of the accidents are non-machine accidents. These may include accidents caused by
   - Flying objects striking the workers overhead,
   - Metallic portion of the hammer becoming loose and flying away from the wooden handle and striking against someone,
   - Objects on the floor, unsafe house keeping facilities (unsuitable shelves, bins, racks, no aisle marking etc.),
   - Oily, slippery floor etc.

3. **Accidents According to the Place**

   These may include:
   - Accidents occurred in stores, foundry, machine shop, installation and building etc.
   - Accidents occurred on the road, traffic accidents, passenger accidents etc.

4. **Accidents According to the Damage Caused**

   In this type, accidents are classified according to the extent of damage caused as:
   - Damage to plant
   - Damage to machinery, material handling equipment.
   - Damage to materials
   - Damage to factory building etc.

5. According to the length of Recovery

According to the length of recovery after the worker is injured in an accident there are following three types of accidents

- First Aid Accidents
- Home Cases Accidents
- Lost Time Accidents

(i) In case of *first aid accidents* the injuries are minor. After first aid treatment the workers are ready to work, no time is lost except the time for first aid treatment.

(ii) In *home case accidents*, medical treatment is first given at factory hospital and the worker is allowed to go home for a maximum of 3 days. No compensation is paid to the worker.

(iii) In *lost time accident*, the injuries are serious. The worker is admitted to the hospital. He is advised to take rest for a certain period. Compensation has to be paid to the worker for lost time accidents according to the "Workmen's Compensation Act".

5.7.4 Preventive Measures (Accident Prevention)

"An injury prevented is a benefaction, an injury compensated and apology". Accident prevention is the work of eliminating the mechanical hazards of environment and the unsafe actions of persons before the accident and the injury occurs.

It is concerned with the control of man performance, machine performance and physical environment. Accident prevention is a vital factor in every industrial enterprises; if it is ignored or practised unskillfully, leads to needless human suffering and business bankruptcy.

Accident prevention brings about a spectacular achievement in the saving of life, compensation, continuity of services, increased production, decreased labour turnover and improved labour management relations.

To be effective in hazard control programme, it must be planned and should be logical. Programme objectives and safety policies need to be established. Responsibility to the hazard control programme needs to be determined.

Accident prevention consists of four major steps. These are:

- Discover the causes,
- Control environmental causes,
- Control behaviouristic causes,
- Supplementary activities.

(a) Discovering Accident Causes

Before any steps can be taken it is essential to find out:

1. The causes of previous accidents and
2. The existing hazards that may cause accident unless corrected.

These activities are necessary not only before starting the actual procedures of accident prevention but also afterwards, for they must be given continuous never ending attention ; otherwise the real efforts of accident prevention will get out of hand. The supervisor's report of accident investigation is the basis of all analysis of past accidents.

After finding the potential hazards by survey and inspection, analysis must be made to select most important hazards to be attacked. The reasons for existence of hazards must be found when these do not yield to corrections. Knowing and finding the hazards is only the beginning. These must be corrected/controlled.

(b) Controlling Environmental Causes

All the environmental causes have something to do with machinery and equipment, with the things one can see and feel. A good layout and working conditions play a major role in preventing many accidents. Improper physical and mechanical environment such as space, light, heat, arrangement, ventilation, materials, tools, equipment, procedures, company policy, routing etc. make it awkward, difficult, inconvenient or impossible to follow safe practice rules:

1. The layout should be such that: (a) Every employee has enough space to move and operate. (b) Passageways between working places, roads, tracks etc. must never be obstructed.
2. The working area should prevent the inrush of cold air, hot air and draughts to the working place.
3. For adequate lighting, ventilation etc. the heights of working room should be about 3 metres.
4. Floors must be non-skid type satisfactorily plane and should have capacity to absorb sounds, vibration etc.
5. Doors and windows should be of adequate dimensions in order to make full use of natural day-light.
6. Select, purchase and make use of machines and process which will produce little noise.
7. Isolate and keep noise producing machines in separate close cabin.

8. Use suitable machine mounts to damp-down the vibration.
9. Use proper material handling equipment, it should also be promptly repaired and adequately maintained.

If there are two or more different ways to prevent certain types of accidents, select proper way for example. If there is a hole in the floor and if there is any danger of worker falling in it and get injured, it is much wiser and cheaper in the long run to eliminate the hole than to place a guard rail around it or to try to teach the worker to stay away. Trying to teach a man to avoid hazard is never ending job requiring constant supervision and discipline. But the elimination of a hazard is an immediate and permanent cure.

Environmental Causes of Accident — How to eliminate them ?

Sr. No.	Environmental Causes of Accidents	Corrective Action
1.	Improper guarding (unguarded, inadequately guarded, guard removed by someone other than injured worker etc.)	(a) Inspection (b) Provide guards for existing hazards.
2.	Substances or equipment defective through use, or neglect (worn out cracked, broken etc. through no fault of injured worker).	(a) Inspection (b) Proper maintenance.
3.	Substances or equipment defective through design or construction, (too large, too small, not strong enough, made with flaws etc.)	(a) Source of supply must be reliable. (b) Inspection for defects. (c) Correction of defects before operating.
4.	Unsafe procedure, hazardous process, management failed to make adequate plans for safety.	(a) Job analysis. (b) Formulation of safe procedure. (c) Job training.
5.	Unsafe housekeeping facilities (unsuitable shelves, bins, racks, no aisle marking etc.)	(a) Provide suitable layout and equipment necessary for good housekeeping.
6.	Improper illumination (poor, none, glaring, headlight etc.)	(a) Improve the illumination.

Contd...

7.	Improper ventilation (poor, dusty, gaseous, high humidity etc.)	(a) Improve the ventilation.
8.	Improper dress or protective devices (management's failure to provide or specify use).	(a) Provide safe dress or personnel protective devices. (b) Specify the use of certain protective devices on certain jobs. .

(c) Controlling Behaviouristic Causes

These can be controlled through the application of

- Job analysis
- Supervision
- Personal work
- Job training
- Discipline
- Physical examination

Proper Placement of Workers: In general, it is much more difficult to control behaviouristic causes than it is to control environmental causes. It can neither be seen nor felt. It is the result of such complicated factors as heredity, emotion, diet and habits etc. For example, a wrong attitude is an important behaviourstic cause that is more closely induced by worry. Many workers worry about current finance problems or the possibility of poverty in old age or the expenses on medical care. The activities such as pension plans, group health and accident insurance and employee credit union have helped to relieve thousands of workers from some of these worries and problems and helped in improving the company's accident record.

Behaviouristic Causes of Accidents — How to eliminate them ?

No.	Behaviouristic Causes of Accidents	Corrective Action
1.	Improper attitude (deliberate chance taking, disregard of instructions, absent-mindedness etc.)	(a) Supervision (b) Discipline (c) Personnel work
2.	Lack of knowledge of skill (New on the job unpracticed, unskilled etc.)	(a) Job analysis (b) Job training (c) Proper placement of men
3.	Physical or mental defect (one arm, deaf, partially blind etc.)	(a) Pre-employment physical examinations (b) Periodic physical examinations (c) Proper placement of men

Contd...

4.	Operating without authority, operating at unsafe speed.	(a) Supervision
		(b) Discipline
5.	Making safety devices unoperative, not using safety devices.	(a) Supervision
		(b) Training
6.	Taking unsafe position or using equipment unsafely. Improper use of tools.	(a) Supervision
		(b) Training

Only discovering the corrective action or remedy is not enough. Unless the remedy is successfully applied, all the previous steps will be useless.

The safety engineer has to direct authority for implementation of the remedies.

Hence he must:

(i) prepare and present his recommendations and suggestions to management so that management is convinced of the importance, and thus obtain active support.

(ii) establish safety organisation.

(iii) create enthusiasm and co-operation at all levels.

(d) Supplementary Activities

The workers should be properly trained to observe safety rules. If necessary, discipline is to be strictly enforced.

Wide publicity should be given through:

1. Posters,
2. Booklets and other literature,
3. Movies,
4. Film strips,
5. Contests,
6. Meetings,
7. Committees,
8. Suggestion system,
9. Employee magazines, Bulletins
10. Safety books, safety training

Welfare and Safety

Welfare activities are associated with economic and psychological growth of employees. In certain areas welfare and safety activities are closely linked together.

These areas of activities may include the following:

(i) Provision of compensation in case of accidents.

(ii) Precautionary measures for maintaining industrial health such as: Reasonable hours of work, rest pauses, housing facilities, education facilities, lunch room and cafeteria, medical facilities, recreational facilities, provision of rest rooms, financial assistance etc.

(iii) Fencing and covering of machines.

(iv) Proper layout of machinery and plant.

(v) Provision of first aid appliances.

(vi) Temperature and humidity control in the work places.

(vii) Proper ventilation.

(viii) Provision of fire extinguishers.

(ix) Provision of personal protective devices.

(x) Good working conditions etc.

General Safety Rules

It is necessary to frame a set of rules to promote safety of employees and to prevent the direct and indirect costs of accident. These safety rules should be strictly followed and administered as a part of safety programme.

While framing safety rules following points should be taken into consideration:

1. The safety rules should be such that it does not cause annoyance to an employee.
2. Safety rules must be clearly defined without any ambiguity.
3. The safety rules must keep pace with changing environments and industrial situations.
4. Safety rules should be such that they should be acceptable to the employees without resistance.

Some of the general safety rules which may serve as a guideline to workers and supervisors are as follows:

1. Power should be switched off before repairing the equipment.
2. Smoking should be strictly prohibited, particularly near chemical or inflammable materials.
3. Personal protective devices like safety goggles, aprons, shoes, must always be used depending upon the type of operations involved.
4. Wire mesh and safety guards must be provided on all rotating parts such as pulleys, gear boxes etc.
5. High voltage equipments and other machines which cannot be properly guarded should be fenced.

6. Pressure vessels and their component parts must be periodically tested, the defective parts should be promptly replaced.
7. Mischievous acts should never be tolerated and defaulter should be punished.
8. Electrical connections and insulation should be checked at regular intervals.
9. Inflammable materials should be stored separately and away from the general stores.
10. Material handling equipments should have unobstructed path for their movement.
11. Defective tools such as hammers, spanners should not be used.
12. Only authorised employees should operate the equipment.
13. Loose dress must never be used while working on a machine.
14. Prompt first aid attention must be paid to any injured person, and remedial measures thereof must be taken.
15. Fire extinguishers should be kept in proper condition and at key places.

First Aid

Inspite of taking all safety precautions and measures, accidents cannot be avoided. An injured worker needs immediate proper treatment. Hence, every establishment should have adequate provisions for first aid treatment. The primary function of implant first aid facilities is to give prompt treatment to those who suffer injury at the work place (before his condition may become critical).

A First Aid-Box must be provided in the charge of a responsible person who must be always available in working hours and should be trained in first aid treatment.

5.8 INTELLECTUAL PROPERTY RIGHTS

Intellectual Property Rights protects the use of information and ideas that are of commercial value. The term "Intellectual Property" covers Patents, Copyrights, Trade marks, Designs, Know-how and so on. The scope of intellectual is growing tremendously. Intellectual persons who create new creative ideas (invention) attempts to seek protection under the umbrella of IPR. Although, the creation of a trade mark has very little to do with intellectual creativity, however it is clear that patents, designs and copyrights are products of intellectual efforts and creative activity in the field of science and technology.

In our country, the majority of intellectual property rights are today founded in the five enactments. i.e.,

i) The Trade Mark Act, 1999
ii) Copy Rights Act, 1957

iii) The Patents Act, 1970

iv) The Designs Act, 2000 and

v) Geographical Indication of Goods (Registration and Protection) Act, 1999.

The law of intellectual property plays a significant role for the cultural and economic development of the country.

The granting of patent monopoly encourages the competitors in the market to manufacture / invent new product or effect improvement in the existing product or in the process of manufacture.

Similarly, industrial design protection encourages people with the creative mind to utilize their talent in developing new improved or economical designs for the product.

The protection of trade mark is intended to provide for better protection of trade marks and prevention of fraud in using the existing or reputed trade mark.

Similarly, copyright is the right granted to the author or originator of certain literary or artistic production whereby he is authorized with a sole and exclusive privilege of multiplying copies of the same and publishing and selling them.

The main purpose of intellectual property rights (IPR) is that no one should be allowed to take advantage of a thing which has been invented or produced by the intelligence, labour, skill, judgment and efforts of others.

Different kinds of intellectual properties can be commercially exploited in different ways.

In case of patents, the patentee may himself commercially exploit the patent or assign his rights or license to the Businessmen/Companies for a lump sum payment or on a royalty basis.

Similarly, the registered designs can be commercially exploited either by assigning or by licensing the rights to others capable of exploiting it on a lump sum or on royalty basis.

Similarly, the copyright can also be exploited.

However, in case of trade mark, the commercial exploitation is only possible by way of registration of the license as registered user. Hence, commercial exploitation of registered trade mark by way of licensing it to others to use if on a royalty basis is not permissible.

5.8.1 Patents

Patent is a grant of right to exclude others from making, using or selling one's invention. It includes right to license other to make, use or sell it.

It is an official document conferring a right or privilege, securing in writing to an inventor for a term of years the exclusive right to make, use and sell his invention; the monopoly or right so granted.

The 'Patent Act' is founded in the enactment "The Patent Act, 1970". The Patent Act provides protection for an invention which must be new and useful.

An invention, in order to be patentable must be capable of being made or used in some kind of industry. In this context, industry should be understood in its broader sense as including any useful, practical activity, and does not necessarily imply the use of machine or the manufacture of an article.

The expression 'invention' has therefore been defined in the Patent Act, 1970 to mean manner of manufacture; machine; substance produced by manufacture. The invention relates to the skill (art), series of action (process) or the particular way (method) or the way (manner) of making a product or thing. It also relates to machine or apparatus by which a thing is made and also the product which is the result of act of making.

The effect of grant of patent is quid pro quo, quid is the knowledge disclosed to the public and quo is the monopoly granted for the term of the patent. Patents and Designs Act sets out that a patent once granted confers upon the patentee the exclusive privilege of making, selling and using the invention throughout India and of authorizing others to do so. This is quo. The quid is compliance with the various provision resulting in the grant of patent.

In case of patent, the patentee may himself commercially exploit the patent or assign his rights or license them to the Businessmen/Companies for a lump sum payment or on royalty basis. In this context "Patentee" is he to whom a patent has been granted. The granting of patent monopoly encourages the competitors in the market to manufacturer new products or effect improvements in the process of manufacture.

Since its inception, the Patent Act, 1970 was subjected to a single Amendment in 1999 to the obligation of India under the Agreement on Trade Related Aspects of Intellectual Property Rights (TRIPS) forming part of the World Trade Organisation (WTO). For the purpose of integrating intellectual property system with international practices, the Act needed another amendment so that it is modern and in accordance with international practices and consistent with the TRIPS agreement. Thus, the Patents (Amendment) Act, 2002 was introduced making far reaching changes in the 1970 Act. It also widened the scope of non-patentability of substances in the nature. Several other modifications were also carried out.

5.8.2 Trade Marks

Trade mark means a mark capable of being represented graphically and which is capable of distinguishing the goods or services of one person from those of others and may include shape of goods, their packaging and combination of colour etc.

In our country, the trade mark act was founded in the enactment 'The Trade Mark Act, 1999'. The Trade Mark Act provides for better protection to the registered trade mark for goods and services, and prevents the use of fraudulent marks on merchandise.

A mark is a part of the brand which appears in the form of a symbol, design etc. It could be recognized only by sight but may not be pronounceable e.g. symbol of Maharaja of Air India, design of two arrows for Delhi Transport Corporation etc. When the brand mark is registered and legalized it becomes a Trade Mark. It is essentially a legal term protecting the manufacturers right to use the brand name.

In selecting a good brand name as a trade mark the various aspects require careful consideration.

1. It should identify the product, its characteristics easily and distinguish from other similar products.
2. As far as possible it should be most descriptive in nature e.g. Mysore Sandal Soap.
3. It should be unique.
4. It should be appropriate for the product concerned.
5. It should be registered so that any other firm might not take advantage of its popularity.
6. It should be helpful in advertisement.
7. It should be short and pointing (i.e. appealing and attractive)
8. It should be easy to print or embossed on packages.
9. As far as possible it should be heart touching so as to influence the mind of customer and catch his imagination (easy to visualize).

Patents, designs and copyrights can be commercially exploited in different ways. However, in case of trade mark the commercial exploitation is only possible by way of registration of the licenses as registered user. Hence, commercial exploitation of a registered trade mark by way of licensing it to others to use on a royalty basis is not permissible. In case of infringement of Registered trade mark, both civil and criminal remedies (imprisonment and heavy fines are available).

Procedure for Registration of Trade Mark

1. Application for Registration: Any person claiming to be the proprietor of a trade mark used or proposed to be used by him, who is desirous of registering it, shall apply in writing to the Registrar in the prescribed manner for the registration of his trade mark. Subject to the provisions of the Act, the Registrar may refuse the application or may accept it absolutely or subject to such amendments, modifications, condition or limitations, if any, as he may think fit. In the case of refusal or conditional acceptance of an application, the Registrar shall record in writing the grounds for such refusal or conditional acceptance and the material used by him in arriving at his decision.

2. Advertisement of Application: When the application for registration of a trade mark has been accepted, the Registrar shall, advertise the application in the prescribed manner.

3. Opposition to Registration: Within three months from the date of the advertisement of an application, the Registrar on application made to him in the prescribed manner may allow any person to give notice of opposition to the registration.

The Registrar shall, after hearing the parties, if so required and considering the evidence, decide whether and subject to what conditions or limitations, if any, the registration is to be permitted.

4. Registration: Subject to the provisions of section 19, when an application for registration of a trade mark has been accepted and either

(a) The application has not been opposed and the time of notice of opposition has expired; or

(b) The application has been opposed and the opposition has been decided in favour of the applicant; the Registrar shall register the said trade mark.

On the registration of a trade mark, the Registrar shall issue to the applicant a certificate in the prescribed form of the registration thereof, sealed with the seal of the Trade Marks Registry.

For the purpose of this Act, a record called the 'Register of Trade Marks' shall be kept at the head office of the Trade Marks Registry.

In this register the following entries shall be made:
- All registered trade marks with the names,
- Addresses and description of the proprietors,
- Notifications of assignment and transmissions,
- The names, addresses and description of registered users,
- Conditions, limitations and such other matter related to registered trade marks etc.

Absolute Grounds for Refusal of Registration

The trade marks shall not be registered as a trade mark if -

i) It is not capable of distinguishing the goods or services of one person from those of another.

ii) It consist exclusively of marks or indications which have become customary in the current language or in established practices of the trade.

iii) It is of such nature as to deceive the public or cause confusion.

iv) It contains or comprises of any matter likely to hurt the religious feelings of any class or section of the citizens of India.

v) Its use is prohibited under the Emblems and names (Prevention of Improper Use Act, 1950).

vi) It consists exclusively of the shape of goods which results from the nature of the goods themselves.

vii) It comprises or contains scandalous or obscene matter.

viii) Its identity with an earlier trade mark and similarity of goods or services covered by the trade mark.

ix) Its use in India is liable to be prevented.

x) By virtue of law of copyright.

5.8.3 Copyrights

Copyrights are also products of intellectual effort and creative activity in the field of fine arts and applied arts or technology. The Copyrights Act has been founded in the enactment 'The Patents Act, 1970'. The Copyright Act confers a long lasting right in literary, dramatical, musical or artistic creation.

Copyrights is the right granted by statute to the author or originator of certain literary or artistic production, whereby he is authorized for a limited period, with the sole and exclusive privilege of multiplying copies of the same and publishing and selling them.

The object of the law is to facilitate, encourage and motivate artists, composers, software programmes etc. to create original works by a system of granting exclusive right for a limited period to re-produce the work for the benefit or consumption of the public. After the expiry of the specific period the work will belong to the public domain and one may reproduce these without permission.

Thus, the producer of an original work is enabled to prevent others from creating or reproducing his work and in this sense, the author gets the monopoly rights in favour. With the growth of science and technology as well as with the growth in inventive and creative flourish in various aspects of literary, artistic, musical and other arts, the need for copyright protection has become all the most important.

The importance of copyright was recognized only after the print media was invented about five centuries back which enabled reproduction of books and literatures in large numbers.

For the purpose of this Act, "copyright" means the exclusive right subject to the provisions of this Act, to do or authorize the doing of any of the following acts in respect of a work or any substantial part thereof, namely:

(a) In the case of a literary, dramatic or musical work, not being a computer programme:

(i) To reproduce the work in any material from including the storing of it in any medium by electronic means.

(ii) To issue copies of the work to the public not being copies already in circulation.

(iii) To perform the work in public or communicate it to the public.

(iv) To make any cinematograph film or sound recording in respect of the work.

(v) To make any translation of the work.

(vi) To make any adaptation of the work.

(vii) To do, in relation to translation or an adaptation of the work, any of the acts specified in relation to the work in sub-clauses (i) to (iv).

(b) In the case of a computer programme:

(i) To do any of the acts specified in clause (a).

(ii) To sell or give on commercial rental or offer for sale or for commercial rental any copy of the computer programme.

(c) In the case of an artistic work:

(i) To reproduce the work in any material form including depiction on three dimensions of a two dimensional work or in two dimensions of a three dimensional work.

(ii) To communicate the work to the public.

(iii) To issue copies of the work to the public not being copies already in circulation.

(iv) To include the work in any cinematograph film.

(v) To make any adaptation of the work.

(vi) To do in relation to and adaptation of the work any of the acts specified in relation to work in sub-clauses (i) to (iv).

(d) In the case of a cinematograph film:

(i) To make a copy of the film, including a photograph of any image forming part thereof.

(ii) To sell or give on hire or offer for sale or hire, any copy of the film, regardless of whether such copy has been sold or given on hire on earlier occasions.

(iii) To communicate the film to the public.

(e) In the case of a sound recording:

(i) To make any other sound recording embodying it.

(ii) To sell or give on hire, or offer from sale or hire, any copy of the sound recording regardless of whether such copy has been sold or given on hire on earlier occasions.

(iii) To communicate the sound recording to the public.

International copyright is the right of a subject of one country for protection against the republication in another country of a work which he originally published in his own country.

In order to adapt the rapidly changing global economical trade scenario, the 1957 Act was recently amended by the copyright (Amendment) Act, 1999. This Act (Amendment) extends the term protection of performers rights from 25 years to 50 years. The Amendment Act provides for powers to government to extend the provisions of the Act to broadcasts and performances made in other countries, provided those countries give reciprocal protection to broadcasts and performances in India.

Offence of infringement of copyright or other rights conferred by this Act : Any person who knowingly infringes or abets infringement of

(a) The copyright in a work, or

(b) Any other right conferred by this Act,

shall be punishable with imprisonment for a term which shall not be less than six months but which may extend to three years and with fine which shall not be less than fifty thousand rupees but which may extend to two lakh rupees.

Provided that [where the infringement has not been made for gain in the course of trade or business] the court may, for adequate and special reasons to be mentioned in the judgement, impose a sentence of imprisonment for a term of less than six months or a time of less than fifty thousand rupees.

EXERCISE

1. Define the term quality and explain the term :
   (i) Quality of design,
   (ii) Quality of conformance and
   (iii) Quality of performance.

2. Define the terms, Quality of design, Quality of conformance and Quality of performance. State the factors controlling them.
3. Fill in the blanks with suitable words.

   (i) Quality is a ------- term and it is generally used with reference to the ------ of the product.

   (ii) Quality is defined as the ------ for use.

   (iii) The quality of design is concerned with the ------- for the manufacture of the product.

   (iv) The quality of performance depends upon -------- and -------.

   (v) The quality depends upon the ----- of a person in a given situation.

   (iv) The quality is dictated by the ------ of the customer.

4. Define 'Quality Control'. State is objectives.
5. Define Quality Control and Statistical Quality Control. State the functions of quality control.
6. What is Total Quality? Explain.
7. Define and explain the concept of TQM.
8. State the elements of TQM and describe them in brief.
9. State the benefits of TQM.
10. State and explain the cause of variation in manufacturing processes.
11. Describe "Process Control" in brief. How it can be determined?
12. Describe the concept of ISO:9000 series standards.
13. Describe briefly the ISO : 9000 standards in general.
14. State the benefits of becoming an ISO : 9000 standards.
15. State the various steps for registration of ISO : 9000 standards.
16. What is Industrial Acts? What is its necessity ? Explain.
17. Define the following as per Factories Act:

    (a) A manufacturing process   (b) Adolesent

    (c) Worker   (d) Machinery

    (e) Occupier   (f) Factory.

18. Explain briefly the different health provisions mentioned in the Factories Act.
19. Describe the welfare provisions under Factories Act. Explain how it will affect productivity.

20. Describe the following in connection with Factory Act:
    (a) Objectives of Factories Act.
    (b) Approval, Licensing and Registration of Factories.
21. Explain the following with respect to the provisions of the Factories Act:
    (a) Hours of work for adults, women and young persons.
    (b) Annual leave with wages.
22. Explain the importance of safety provisions in case of machinery, hoist and lifts and precautions in case of fire as mentioned in Factories Act.
23. Factories Act helps productivity. Justify the statement with reference to few relevant provisions of the Factories Act, 1948.
24. Describe the role of Intellectual property rights for the cultural and economic development of the country.
25. Describe the following property rights in brief (any one).
    (i) Patents
    (ii) Trade marks
    (iii) Copyrights.

www.ingramcontent.com/pod-product-compliance
Lightning Source LLC
Chambersburg PA
CBHW081221170426
43198CB00017B/2681